ARKO

ARKO
MY GAME

KEN ARTHURSON

WITH IAN HEADS

IRONBARK
Pan Macmillan Australia

First published 1997 in Ironbark by Pan Macmillan Australia Pty Limited
St Martins Tower, 31 Market Street, Sydney

Reprinted 1997

National Library of Australia
Cataloguing-in-publication data:

Arthurson, Ken.
Arko: my game

ISBN 0 330 36033 7.

1. Arthurson, Ken. 2. Australian Rugby League. 3. Rugby League football—
Australia—Management. 4. Football managers—Australia—Biography. I. Title.

796.3338092

Typeset in 11/13pt Sabon by Post Typesetters
Printed in Australia by McPherson's Printing Group

CONTENTS

Arko

This book is dedicated to the game that was rugby league—and to the hope that one day soon it will rise again to reclaim its rightful place in Australia's sporting life.

Equally I dedicate the book to the football fans of Newcastle whose unfailing strength and support and loyalty for the ARL cause gave me the strength to carry on during the bad times of seasons 1995–96. In times of great uncertainty, they were the true believers.

INTRODUCTION

There are no doubt people in the game of rugby league who reckon I've had more than enough to say over the years. Frankly, as I faced an endless barrage of press conferences and questioning in the long and gruelling months of 1995–96, following the hijacking of the game by News Ltd, I was pretty much thinking that way myself. I figured that if I never heard (or mouthed) the names Ribot, Cowley, Murdoch, Packer, Lindsay, Carden, Morgan . . . and plenty of others again, that would be soon enough. And if I never saw another microphone or camera or reporter's pad, that would be fine by me, too. The wear-down factor was one of the reasons I got out of football in 1997. My health was not great, and there was some life I had missed out on. I had had enough.

But I felt on the day of my departure from Phillip Street late February 1997, as I emptied the drawers of my desk on the fifth floor, glancing now and then at the old familiar photos on the walls, that there was still much left unsaid. Essentially, it was the reason I chose to become involved in this book. My official connection with the game of rugby league had been a long one, near enough to 50 years at a high level. I had experienced deep troughs and soaring peaks. There had been dramas and triumphs, tears and laughter. There had been some good fun. And good mates. There had been great football. There were stories to tell . . .

Arko

I am thoroughly aware that there will be those who will choose to decry my view of rugby league's passing parade. In the past two years particularly, I have made enemies in the game. Long before that I accepted the reality that my life in football would be a little more challenging than most because I happened to be associated with Manly club—a place which has been increasingly resented down the seasons, by others jealous of Manly's front-running efforts in the area of professionalism, recruitment, and their single-minded search for success. Manly became very unpopular simply because they made the mistake of trying to be the best.

Over the years I have paid the inevitable price of those in Australia who achieve positions of influence and some success in their working lives. As an ex-halfback I am a little short to be a tall poppy, but there have been times when I felt I was caught up in that syndrome, with people trying to lop me off at the knees. I have been accused of being manipulative, of playing favourites, of being a politician wearing a footballer's hat, of influencing referees. I stoutly deny the charges, all of them—although perhaps I do have an Achilles' heel. I confess freely that I suffer terminally from the condition of deep loyalty to the things I love—such as the club which has been part of my life for most of my life—and to the game of rugby league itself. In those things I wear my heart on my sleeve.

And has that condition of loyalty to things or people cared for ever blinded me, causing me to make decisions that perhaps I shouldn't have made? I firmly believe not. Sure, I've cheered for Manly in matches when I was chairman of the League, and had people pull me aside and whisper that I should hush up in the interests of public 'perception'. And sure, I have watched over the career of someone such as Bob Fulton like a proud father, and been criticised for it. I don't apologise for any of that. Manly club has been part of my life for half a century. I love the place, have been part of its growth. I can't exorcise that. And Fulton, the champion player—the best I have seen—and champion coach too—the fact is he *has* been like an extra son to me since I brought him to Sydney in his teenage years and I have taken great pride in his successes.

And yes, I have supported and encouraged Manly club's players over the years—but never unfairly. If Manly players or coaches deserved to get picked for some team or other, they generally got picked. If they didn't, they didn't. No other club was different in that way. When I became chairman of the League in 1983 I made myself a promise that any decisions in which I was involved would be based on only one condition: that they were made for the good of rugby league as a whole. After the 14 years 1983–97, I can rest easy, secure in the knowledge that I stuck resolutely to that self-imposed condition.

This book presents a very personal view of rugby league's evolution in the post-war years. The story is told exclusively and by considered design from *my* perspective, through my eyes—as player, coach, club secretary, NSW and ARL administrator. And it is told honestly, the stories presented exactly as I know them to be. If along the way there are differences from this view or that, well so be it. I can only tell my tales based on what *I* know to be the facts.

I am torn apart by what happened in 1995 to the game that has been my life. The chance to open up and give an insider's view of the Murdoch raid of April '95 and what effect that had on rugby league, was a powerful motivating force for me to decide to sit down and write my story. I still find it almost impossible to believe what took place, how greed and corporate ambition could prove such a swift and deadly combination in dismantling a game which for so many Australians had been as certain and as comforting as the rising and setting of the sun for almost 90 years, and which was in its most successful-ever phase. The Super League raiders talked their bullshit talk of 'vision'. As this book goes to press, they should be talking instead of 'ruin'. Because that's what they've done to a wonderful game—or damned close to it.

Rugby league is a tough old boot, and maybe it will survive . . . and one day again even thrive. I hope so. But the blood of this sport that meant so much to so many people is on the hands of Morgan and Ribot and Neil and Murdoch and the rest. I don't know how they can live with themselves.

I know I couldn't if I had done what they have done.

Ken Arthurson, June 1997

1

THE
BEGINNING
OF THE END

The words are burned into my mind, imprinted forever. In a private box high above the Sydney Football Stadium, Kerry Packer, supreme chief of the Channel Nine network and peripheral empires, reached out his hand to me. 'Son,' he said, 'I give you my assurance that I will be doing no deal with News Ltd without your approval and if I get knocked over by a bus tomorrow those two guys have heard me say it.' The big fella gestured towards his son James, and his right-hand man, PBL head Brian Powers. Standing alongside, John Quayle, general manager of the NSW Rugby League and chief executive of the Australian Rugby League, heard every word of it. Nick Politis, chairman of Sydney City Roosters and boss of one of the most successful car sales franchises in the world, was to tell me later that he too had heard the assurance.

It was the afternoon of Sunday 5 February 1995. Below us on the SFS's green spaces, teams from most corners of the globe were engaged in fast, furious battle in the annual Coca-Cola World Sevens. Everything *looked* normal. But, of course, it wasn't. The following morning the delegates of the Australian Rugby League's 20 clubs were to meet at the game's Phillip Street headquarters to hear a submission from Rupert Murdoch's News Ltd. At the heart of it were the two words that had dominated newspaper headlines for months, and brought me hurrying back from England in late 1994 to help shore up our forces against the predators who had arrived at the gates. Those words . . . *Super League.*

I chose to begin this book on 5 February 1995 because it was on that day that the seeds were sown for my departure from the game I love. For me, it was the beginning of the end. I was to stay almost two more years at the helm of the Australian Rugby League, fighting a fight I believed in, confronting more stress, more pressure, more anguish than I had in the entire previous half century of my time in football. In the midst of the battle, I stood transfixed one day, almost too afraid to move as pain knifed through my chest. That night, super sensitive to every tiny pain, I kept thinking that the next breath might be my last . . .

February 5, 1995 was an extraordinary day in my life. In the morning I had rung Ken Cowley, News Ltd's managing director, to tell him that I wouldn't be supporting his company's Super League plan the next day. I called Cowley early, around 8 o'clock. I want to make it quite clear here that at that time I had *not* spoken to Kerry Packer, who had been overseas and was rumoured to be on his way back. I was up early that day, and out—the Super League thing dominating my thoughts. As is often the way on a long walk, clarity came as I paced along. I could see merit in the plan that the Super League proposal represented—that much-discussed vision of an elite super-competition beamed to a vast world audience. But we had our successful competition in place and a plan for the future, too. Four new clubs were just about to play their first games in the Winfield Cup (Auckland Warriors, Western Reds, North Queensland Cowboys and South Brisbane Crushers), representing the greatest expansionary leap in the game's history. Already at Phillip Street we had decided to give the 20-team format two years to settle in, and at that point to begin the hard steps towards 'rationalisation'—the reducing of the number of Sydney clubs. Our television arrangements were firmly in place with Channel Nine and through various world networks the international 'reach' of the game was already substantial. To link with a company of the stature of News Ltd, with whom we already had strong marketing links, had its attractions, but the fact was they needed us more than we needed them.

I rang Ken Cowley early that morning and told him of my decision—that I wouldn't be backing the Super League plan that was to be put to the ARL clubs. I told him too that I wouldn't be standing in the way of the Monday presentation, and that I believed it should go ahead, with the clubs to make their own decision. But there would be no support from me. It was during our conversation that Cowley is supposed to have offered one of the most famous quotes of the Super League wars that ensued. The story goes that when I told Ken I had been out walking my dog, and that during that time made my decision not to support the Super League concept, Cowley responded: 'What's your dog's name? Kerry?'

Well, if Ken Cowley said that, I didn't hear him. If he claims he said that, well I've got to accept that. But I didn't hear the words—and if I had I would have repeated what I had already told him, that I hadn't spoken to Kerry Packer that day, or for some period before. In fact I said to Cowley early in our conversation, 'I don't want you to think that I have spoken to Packer about this, because I haven't.' The decision I made that morning was based on what I believed, and knew to be right, not on some fabled 'direction' from Packer or anyone else.

In Roy Masters' recent book *Inside Out*, Cowley is quoted as saying that I had 'definitely' rung him on the *Saturday* morning, not the Sunday. There is an inference that my call had come after I had received 'riding instructions' from Packer. I refute both claims absolutely. I rang Cowley on the Sunday. I had not spoken to Packer.

Here is exactly where I stood in February 1995: I saw some positives in the Super League proposal and I felt that if we got to a situation where we had the full weight of News Ltd behind us, with them doing a deal with Packer, then I could see the game going ahead like wildfire. But whatever happened had to be *under the control of the ARL*, and those words became my mantra in the months ahead. Also, it had to be done with the full consent of the clubs. But the decision I reached and which I conveyed to Cowley, was that I felt there was no way I would do anything to influence the clubs in the decision they made. There was no way I was going to be party to the taking-away of the identity of great and loyal clubs who had been part of rugby league for years longer than anyone's memory.

I told Cowley I would try to ensure that the case was put fairly and squarely the next day, but no more. He was very disappointed in my declaration that I wouldn't be supporting the proposal. I said to him: 'Ken, I have rung you out of respect. I didn't want you to come to the meeting believing that I was going to support you, when I wasn't. I hope you decide to still come to the meeting. I still think it is a good idea.'

He responded with the words, 'Let me think about it.'

My conversation with Packer at the Sydney Football Stadium came hours later, when he turned up at the World Sevens, obviously hell-bent on protecting Channel Nine's rights to the game and on keeping the Murdoch bid for a large piece of the action at arm's length. John Quayle and I went to Packer's box at the Stadium. In the box that day, to the best of my recollection, were Kerry Packer, Quayle, Channel Nine's David Leckie and Brian Powers, James Packer and Nick Politis.

Packer made his position very clear. There was no way he was going to agree to let News Ltd take any position in the game or any control. He'd back us to the hilt on that. By this time the Super League issue had been widely aired in the media. We had received the first off-the-record sniff that something was afoot as early as mid-1994, and the stories had begun to appear around then in *Rugby League Week*, the *Australian*, then progressively across the whole spectrum of the media.

In Packer's box at the SFS that day I said to him: 'Kerry, I'm genuinely concerned about all this.' I went on to raise the issue of a document presented by John Singleton to Canterbury CEO Peter Moore some time before. Purporting to be a blueprint for the game's future, the paper proposed a radical reduction in the number of Sydney teams. Moore had shown me a synopsis, based on the original document. I said to Packer: 'I wouldn't have thought that John Singleton would have put forward a proposal like that without your knowledge.' Packer didn't answer that, and I pressed on. 'What I am getting around to,

Kerry, is this: I wouldn't like to think that you would do a deal with News Ltd and leave us out in the cold.'

It was then that Packer uttered the words I would never forget, assuring me he would be doing no deal with News Ltd. I put out my hand and looked him square in the eye: 'Thank you Kerry, I appreciate that,' I said. I would have bet my life on Packer honouring that pledge.

That day at the Sevens was full of tension, with the football barely a distraction from the main subject at hand—Super League. Through the day the former League president Kevin Humphreys was also campaigning strongly for the ARL cause. I left the ground late that afternoon with a real sense of relief, knowing that whatever happened in the days and weeks ahead, at least we had the full support of Kerry Packer. After all, we were up against one of the world's most powerful and influential men in Rupert Murdoch, and it was a substantial comfort to know that we had a big gun in our corner too.

The punchline to all this, of course, is that on 24 November 1995 Super League announced that Packer's Channel Nine had secured the free-to-air rights to telecast Super League. This came in the midst of the bloodiest fight in the game's history. With Optus Vision and the ARL, Channel Nine had been in the trenches for months fighting the Murdoch invasion. Suddenly, in as long as it took for the press release to roll through the fax machines, Packer's Channel Nine was in bed with the enemy. That first deal fell through in the wake of squabbling between the billionaires Packer and Murdoch, during which Murdoch called Packer a 'welsher'. A year or so later he was back to being an honourable, upright, business gentleman in Murdoch's eyes. As it turned out there was nothing to telecast anyway in 1996, with Justice James Burchett's Federal Court decision KO-ing Super League's plans—in the short term, at least— and sending the matter deeper into the legal mire.

In early 1997, with Super League up and running, Channel Nine reforged their arrangement with News Ltd over free-to-air rights. Worse, they did it via a vehicle that had been a jewel in the ARL's crown—Monday night football, an innovation that had been a considerable ratings success. This was hard, cynical business at its worst and most immoral—a bitter disappointment to all of us at the ARL. I am aware that many people at Channel Nine were privately angered and disappointed too. They knew of the fight we had fought, the toll it had taken, and the wonderful loyalty and camaraderie it had generated among genuine ARL people determined that Murdoch would *not* steal their game.

I felt twice betrayed—by the November '95 decision and then by the early '97 confirmation of the Channel Nine–Super League deal. On 20 June Packer's PBL forged a deal with News Corporation and Telstra aimed at benefitting Foxtel. PBL had gone full circle, deserted Optus and thrown its weight behind Foxtel. I felt betrayed especially, because of the faith I had had in Kerry Packer's words of February '95. I had known him for a number of years by then, and the early association had grown into a genuine friendship of some warmth. There were many times over the years I had defended Packer. Once, I almost came to blows with a Packer critic in his defence. And I recall a day years ago when Kerry was in the depths of despair—it was at the time of the Royal Commission and the 'Goanna' publicity— when Bob Fulton and I went to lunch with him at the Wentworth Hotel, as mates do when one of their own is doing it tough.

At the ARL Christmas party soon after Channel Nine's first 'deal' with Super League, I made my feelings on the matter very clear to David Leckie and James Packer. Kerry rang me a week or two later when he got back from overseas and the conversation, to the best of my recollection, went something like this:

Packer: 'G'day, how are you?'

Arthurson: 'Well, I'm not too good.'

Packer: 'Why, what's up?'

Arthurson: 'Well, to tell you the truth I've seen better times. That agreement that you guys at Channel Nine have come and out and done with Super League after all that has gone on . . . well, it's not exactly the best of timing. It's put us in a very awkward position.'

Packer: 'I didn't look at it that way—it's just a conditional type agreement that doesn't matter very much.'

We obviously saw things very differently. I regarded Channel Nine's decision to shake hands with Super League to the detriment of the ARL, after all that had gone on, as a breathtaking piece of corporate treachery. I knew such a decision wouldn't have been made without Kerry Packer giving it the nod. And that hurt most of all.

For me, the Channel Nine–Super League deal in 1997 was the last straw. I had already made up my mind to retire from the game at the *end* of '97, and had begun the path towards that by stepping down as executive chairman of the ARL. When John Quayle left the game, my thoughts were to stay on, and help nurse the new general manager, Neil Whittaker as it turned out, through the difficult early months.

But I had been worn down, perhaps more than I knew. The health scare I had suffered in 1995 had shaken me, and brought a strong direction from my doctor—to take my foot off the pedal. So many bad things had happened. Eating away at me, even after two years, was my distress, and in some cases disgust, at the treachery, deceit and disloyalty shown by individuals and entire clubs who had dumped the ARL cold in their mad grab for Murdoch's cash.

Now Kerry Packer had done business with the enemy, too. Packer, whose determination to preserve his TV rights to rugby league, supported by his pledges of support to the traditional side of the game, had contributed so much to what happened in 1995: to the ARL going onto a war footing, ready to fight to the death. I only wish there had been some supreme being around in early '95 who could have cracked Murdoch and Packer's heads together, and got them to work out a deal right then.

Just imagine what a game we would have now if the hundreds of millions of dollars wasted on rugby league's crippling, internecine war had been injected in a positive way into the game. We would have nothing short of the finest, best-promoted game in the world, instead of the fragmented, fading, ill-tempered shadow of a great sport that is 1997's legacy of the Super League wars. In my early retirement I can do no more than hope that a settlement to benefit the game can be found one day before too long. What I *know* is this: that fearful damage has been done in the interest of pay TV ambitions. That ambition, married to the dark and treacherous deeds of ARL people and clubs working against their own game, have combined to give give rugby league the worst years of its 90 seasons of existence in Australia.

So, as you can see, this story of a life in football starts at the end, rather than the beginning. It begins in the worst of times, rather than the best. And with teeth gritted, I'll get back to all that further along the track before the ref blows fulltime on these pages, and offer you my personal snapshot of the Super League nastiness.

But meanwhile, there is the small matter of the panorama of 50 years of joyous involvement in this game they call rugby league. The days of my life and the game of league have virtually been inseparable since we first discovered each other on an unfenced playing field one winter's day, long ago.

Let me tell you about it . . .

2

THE KID
FROM
TIGERTOWN

To kick it off, some news that I know will come as a huge shock to many people—the revelation that I was born deep in the heart of Tiger country, in Glebe, in Sydney's inner-west. On the first day of October, 1929. And I can also tell you that the Arthursons, Ken and Mary (nee Crowe), son Kenneth Richard and daughter Jean were most certainly not silvertails. We were a battling Aussie family of the most basic kind, both my parents second or third generation Aussies—Mum of Irish descent, Dad of Scottish. Money was desperately short, and life a week-to-week battle just to get by. We lived in rented houses in the most modest circumstances you could imagine, my father picking up work where he could, for a long time working on the roads.

I don't recall the Glebe days, and only through a distant mist those that followed, when we shifted for a short while to Leichhardt (still in Balmain Tigers country!). I remember years later a great old pal of mine who had followed Balmain all his life stumbling on the knowledge that I had been born in Glebe. 'Well, I *knew* there was something all right about you,' he said.

My first formative memories really are of our next home— Bondi by the sea. We moved there when I was just a little bloke, to a small flat above some shops in Curlewis Street. Beneath our north-facing window the toastrack trams rattled

Arko

noisily by, carrying their armies of picnickers and beachgoers to and from Australia's most famous beach. Those trams became part of my young life. I became an expert tram 'scaler', leaping on and off the running boards at all speeds, and superbly skilled at dodging the red-faced conductors who we tormented. Our flat was tiny; literally, you couldn't have swung a cat in it. Money was almost non-existent. Dad was out of work plenty of times and Mum would pick up occasional cleaning or washing jobs to help out—and resolutely walking to Bondi Junction to save tuppence on the tram. There were weeks when we didn't even have the rent money and I can remember times when we sat in the house as quiet as little mice as the landlord hammered on the door, looking for his money.

Life wasn't easy for my father. I know that he carried an extra load, apart from the difficulty, serious enough in its own right, of getting work in the Depression years. As an 18-year-old he was fighting in the trenches in World War I. On a day he would never forget, his 17-year-old brother Donald, fighting alongside him, was killed by an enemy bullet. I don't think Dad ever got over that. Yet he involved himself thoroughly in life; he was a great organiser, a Labor Party man who was a big supporter of working class stalwarts like Eddie Ward and Jack Lang. My father wasn't a footballer, but he became more and more interested in the game as the years went by. When the Arthurson family moved later to the northside, he became treasurer of the Manly Junior League and founded a club at Balgowlah. He was a founding director of the Manly Leagues Club when it first opened its doors in 1957 and today there is a trophy named after him—the Ken Arthurson Shield.

Mum was the nicest, kindest woman I've ever met in my life. On reflection, I can't even imagine just how much she must have gone without to try and make life just that little bit better for my younger sister Jean and me. In our years at Bondi, I went to Bondi Beach Primary—just across Campbell Parade from the beach. My classmates there included a man who was to become a jazz legend in Australia, Don Burrows, and John Utz, who grew to be such an outstanding businessman and whose life intersected with mine via football many years later. It was only recently that I discovered Brian Bevan—the skinny winger who left Sydney to build one of the most astonishing of all rugby league careers in England—had also been a pupil at Bondi Beach Public around that time. I can only remember seeing Bevan play on one occasion—a reserve grade game with Easts. He was fast and tricky, but I think there was a general and growing amazement as the years went by and news of his freakish deeds in England filtered back.

My mother and father enrolled me in the Bondi Swimming Club and there I also learned to box and wrestle. Wrestling was big news in those days and at weekends all the famous wrestlers in town would congregate down at the beach. I can distinctly remember the thrill one day at the sight of Chief Little Wolf, one of the real headliners at Sydney Stadium, strolling nonchalantly down the promenade.

After primary school years at Bondi, I graduated to Randwick Boys' High. And it was there that I first played rugby league—as a member of the school's five stone seven (39.5kg) team. I would have been about 12 and I still hold one memory of the very first game I played. It was at Queen's Park, adjacent to Centennial Park, and we wore black and gold . . . there's that Balmain link again. My uncle, Arthur Crowe, came along to run an eye over me. I haven't a clue where I actually played in the match—it might have been wing. But I still have a clear memory of getting the ball for the first time, and of putting my head down and running as hard and fast as I could. I didn't try to step or swerve or anything fancy like that, just went straight ahead like a (small) bull at a gate. Whatever happened out on Queen's Park that day, whoever won or lost—I know I was smitten. I had found my game.

Virtually from that day, both as player and fan, rugby league was my sporting life. The War, however, played havoc with the lives of most people at that time, and so it was with my new found passion for rugby league. For whatever the specific reasons may have been, and I suspect it was much to do with the night the Japanese midget submarines came into Sydney Harbour and sunk the ferry *Kuttabul*, Mum took Jean and me out of Sydney and to the safety of the bush. For a year, I lived in Grahamstown near Tumut, a town which had produced famous league men in George Treweek and Tom Kirk. Mum's parents hailed from down there and with fear and uncertainty in the air in Sydney, she felt it was the best thing to do for her family. She came from a real rugby league family, the Crowes, several of whom were top footballers in the district. For a year of my young life, I went to school at nearby Adelong High, riding to school each day on horseback. Back in the Gold Rush days in the middle of the last century Adelong's (or Grahamstown's??) population had been up to around 20,000. But those days were long gone and it was a sleepy town of 300 or so during my brief stay there.

One day not so long after my return home, my parents confronted me with shattering news—that we were moving . . . to Manly. Jeez, I was upset, in fact there have been few things in my life that have ever jolted me as much as that. Bondi was home to me; my pals were there, my life was there. I didn't want to go way across the bloody Bridge to some place a million miles away.

But we moved, and I suspect it was for reasons to do with money. Cheaper accommodation was available over the northside at that time. For us it came in the shape of a very small flat near Fairlight, with one bedroom and a tiny annexe cut off by a curtain, where I used to sleep. I was 13 or 14, and for a while I was about as sad as a young bloke can be. Being back in Bondi, going back to Randwick High—they were the things with which I was comfortable, the things I wanted.

The sporting life at Randwick had appealed to me greatly as well—the football most of all. But I was a good swimmer too—I had learned well at Bondi. Near the end of my stay at Randwick High I won the Combined High Schools breaststroke championship at the famous North Sydney Olympic Pool. I went on to the State titles, but they went a bit too quickly for me there. Boxing was another sporting love, I did a fair bit of boxing myself and the pale-skinned southpaw Vic Patrick was my special idol. I saw Patrick fight, but the small problem of no money meant that my interest in the fights was mainly via an ear to the family wireless on a Monday night and a scrapbook in which newspaper clippings were lovingly pasted.

But with me, it was always going to be rugby league. As a Bondi Boy I fell in love with the local side, Easts. Five eighth Wally O'Connell was my football hero and to get to play with him later, as I did at Manly in 1951–52, was an absolute privilege. I used to go to all the Easts games—at the Sydney Cricket Ground and the Sydney Sports Ground—and Wally was always the centre of attention. He was a marvellous, marvellous tackler—a model for anyone . . . then or now. They used to talk about 'little' Wally but there was more to Wally than people figured. He was short, but chunky—a powerful, compact package, playing his football at pretty close to 13 stone (94kg).

Wally O'Connell became a guiding light in my life. He was a highly principled bloke and when we were together at Manly, I learned so much from him. He taught me plenty about football, and a lot about life—and the friendship formed then endures today.

When Easts won the competition in 1945 I was living at Manly, but was still a died-in-the-wool Tricolours' fan. Manly then were still a couple of years short of entering a team in the Premiership. I was at the '45 final when Easts' lock Dick Dunn scored 19 points to get the Tricolours home 22–18 over Balmain. It still seems strange to me that a later revolution of the merry-go-round of life brought me into close contact with Dick Dunn—over the long period of years that we worked together as administrators on the NSW and Australian Rugby Leagues. I admire Dick greatly; he's a wonderfully upstanding, honorable gentleman of the game. Rugby league's successes over the years have been built around the input of men such as Dick Dunn.

It was rugby league more than anything else that eased me into acceptance of a new life at Manly. At Manly High I was soon playing in the under five stone seven's team. I was a skinny little bloke; I would have been lucky to make five stone (36kg), wringing wet. At weekends, I expanded my 'career' still further in 1945 by joining the team from Freshwater Surf Club, and in that first year we won the D grade competition, beating Queenscliff 59–6. I remember the game well because they led us 6–0! In 1946 we had a remarkable ongoing battle with a team from Christian Brothers Old Boys. Both of us beat all the other sides easily, but every time we played, we finished up in a draw. In the final, at fulltime, it was 6-all and we played on. In the extra time both of us scored again, and the match was still deadlocked. Then, with a minute or so to go, we scored under the posts and won the game, 14–9. In fact, I scored the winning try, which was quite a thrill for a blow-in from the eastern suburbs. So it was after all that, and with not a struck match between us and the Old Boys side, that we went through the season undefeated.

It was at Freshwater Surf Club one weekend in 1947 that I became 'Arko'. It happened this way: I was a good beach sprinter, the best at the club, and after a particular Sunday on which I had won the club's beach sprint title, I eagerly sought out the newspaper the next morning, and thumbed through the results. And there it was, under the surf results: Freshwater, Beach Sprint, First: K. Arkansas. Arkansas! The boys at the surf club picked it up in a flash and before you could blink, I was . . . *Arko*. I have been known as Arko ever since.

Gradually, I settled into life in Manly. With its detachment from the 'big smoke' and its holiday air, the place soon enough had me under its spell. My attachment to the peninsula—'God's Country', as many of the locals call it—has never waned in all the years since. As a kid, accepting day by day that the move across the Harbour hadn't been such a bad one after all, I quickly got into the swing of things. With a pal from school, Dick Eve, I used to dive for coins off the Manly Wharf. People would throw change into a spot we knew as the 'Deep Hole' which was about six metres deep—and we'd be after it. The Yank servicemen made life even more exciting by hurling coins into the Harbour—*outside* the shark net. At the end of the day Dick and I would halve the pot. In my young summers in Manly it seemed that I spent my whole life in the water.

In winter, it was football. In '47 I was a member of the Freshy C grade side that won the title. Then when the 'A's were beaten in the preliminary final and had the right of challenge, I was called up into the A grade grand final. We won that, and so I had the bonus of playing in two premiership-winning teams in the one year. I went on to captain Freshy 'B's in 1948 and again in 1949 when we didn't lose a match. From my greenhorn beginning as a winger (I think) in my Randwick High days, I had by then graduated to half or five-eighth, with half back gradually emerging as the position which would be my speciality through a short, but interesting, career.

And so it rolled from there, steady progress up the football ladder for a young bloke who loved his weekend footie more than anything in the world. For we kids of the district there was an extra incentive now, too. Manly was elevated to first grade premiership status in 1947—as a sort of 'splinter' club off the major northside establishment, North Sydney, providing the inspiration we needed, and building district pride. I remember Manly's arrival on the bigger stage very well. I was a bit too young to be actively involved, of course, but my father, with some prescience, enrolled me as a club member, right from the start. Five bob a year I think it was and I've been there ever since.

Working my way through the district's junior representative sides, I arrived at the top rung in that structure, the President's Cup. From there, in 1949, the senior club called me to grade football. But it was a different world in those days, a world in which kids just played the game for enjoyment and formed wonderfully close bonds with their junior clubs. So when Freshwater convinced my parents to convince Manly Warringah *not* to call me up that year, well, I wasn't too upset at all. But I had ambition, sure, and it was with a great sense of pride that I became a 'Manly' player the following year, 1950—buzzing with excitement as I first pulled on the maroon and white jumper which was to be so much a part of my life for all the years that followed.

3

MANLY MAN

I left school at 15 as many kids did in those days, armed with the Intermediate Certificate I had earned at Manly Boys' High. Back then, there was no such thing as the luxury of a year off after school days; I went straight to work, joining the PMG (Australia Post, these days). At the modest stipend offered of one pound, 13 shillings a week, I became a junior postal officer, which sounded quite impressive when people asked me what career I had taken on. In the fair dinkum department, I was a telegram boy, and the tough area around East Sydney, Kings Cross and Darlinghurst was my 'beat'. I worked nights, so as you can imagine, I saw some colourful sights in that raw, rough part of the world. They were days when the legendary hard man Frank 'Bumper' Farrell ruled the roost at Darlo Police Station. In and around the crims and the cops and the street girls I whizzed on my PMG bike—wide-eyed and quick enough to scoot away from any trouble.

I was a telegram boy for a couple of years, enjoying what I was doing, but ever dreaming of the weekend, and football. Then late in the '40s, I moved on from the PMG, to become an office boy at the smallgoods manufacturer, Thomas Playfair's. After a while, I graduated to a clerical position, and as a junior clerk I got to know my way around the place. Most of all I used to enjoy mixing with the blokes in the factory—and there were some bloody hard men among them. It was there that I first met Peter McLean who I was to meet again on a different arena somewhat later. Peter became captain of Western Suburbs club and our paths crossed more than once on the football field. I can still picture him and some of those other big tough blokes at Playfair's, lumping beef carcasses around as if they were made of cotton wool.

The Playfairs who owned the place were very much rugby *union* people. David Playfair, a good union player and surf swimmer, gave me a lift home one afternoon. I can still remember the roaring argument that developed over the respective merits of league and union. Things got so heated at one stage that I was on the verge of getting out of the car and walking the remainder of the journey. Oh yeah, I was a true believer all right. Even then.

I'm sad to say that I haven't still got my first Manly jumper from 1950. Either the moths got it long ago, or maybe it was an over-enthusiastic spring clean-up. I can't remember. What I do know is that it meant the world to me back then. At football clubs in those sandwich-and-cup-of-tea days, that was about *all* you got—the jumper. You had to provide all the rest of the gear yourself, and wash it all after the days you had been rolling in the mud at some forlorn suburban ground.

In my first year there, none of us had a car, except for one of our forwards Sandy Herbert, who had an old battered ute he used at work. For the rest of us, the travelling to and from training was by public transport. It's a little different in the players' car park these days; nowadays you can't move without bumping into a BMW or a four-wheel-drive. But if things were relatively primitive, the fun factor was never less than high.

Training in those days was just a bit of a get-together on Tuesday and Thursday nights, some ball work in the gloom. The lighting set-ups at grounds then weren't quite as sophisticated as they are today. There wouldn't even be a beer after training. They were the days of six o'clock closing, and all the watering holes would have their doors well and truly shut by the time we had finished our run. On match days we'd meet the coach half an hour or so before the game and have a yarn. Life was simpler then.

I recall one early training afternoon at Brookvale Oval on which my great mate Gordon Willoughby, who had come across from Norths in '47, and I were the only blokes in the dressing room. Suddenly the door swung open and in came Sandy Herbert brandishing a live green grass snake. He had somehow acquired it at the Royal Easter Show which was in full swing at the time. Now, the list of things that footballers seem to share a fear of would include: flying, not getting paid as much as they reckon they should be paid . . . and snakes. Gordon and I were certainly terrified of the bloody thing. With Sandy twirling the damned thing around his head, giving every indication that he was about to throw it, we both took off, hurtling across the oval. The only problem was that we were both stark naked. I'd like to think that was a ground-breaking moment in rugby league history—the game's first streak.

Football season 1950 arrived—and I played the first three third grade matches for Manly. On the Tuesday night team sheet the next week I was listed in reserve grade. Then, towards the end of the season came the call-up I had hoped for; for three matches which filled me with enthusiasm and hope for the future I became a premiership first grader.

Manly's 1950 season was nowhere near what it should have been. In a spirit of great anticipation and expectation that year, the club had signed champion Test five-eighth Wally O'Connell as captain-coach. But politics reared its ugly head as it was (and is) prone to do now and then in rugby league. After the 1948 Kangaroo tour which was an outstanding success for him, Wally had joined a South Coast club in 1949. When he attempted to take up his new contract at Manly in 1950, his former club Easts appealed to the NSWRL's Residential and Status Committee which ruled that he was not qualified to play for Manly, and must return to Easts. Wally O'Connell is a man of principle, and there was a strong principle involved in that long-ago dispute. Refusing to buckle, he declared he would stand down from playing football in 1950, and be non-playing coach of Manly. It was a brave and honorable decision, although one which cost O'Connell a certain place in what was to be an historic Australian Ashes victory over Great Britain.

Manly paid for the League's intransigence too. With Wally on the sidelines and not on the paddock we had a moderate year, finishing down the ladder and well out of contention.

The bulk of my season—played out in the lower grades—was under the direction of two different coaches named Mullins. I started out in Thirds under Reg Mullins, a wonderful bloke, although I didn't have that much to do with him as a football coach. My step up to the Seconds linked me up with George (Barney) Mullins (no relation to Reg), a former Balmain player. Gee, he taught me a lot about football. We had a series of moves that he had devised, clever intricate patterns that really made you think about the possibilities of the game.

I remember my first game in first grade. It was against Parramatta at Brookie, I didn't play well and we lost, 18–5. An inauspicious debut. Frankly, I was overawed that day, although coach O'Connell had already begun in his skilful way to instil the necessary confidence in me to begin the process of making me believe in myself. I played five eighth that day, marking a balding, older bloke who probably ended the afternoon figuring the kid in No. 6 opposite him hadn't presented him with too many problems.

It was a beginning and, pleasingly, I was able to take the next step as a fair dinkum first grader in 1951. My story is the story of countless players down the years—of a door opening for me unexpectedly, of an opportunity taken. In the first match of 1951 against St George, Manly's first grade half Perce 'Peblo' Pritchard was injured, and the next Tuesday night I got the call-up. I never played lower grade football again. In the next two seasons of a career which, as chance had it, disappeared as quickly as it had begun, I played 45 first grade games for Manly, 57 in all grades—and loved every moment of it.

4

GRAND FINAL DAZE

I suppose you could say that my fair dinkum big-time football career lasted three years and two-and-a-half matches. I'll tell you about the three years first. A confirmed halfback by then, I became a permanent member of Manly's first grade team in 1951, the year that Puig-Aubert and the fabulous Frenchmen brought a football revolution to our shores. It was the fifth year of Manly's senior premiership life and for a young footballer of ambition, a great time to be alive.

Called to first grade after the opening game of the year, I didn't miss another match, going all the way with the team to the grand final—a thrilling and unexpected experience for both the club and the district considering our tender years. For my efforts I received the princely sum of 202 pounds which doesn't sound much in these days of $800,000 a season contracts. But I was happy; I had a Manly jumper, a first grade spot and a few quid to make life just that little bit better.

The Manly achievement of '51 was something very special, though lost in the mists of time these days. We were so new as a football club, and yet on a formula of talent, spirit and good coaching we went all the way to the grand final. For us, the season was just one week too long. The red hot Souths side of that time were three-to-one-on favourites to take the title before the semis kicked off. They had streeted the field during the season, mustering 33 premiership points to our second-placed 22. But in a brawling semi final match there came a huge upset, with St George smashing the Rabbitohs 35–8. Our equally dominant victory over Wests in a semi (37–9) left us to face Saints in the final—with minor premiers Souths sitting back with the right of challenge in the grand final.

The nature of the final, in which the two sides battered each other from start to finish, effectively killed the chances of either in a grand final. As it turned out it was Manly who got through, bringing off an 18–8 victory over St George in what was undoubtedly the singular outstanding triumph of the club's young life to that point. But the price was heavy. Our captain-coach Wally O'Connell snapped his right wrist in the final, and so was out of the grand final, and Gordon Willoughby was dragging a serious leg injury and was strapped up like a square-gaiter when he took the field in the grand final. In short, we were ripe for the picking . . .

And boy, didn't Souths do a job on us. With winger Johnny 'Whacka' Graves running in four tries, they smashed us 42–14 and won their second successive premiership. For the first time ever the grand final was played on a Sunday, at Sydney Sports Ground—with the SCG being off limits, owing to preparations already being underway for the cricket season. For us it was a bitter–sweet occasion—to get as far as the premiership decider, then to take such a towelling.

But it was no disgrace to fall to a team like South Sydney. They were a sensational outfit, laced with so many great players, and playing their traditional style of free-running football about as spectacularly as it could ever be played. I admired them greatly—Churchill, Graves, Cowie, Purcell, Hammerton and the rest. I especially admired Jack Rayner, one of the game's all-time great captains and a man who led by example. There is no doubt that I was influenced by the Souths' style when my own coaching career began later in the '50s. It is a source of pleasure to me that the Manly style has always been a free flowing one, of great crowd appeal. And I know that my own embracing of that style as a coach came from the Souths' example of the early '50s. I thought they were a terrific team and I loved the way they played: the free movement of the ball; the switching of the point of attack; the constant sense of adventure in their football.

Our home ground in '51 was Brookvale Oval, just as it is for the Sea Eagles today. But it was a vastly different place then, a basic, no-frills suburban ground. I especially remember a game against Souths there in season 1951 on Anzac Day. The crowd was huge for that time, a record 9,447, with people four and five deep on the sidelines (the ground holds 28,000 or so these days). The match is part of South Sydney legend owing to the fact that 'Whacka' Graves twice had to clear a channel through the mob as he lined up touchline goal shots. On the second occasion a wag in the crowd challenged him: 'I'll bet you won't kick this, Graves!' The colourful Whacka accepted the wager—and ran down the lane of spectators to kick the goal. They beat us 29–17.

The Sydney Cricket Ground was the game's Mecca. To get there for a Saturday 'match of the day' was an achievement in its own right and any player who walked through the gates there knowing he was about to get the chance to play on its famous ground would immediately have a great sense of occasion. We got our share of games there in the early '50s and I thought it was just terrific. But you paid a price for playing on the SCG. On the muddy days—which seemed plentiful at that time—the smell rising from the sticky Bulli soil was appalling. It would stay in your nostrils for days. And the ground was pure poison. You could bet that any cut or graze you suffered would become infected, and stay infected. In the showers after matches blokes would be scrubbing furiously at their grazes and cuts, determined to get the mud out. It rarely worked. But it was a grand, special place for all that. On the occasional times I go back there these days, I still get a buzz.

The memories flood back when I think of our Manly side of the early '50s. I think of the hard men of our rugged forward pack—the front row of Roy Bull, Kevin Schubert and Freddy Brown, a second row of Sandy Herbert and Jack Hubbard—a bloody great player—and with Georgie Hunter at lock. I think of our five eighth O'Connell, my idol . . . and Gordon Willoughby, such an athlete in the centres, with Warren

Arko

Simmons alongside . . . and Ronny Rowles, a fantastic goal-kicker, and fullback Ron Beaumont.

And I think of our fleet-footed freak of a winger Johnny Bliss. Bliss was a magnificent beach sprinter—no-one could beat him on sand—but unlike some other speedsters from the surf clubs, he was just as quick on grass. Light of frame, and razor sharp to grab any opportunity, he could run like a deer. And Blissy had fast feet. I don't think I've ever seen a player who could get into top gear so quickly. He would go from zero to 100 miles an hour in the blinking of an eye.

Speed was a great feature of the Manly sides of that era. Gee, we had some fliers. Johnny Bliss may have been the quickest of them, but there would have been no guarantees when you lined him up against blokes like Brian Allsop and Nick Yakich, both sub ten second 100 yard runners.

Speed has always been a great talking point in the game, ever since they first kicked a ball in Australia back in 1908. I don't think there's any doubt as we head towards the next millennium that the *game* itself is faster than ever before. But I doubt that today's quickest, with the possible exception of Parramatta's Shane Whereat, an accomplished professional athlete, would get anywhere near some of the fliers of the past— blokes like Bliss, Ken Irvine, Mike Cleary, Dudley Towers, David Irvine, Brian Allsop and quite a few others. It is a peculiar development considering we now have a decidedly faster game but one in which the quickest men lack the blistering pace of players of 30 and 40 years ago.

I digress. As was the way of things back then I probably had more to do with our hooker Kevin Schubert than just about anyone else in the team. Schubert was a wonderful player, and *very* demanding in what he wanted from his halfback. You had to put the ball in the scrum *just* right or you were in serious bother. We had all sorts of tricks, hand signals and the like, so that he knew exactly what I was doing as I approached the scrum to feed the pill in. There were so many tricks of the trade, so many different ways to approach the conundrum of the rugby league scrum. Halves and hookers have always been wily critters, and especially in those days, when scrums were such a contest.

Schubert and I worked endlessly to fine-tune our partnership; he was a terrific player, one of the first of a new breed of No. 12s who were damned good *footballers* as well as good hookers. Just before the era which took in my career I had of course heard of the 'old style' hookers—the blokes who used to sit in armchairs smoking pipes between scrums, but who were absolute wizards at getting the ball once the scrum packed down.

The scrum, frankly, has been a bloody headache in rugby league ever since the game was first played. It is a fine ideal—a fair contest between two packs to decide possession. But it was never really that; most often it was an ugly seething mass of arms and legs with the blokes wearing the No. 7 and No. 12 jumpers doing whatever they possibly could to stretch the rules—and win the ball. I have read the horrifying statistics of years gone by, of matches in which there were 60 or 70 scrums. Can you imagine that? I firmly believe that the game has evolved the right way—that, although the scrum in 1997 is no more than a very pale shadow of what it once was, it is also thoroughly in tune with what the public want. The last thing the fans want to see is a great heaving mass of bodies, collapsing and reforming. The scrums these days with a quick put-in and an almost certain result are in line with a faster and more open game which has to make itself as attractive as possible in the highly competitive bidding for the 1990s entertainment dollar.

My last year in Sydney football, 1952, started with immense promise. As grand finalists and one of the gun sides we started sensationally, and won eight of out first nine matches. We were beautifully placed to head on to the finals—and beyond. But injuries progressively disjointed us, with myself on that list and defeats in four of our last five games left us stumbling into a play-off with North Sydney for fourth spot in the semis. We took a walloping in that, 36–8 and so departed meekly from a season which had offered much. I played 18 of 19 first grade games, got some wraps and was looking forward to a long and fruitful career as a rugby league player.

But things can change, and quickly. Near the end of the year the former Test front rower and larger-than-life league character Ray Stehr had a yarn to me about moving to the country in

Arko

1953. Stehr was coaching the Country side then and put forward the case for me being able to enhance my career by a season or two in the 'bush'. Being a man of some action, Stehr arranged for the Parkes Club in Group 11 to make me an offer. It was no easy decision for me and especially so when Manly tried to talk me out of it—and offered me an upgraded contract. But the idea of a move had appeal; I was a player of some ambition, desperate to do well, in fact, and the thought was there that representative football could be a chance for me if I did well in the country. I could see it as a stepping stone, and so I contacted Parkes and said 'yes'. I had a picture in my mind—of being Country Firsts halfback and having a shot at the Sydney 'crack' whoever that might be. Keith Holman almost certainly. Country against Sydney . . . one on one. It provided a chance—and that's what I was looking for.

So, I packed my bags and went bush, taking the train west one day in the late summer of '53. For a time I boarded at the Cambridge Hotel and then I moved in with a couple of terrific people, Alan and Molly Petty, with whom I'm pleased to say I still have a wonderful friendship all these years later. The people of the town were just superb to me, and nothing has ever changed on all the trips I have taken back there over the years. I must say the weather can be a bit rough, though. Who could forget the extraordinary Australia–France Test played there in 1990? A simply unbelievable night of snow and ice and freezing wind—yet the loyal league fans of Parkes and surrounds still turned up in numbers, some 9,000 of them.

Yes, they are terrific people up there and I love them dearly for the kindness and compassion they showed me way back in '53 in the aftermath of a dreadful day. In a single moment on Parkes' Pioneer Oval, my football career ended. To this day, I can only be thankful that it wasn't my life. Probably any thought of the town of Parkes should chill me to the bone after the destruction of my ambitions and dreams there on that day. But it doesn't; I'm always happy to go back. What happened to me was no more than a bad bounce of the ball—although one that sent my life in a dramatically different direction . . .

5

THE DAY IT RAINED FOREVER

I can remember it as clearly as if it was yesterday. A scrum on half way, ten or 12 metres in from the sideline. A balmy early autumn day in 1953 at Pioneer Oval, Parkes. At halfback I gathered the ball which our hooker Ian Walsh (bound for later fame at the highest level) had won from the scrum and headed right, towards the blind side. I ran straight for the opposition winger, at the same time calling our winger to 'come inside'. As he did, I turned and dummied to him, then held the ball and accelerated *past* the opposing wingman and off down the touchline. If I had passed the ball that day my whole life may very well have been different. Of all the things that have happened to me over the years nothing has ever been (or surely will be!) more dramatically indicative of the truth that a life can change in a single moment, on a single decision, than on that afternoon in Parkes . . .

I had been in the town only a short while, played a couple of preliminary games, and been happy with both my form and the prospects ahead. This day was the first real 'test'—an inter-group match, from which the Western Division team would be drawn for the annual Country Championships. And from that tournament would come the Country sides to play City. This day was stage one in the Ray Stehr–Ken Arthurson plan.

And there I was in full flight down the right flank, the wind in my hair, the crowd cheering. The winger I had fooled with my dummy pass had turned quickly and was in hot pursuit. I was quick . . . but so was he. Close to the tryline, the opposing full-back came at me hard from the left hand side. I veered in towards him, then out—an old and trusted weapon in the armament of many wingers. His hesitation was enough to get me around him and sliding for the corner for the try. I made it with a foot or two to spare inside the corner post, but the confrontation with the fullback had slowed my pace and the winger was on me now.

As I slid low across the tryline, the bloke chasing me launched himself through the air in a crouched position, knees forward. In a moment frozen in my memory, they arrived together—my head and his knees—on ground made concrete-hard by a long dry spell. The timing was unbelievably bad. If my head had been an inch or two above the ground it may have been OK. Instead, I was trapped in the critical millisecond between hard knees and equally hard ground. In the times I have talked about it since—and that's not something I particu-larly enjoy doing—I have likened it to the act of smashing a kerosene tin on cement, with a sledgehammer. It happened in the blink of an eye—with great speed and great force, a classic footballer's nightmare of something going terribly wrong.

The rest is a haze. I only remember getting to my knees, and not being able to rise any further, and a booming voice from the nearby oval fence: 'Get an ambulance from the hospital!' They laid me back on the ground on the spot where I had scored the try, made me as comfortable as I could be and waited for the ambulance which rushed me to Parkes Hospital, where I was to stay for three weeks before being transferred to Sydney.

I had suffered a severely depressed fracture of the skull, my head misshapen like an orange dropped from a ten-storey build-ing. Fellow Parkes player Ian Walsh's later quote on the injury was enough to make you wince: 'He had a hole in his head into which you could have put a cricket ball.' The depression in my skull that I suffered that afternoon remains to today. So bad was the injury that in hospital I was given 48 hours to live. The Bishop of Wilcannia held a special Mass, offering prayers that I might somehow pull through.

It was a shocking, life-threatening injury—far worse than I realised at the time. I was in wonderful physical condition in those days and within ten days of the accident I thought I was travelling well when I could sit up for an hour or so and play cards. But it wasn't that easy. After a long rehabilitation punctuated by headaches and dizziness, they cut open my head again in a major operation in the Masonic Hospital in Ashfield, removing fragments of bone which lay against my brain. If just one of those shards had penetrated the brain, well, I wouldn't be telling you this story today . . .

On the night of the accident, Western Division selectors picked their team for the Country Championships. Unknowing, as I lay in my hospital bed, I was named as halfback and captain. And d'you know what? That year Country beat Sydney 28–27 in the annual tussle—and half a dozen of the Country boys won themselves State jumpers. Ray Stehr's plan had worked pretty close to perfection . . . except for one thing: I was finished as a footballer.

The Parkes *Western People* of April 27, 1953 carried this report of my misfortune:

> Ken Arthurson, coach to the Parkes first grade league team, was admitted to the District Hospital yesterday suffering from a fractured skull sustained while he was playing with the team at Pioneer Oval. The game between southern zone and northern zone was in the early stages when Ken fell over the goal line and another player, who was following him, fell on top of him, striking Ken's head with his knee. The ambulance, which was in attendance, rushed the injured man to the District Hospital. Arthurson, who has been living at the Cambridge Hotel, came to Parkes from Manly, Sydney, about three weeks ago and yesterday's match was the third in which he had taken part since his arrival here. He is likely to have a prolonged stay in hospital.

Funnily enough, I had a mate in the hospital the following week. Ian Walsh broke his leg in a club game the next weekend—and finished up in the next bed. And the bloke who did me the damage, whose name I have long since forgotten, came to see me to try to put into words his regrets and concerns, never an easy thing. I never blamed him for what happened. Sure, he was out to get me because I had beaten him badly with a little sleight of hand that had come off. But he had never intended for it to finish like *that*. I never saw him again. Once or twice I allowed myself to wonder about his career, about how it had worked out for him.

Mine was certainly over in that fleeting moment. The doctors and specialists warned me that to play football again was to take an unreasonable risk. 'Don't even consider it,' they said. Well, I can reveal here for the first time that in fact I *did* play a couple more games of football—though nothing at a serious level. I recall in the mid-'50s playing a match for Manly Police against the Vice Squad. Just don't tell the doctors.

But in reality, it had effectively all ended for me in a crunch and a flurry of dust on a country field. It wasn't an easy thing to live with; to wake up one morning at 23 years of age with a pounding headache and begin the process of accepting that all the ambitions you ever had in the game you loved—to win a premiership, to play representative football . . . maybe even Test football—were gone. A door had slammed shut on my life, but the old cliché about another one opening is generally true, and so it was with me.

Back at home at Manly when I was well enough, I faced a new start. The funny thing was I still had ambitions bubbling away in me concerning football and that had more than a little to do with me turning to coaching. It happened in 1954 when I had regained my health and enthusiasm after the trauma of the previous year. Manly took a punt and appointed me third grade coach, and a very odd year to get into coaching it turned out to be. Season '54 was the one in which Manly—by now the Seagulls—made a bold decision to take a completely different approach to coaching and to virtually introduce 'coaching by committee'. It was a time of experiment and change in Australian sport and two of the men at the cutting edge of the revolution, Professor Frank Cotton and swim coach and pentathlete Forbes Carlile, were co-opted onto the Manly coaching panel. Ray Norman, who gained much deserved renown for his book and film, *Football Fundamentals*, was the head coach, and the much-respected Frank Hyde, ex-star player bound for great things as a commentator, was part of the coaching squad, too. Bruce Ryan the ex-GPS sprinter and Newtown winger had the Seconds. Frank Hyde recalls that we were known collectively as 'The Pink Pill Boys'.

Professor Cotton and Carlile were into all sorts of experimentation in sport, based around such things as the importance of correct diet and hypnosis. Both no doubt had an influence on the success that Australia was to achieve two years later at the Melbourne Olympics. Ray Norman was a technically outstanding coach—and the school team from Rose Bay Public that he used for his film outlining the fundamentals of the game was his pride and joy. They were indeed a model team, wonderfully skilled in playing the game the 'right' way. But I recall Reub Hudson telling me he went down one day and watched them play a tough outfit from Plunkett Street. The boys from Plunkett Street put on the hard stuff from the kickoff and by fulltime had not only won the game handsomely but had also belted the s—— out of the Rose Bay boys. I always thought there might be a message in that.

The coaching-by-committee experiment in '54 wasn't any runaway success. But it wasn't a failure either. The Firsts missed the semis by only a point and the Reserves won the competition. My boys had a struggling year, marking a modest introduction to coaching by yours truly. But they appointed me to the Thirds again in 1955, another struggling year, and then to the Reserves in 1956, which produced my first real taste of success as a football coach. Highly competitive from the start, we went all the way to the grand final—to a desperately close 10–6 loss to South Sydney there.

The administrative career which was to sweep me on to bigger things—heights I never even began to dream of—had kicked off by then, too. Essentially, that all happened without my knowledge. Back in '54 Gordon Willoughby, unbeknownst to me, had nominated me for a place on the Manly committee. Gordon must have spotted something about me that I had no clue about myself. The truth was that I had not the slightest interest in throwing my hat into the ring for the committee.

Arko

When I learned about my nomination, I confronted Gordon, as close a pal then as he is 40 years on today.

'Jeezus, what have you done to me?' I asked him.

'I want you to stand—and I think you should,' said Gordon.

So I thought about it for a while, left the nomination there—and got the nod. I've been an official ever since, well, until February 1997 that is, when I decided that the background noise I was hearing was the ref blasting on the fulltime whistle. Then, I knew it was time to go.

The coaching segment which was the sandwich filling in my long years with Manly—player, coach, then administrator—was a time of great enjoyment. In all, I coached Manly teams for eight consecutive seasons, my own enthusiasm and ambition nicely tuned to that of an exuberant young club hungry for early success. For me, coaching got *very* serious early in 1957 when a letter arrived confirming that I had been appointed first grade coach for that year's season. It all came as something of a shock. After all, the man I had beaten for the job was something of a legend—the great five eighth and ex-Australian player Pat Devery who had coached Manly in 1956. The letter confirming my surprise appointment was couched in the slightly old-world language of Manly's secretary Jack Munro. Dated 1 February 1957 it read:

> *Dear Sir,*
>
> *I have to acknowledge your letter of the 21st ult, making application for the position of non-playing coach for the first or reserve grade team for season 1957.*
>
> *I now have to advise you that the letter was dealt with by the committee of the club, last evening, and as the result thereof you was (sic) selected to the position of first grade coach for season 1957, on the terms set out in your letter, viz, a first grade player's bonus.*
>
> *Congratulations on your selection.*
> *P.S. Training will commence at Brookvale Oval on Tuesday 19th February.*

I had just turned 27 when the mailman delivered me the official confirmation of news I had already heard on the grapevine. I was equally thrilled and daunted by the prospect. After all, I would be coaching blokes older than myself, hard heads who really knew the ropes. At 27 I was (and the record remains), I believe, the youngest-ever non-playing coach of a first grade team in the Sydney premiership history. I think Phil Gould was 30 when he won the premiership with Canterbury as a first-term first grade coach in 1988. Back in '57, at 27 years of age, I figured I was ready for the challenge. I knew fitness would be a big part of it and the more I thought about it, the more I reckoned I could do something with them.

6

COACH ARKO

In March 1957, the fine old Sydney *Sun* sportswriter W.F. 'Bill' Corbett, a member of an illustrious newspaper family, wrote a story in which the new Manly coach set out his hopes and dreams. It was the first time I had been interviewed as a first grade football coach and I responded this way:

> My coaching idea essentially is to indicate a pattern of football to be applied throughout the season. I will make sure that the players are properly conditioned. Biggest features will be team spirit and co-operation of all the players. Speed, open football and fitness are my aims.

Well, for the five years that followed, I think that pretty much said it all. My approach was an intertwining of two strands: firstly, all that I had learned from Wally O'Connell, a man I greatly respected and secondly, the adventurous South Sydney style that I admired so much. I reckoned that was the way to play football—to let the ball run fast and free, albeit within a framework in which the blokes fully addressed their obligations in defence. But I didn't want anyone in the side who wasn't prepared to 'use' the ball. I was chuffed in 1957 when the side was afforded the tag 'The Flying Seagulls'. That year, for the first time at Manly, we adopted a synchronised system of coaching through the grades. Any player called up from the Seconds (coached by Neville Pearce) or the Thirds (coached by Bill Crowley) could immediately slot into the first grade pattern.

To provide incentive and build a 'hunger' in the team we considered in 1957 and then introduced for the 1958 season a new pay deal, one that I pushed through the committee. For our players there were no sign-on fees or guarantees, apart from a one-off payment to imports, but we offered good money for achievement—30 pounds for a win, 20 pounds a draw and 15 pounds a loss. It is still the best way. Players contemplating vast sign-on fees stretching over many seasons inevitably have to battle the temptation of sliding into the comfort zone. Incentive money—you get paid when you win—certainly adds an edge to any sporting team.

1956 had been a moderate year (seven wins in 18 games) and there had been no off-season buying programme to give fans much basis for hope that 1957 was going to be any better. But I was full of personal hope and youthful enthusiasm—and set my goals high, to achieve whatever we could with the players on hand. We had a new look to go with the new spirit—a flashy maroon jersey with a big white seagull on the chest and two white stripes down each arm. The Seagulls who later became Sea Eagles have changed their plumage from time to time. We started with maroon jumpers and a white V, then switched to a broken bars design—before the big bird appeared on the front in '57. I knew that fitness was always going to play a big part that year and we worked bloody hard in that area. And being something of a fitness fanatic myself, I didn't ask the players to do anything that I didn't tackle myself. It took a bit of getting used to—directing senior blokes like Roy Bull, our skipper George Hunter, a real hard man from Kurri Kurri, and Rex Mossop—but to be honest, I relished the challenge. It was a season in which we sort of sneaked up on them. Expectations outside the club weren't too high, but we started well, losing only one of our first five games—and that to the premiers St George—then went right on with it.

In fact the Saints were the only team who had our measure in what turned out to be a magic season. We went all the way to the grand final—our three finals games drawing an aggregate of 136,309 fans to the Sydney Cricket Ground, an indication of the sort of crowd appeal our free-running style attracted during the year. On the big day they were far too good for us, winning 31–9 after we had held them to 9–4 at halftime. For their efforts the Manly players earned themselves record bonuses of 326 pounds . . . and so did the coach.

I stayed for five fruitful and wonderfully enjoyable seasons as Manly first grade coach, and this was the record:

1957   23 premiership points (second on the ladder). Finished second.

1958   23 points (third). Finished fourth.

1959   22 points (third). Finished second.

1960   20 points. Finished sixth.

1961   20 points (third). Finished fourth.

They were exciting seasons, filled with hope, all of them, and each one progressively adding to Manly's appetite to take the big step—and win a premiership. Probably we were unlucky. It just happened that the emergence of a Manly team of consistent performance and ability coincided with the rise and rise (and rise!) of a true footballing juggernaut in the team from St George. In those years we often threatened them, beating them on occasions, but could never master them when the chips were down. I suppose we consoled ourselves with the thought that no other team could manage it either.

Twice we ran into them in grand finals (1957, 1959) and twice they were too good for us. Without a doubt, Saints were the best club side I saw in my years in football. Very likely they were the best ever. Simply put, they 'jumped' the field. They had the first Leagues Club in town, they had wise men who came back from England bringing winning ideas with them (Ken Kearney, Harry Bath) and they had a simply outstanding recruitment programme, built on a policy of identifying 'gaps' in the side a couple of years ahead . . . and then filling them with the likes of men such as Brian Clay, Johnny Raper and Kevin Ryan. In '59 we went in as considerable underdogs against them, but still with hopes high, even though Saints had gone through the season unbeaten. Our preliminary final win over Wests (14–13) had us ready for the big day, but Saints were just too good and too tough, and beat us 20–nil. The bookies were giving us 10-start at even money. It was the day of the famous Rex Mossop–Harry Bath fracas, which resulted in referee Darcy Lawler giving the pair of them first use of the showers. Rex showed all the courage in the world that day. Against Wests in the final he had his cheekbone smashed when the big blond Magpies prop Mark Patch caught up with him in an off-the-ball incident. Rex's problems with the injury were highly publicised during the week leading up to the grand final and from the kickoff, Saints targeted him. It was a tough, cruel game in those days. It was about ten minutes from the end when 'The Moose' decided he had had enough and he and Bath singled out in one of the most notorious one-on-one scraps seen at the old ground. With the words, 'Righto, you two gentlemen—piss off!' referee Lawler despatched the pair of them to the dressing rooms once he had finally regained some semblance of order. Mossop and Bath these days are the best of mates, rugby league being that sort of game.

In recent years I read with interest speculation about alleged 'hot' matches in that era. Noel Kelly's book *Hard Man* contains a sensational claim that Western Suburbs had been robbed by referee Darcy Lawler in the grand final of 1963. Kelly and other Wests players including Jack Gibson were privy to information that Lawler had effectively backed St George to win the match, via an outside agent. These are not happy claims for the game of rugby league—but such things, of course, must be confronted.

I have no inside knowledge of the events of 1963 but I will just say this: that I hold to today the most profound doubts about circumstances surrounding the semi final we played against Balmain in 1961 . . . under referee Darcy Lawler. It was a brute of a day—a match played in quagmire conditions, the ball chased this way and that by a swirling wind. We faced the breeze in the first half and did a mighty job, grafting out a 5–2 lead thanks to a brilliant kick-and-chase try by our fullback Ron Willey. But at halftime something alarming happened. As I came back to the dressing room Jack Gibson, then a front rower with Wests, pulled me to one side.

'Ken, there's some disquieting news,' he said. 'The betting indicates that you're "off".'

I said to him: 'That doesn't make any sense: we're ahead 5–2, they're a man short (Balmain's Bob Boland had been taken off injured in the first half) and we're running with the wind.'

'I'm just telling you what's going on,' said Gibson.

Anyhow, we went back out into the mud in the second half and got beaten 10–5, thanks to a string of penalty goals kicked by Keith 'Golden Boots' Barnes. Penalties in the match ran against us 16–7 and the second half seemed a never-ending blast of Lawler's whistle accompanied by his arm going up in Balmain's direction.

Coincidence? Well, I don't know for sure, and I'll never know. My preferred position is to *not* believe something untoward happened that day. Over the years I've heard many stories of referees favouring this team or that, but I've got to honestly say that I don't know of any time that a ref has been 'crook'. But on this muddy, miserable day at the SCG . . . well, I had my doubts. I'll just leave it at that.

I noted in gathering material for this book an interesting item that appeared in Bill Corbett's column 'Sports Diary' in the Sydney *Sun* on 13 December 1957. It read:

> The sky's the limit for signing on rugby league players. Bids and counter-bids are mounting so much each season that club secretaries have been contemplating a meeting to put a limit on the ante. A lot of good that would do—the bartering would all go underground. The clubs can't squeal when they're so willing to deal out the money.

Forty years ago it was when Bill wrote that—and nothing's bloody well changed. Amazing really, that no-one seems to have learnt after all this time, and that the steep inflationary spiral just keeps heading upwards. I've been saying since the early 1960s—from when I became Manly secretary in 1963—that unless there is eventually some way of curbing player payments, unless some sanity eventually prevails, then we are heading for disaster. The fact of it is, then or now, the game just doesn't generate enough money to pay the players the disproportionate sums they are offered. That is especially the case in the aftermath of seasons 1995–96 when player contracts soared to stratospheric levels as unholy war broke out between the ARL and Super League.

Like everything in life, rugby league payments need a firm system of checks and balances. Yet the problem that was evident to Bill Corbett 40 years ago is still unsolved today—notwithstanding the genuine efforts that have been made over the years. As the ARL clubs headed into a future clouded into some uncertainty they settled on a salary cap of $4 million for each club. But almost as soon as the figure was set, the quibbling began. The thing about it is this: they can make it $8 million as far as I am concerned, but all that would mean is that instead of giving players $400,000 a contract, they'd give them $800,000. The spiral is ever upwards, vicious, and very likely to send clubs broke. Payments to players in the 1990s have got totally out of hand. It's just ridiculous. There was a point reached in 1990 at which we felt we may have reined them in with the imposition of a salary cap in conjunction with a player draft. But, even though it is the platform on which some other games build their programme (AFL and NFL), there was a small group in league who decided they had to oppose it. In having it thrown out—even though just about everyone agreed that it was unquestionably for the greater good of the game—they did rugby league an immense disservice.

The thing that worries me now is that success-hungry officials are close to killing the goose that laid the golden egg—the Leagues clubs that have underwritten football for years. For many years the licensed clubs have supported football clubs to an enormous degree. But they just can't give *all* their profits to footballers and one day soon it may reach the point where members jack up and say: 'Hang on—this is *our* money, and you've gone too far.'

The problem is quite simple—to identify, anyway, if not to fix. It just involves football clubs paying players too much money. Nothing else. It has been said many times that league is the most heavily subsidised game in the world. Unless commonsense arrives at some time . . . well, I don't know where we're heading. And things are getting tougher. Over everything that will happen in Australian sport in the years immediately ahead, the shadow of the 2000 Olympic Games hangs heavy. Sponsorship money once available in other areas will no longer be there. Yet clubs continue to throw vast fistfuls of money at players in that endless search for 'instant' success. Even News Ltd with their seemingly bottomless pit of money are starting to look askance at the mounting costs of being involved in football.

It's fascinating in 1997 to reflect on Bill Corbett's words from 1957 and ponder a sad reality: that the messages about fair dinkum, sensible, responsible management of football clubs—in line with the game's finance-generating possibilities—have not even yet sunk in . . . after all these years.

Driven by the ambitions of the Wests' 'millionaires', inflation was at full gallop in the game at the time I made my next big decision. There is a conveniently forgotten irony from those years. In more recent times I have copped more than a little flak over Manly Club's buying policies—over the players we signed from such clubs as Souths and Wests. But the undisputed fact of it is that it was Western Suburbs who kicked off the era of the big-spending clubs, building what became known as the 'Million Dollar Team'. Wests recruited widely and enthusiastically, mustering some of the great players of the era—Dick Poole, Harry Wells, Ian Moir, Peter Dimond, Darcy Russell, Arthur Summons—into black and white jumpers. Inflation and active recruitment were upon the game long before Manly swung into gear . . .

In 1961 I quit as Manly coach. I figured that five years in the business was quite long enough—by then everyone knows everyone else a bit *too* well. So I pulled the plug and took the next step—I became a club official.

As we headed into the premiership finals that year I penned some words for the Sydney *Sun* which summed up the gnawing hunger that existed within the Manly club. I wrote:

> It must surely be Manly's turn to crack the rugby league jackpot with a first grade premiership win after all our near misses. We have done everything but win the premiership . . .

A couple of days later Balmain beat us 10–5 in that highly contentious semi final in the mud. We had missed out again, and my coaching career was over.

7

THE HON.
SEC.

Jack Munro who preceded me as secretary of Manly-Warringah club was an official of the old style. In his later years Jack was rather portly, to put it gently, and there was a joke within the club that Manly training used to consist of twice around Jack Munro, then home. He was a wonderfully loyal servant of the club, a meticulous old guy. I used to marvel at his memory, his grasp of detail. One day, I learned his secret: Jack plunged a hand into a coat pocket and came up with dozens of scraps of paper, each one containing some piece of currently pertinent information. Jack was also secretary of Freshwater Surf Club, although not a man of much *direct* athletic involvement himself. In fact on the day of his funeral in 1963 when the hearse bearing Jack's coffin broke down they hoisted the coffin out of the back and put it in the club surfboat. They reckoned that was the only time Jack was ever in a surf boat—even though he had been secretary of the club for many years.

In 1962, following my retirement as first grade coach, I became Manly treasurer. My working life, running parallel with my football involvement, had changed markedly by that time. I had left school after completing my Intermediate Certificate, but realising the advantages higher qualifications could bring me, I went to night school—and gained my Leaving Certificate. Thus armed, I joined the Public Service, firstly in the PMG

Department and then, on appeal, into the Department of Trade. It was a place of what they used to call 'accelerated promotions'—days in which import licensing was a fact of business life—and many of us were experts in that field. But when the system of import licensing folded up, there was a great deal of casting around to decide what they were going to do with we Department of Trade people. Many were shipped off to Canberra. But in a great stroke of personal good fortune, at that time the Attorney General started up the Australian Police College at North Head and I was offered the position as Administrator of the College. Geographically, and job-wise, it was quite a windfall—and I grabbed the chance.

It was the early 1960s and a time of considerable change in my life. I was no longer a football coach, I now had both a new career, and a family to attend to. In 1952 I had married Judith Tobin. In the years that followed came the arrival of three children, Susan, Stephen and Mark. Judy was to die, far too young, in 1986—a tragic and jolting event in the lives of all of us, and a reminder of how fragile life is.

In 1963 there came another change in my life. On the death of Jack Munro, who had been Manly secretary for the duration of the club's life, I was elected club secretary. I can't remember the wage—although the word 'modest' comes to mind. In collecting material for this book though, an interesting note came to light, listing in handwriting unknown the salaries of club secretaries in 1967. Mine was a 'package' of $110 a week—a salary of $80 a week, an allowance of $10 and a car allowance of $20. Top of the tree in the wages department were Charlie Gibson (Souths) and Merv Cartwright (Penrith) both dragging in the vast sum of $130 a week. Somehow it all pales into insignificance in the wake of the huge and ridiculous amounts thrown around at the height of the Super League madness. My full time appointment as secretary was the next step towards the career in football that lay ahead, and also to my first established link with Phillip Street and its workings. League headquarters.

As club secretary, I became a Manly delegate to the NSW Rugby League, and a regular at the Monday night meetings in the big old committee room on the first floor. I loved those nights, loved the cut and thrust of the debate, the mateship that existed among the delegates. Those Mondays always followed a pattern. We would meet in the downstairs bar of the Leagues Club, have a beer or three, and thus fuelled—to varying degrees—climb the dingy stairs to the meeting. I just missed the era of H. Jersey Flegg, a real old-style hard man by all accounts. Bill Buckley was the NSWRL president when I first went to Phillip Street, a tough, direct bloke who I admired a great deal. It always worried me, and still nags at me now, that Buckley had the wrong perception of me. I remember years ago some-one telling me—it might have been Ken McCaffery—of Buckley's opinion of Kevin Humphreys and myself—'the best two young delegates we have in the League'. But Buckley went on to venture the opinion that Arthurson didn't like him very much. It was only a small thing, but it worried me greatly. Not only did I like Bill Buckley—I really respected him.

I honestly don't know how he formed that view, although I must say some fierce and angry debating took place down there—maybe it stemmed from something said in the heat of the moment one night. The fact was that blokes like Kevin and myself—the 'young bulls'—used to have some shocking clashes with Bill. I think Bill probably formed the opinion that we were crooked on him—which we weren't. Jeez, it used to get heated down there, and now and then the odd punch would be thrown. I was there on the night of the infamous blue in which two red-faced officials wrestled through the committee room doors and spilled out into the corridor. And on one awful night Easts' delegate Jack Lynch died on the floor of the same com-mittee room after suffering a heart attack. I can still picture in my mind the sight of Parramatta's Jack 'Colonel' Argent work-ing desperately over Lynch, trying to revive him.

I learned a lot about rugby league and rugby league men on those long Monday nights at Phillip Street. No matter how fierce the tussle had been during the meeting itself, afterwards a keg would be tapped in the tiny bar in the corner, snacks wheeled in and peace and mateship in a shared interest would prevail. The night would end invariably the way it does after a good hard football match—some yarns and conviviality, an ale or two and some pleasure in an experience shared.

In May 1965 came further progress in my career—appointment as Manly's first fulltime secretary. Among my souvenirs I still have the letter of application I sent in for the job. It reads in part: 'You may be assured that I shall at all times conscientiously and diligently discharge my duties in the best interests of the club.' On the evening of 24 May 1965, I got the nod, making the big decision the next day to take the punt and leave the security of the Australian Police College. My appointment to a fulltime role at Manly followed hard on the heels of that of Frank 'Fearless' Facer, the game's first fulltime secretary (at St George).

My first appointment from 'in town'—Phillip Street—came that year too. I was given the job of co-manager, with Eric Cox, of the NSW team on its campaign in Queensland. We had a sensational team that season with the likes of Langlands, Gasnier, Irvine, Raper and Coote—and we bolted in to win the series 4–nil. There was something said on that campaign that has always stuck in my mind. It came after an additional game we played on tour—against North Queensland in Townsville, which NSW won 55–7. The next day NSW coach Harry Bath offered the opinion to the local papers that Queensland was behind the times in rugby league, and that training routines and methods of play needed to be updated. In Brisbane, the then Queensland coach Bob Bax was asked for his opinion on Bath's comments. 'Let's swap teams and see who wins then,' said Bob simply. Not a bad comeback.

I doubt if any new appointee was ever keener about a job than I was about being Manly secretary. I was constantly on the prowl for players—I didn't care where I had to go or how far I had to travel to see a prospect, or what sort of hours I had to work. When I think about it now I figure that I was truly driven. It seemed that we at Manly had been to the brink on so many occasions in our quest for a premiership. As a coach I had got close—but not close enough. Now I was in a position to bloody well make sure of it . . .

It was in 1965 that I made my most important signing in football—and the most important in the history of the club. I was well aware of Bob Fulton by then, although the first phone call from the coast that drew me to him is lost somewhere deep in my memory. I had watched him play as a schoolboy down the South Coast, and quickly realised that he was special. When I finally decided it was time to pounce, I had to negotiate a small minefield. A great mate of mine, Jackie Lumsden, was defiantly of the opinion that another South Coast player, Alan Maddelena, was a better prospect than Fulton. Jackie's advice pointed us firmly that way. But even though I knew Maddalena, who could run like a greyhound, was a fabulous prospect . . . I had no doubt that Fulton was going to be even better.

I knew too that he wasn't going to be easy to get. The chase for players of quality was as fierce then as it is now, and I knew I has going to have to get the jump on blokes like Charlie Gibson (Souths), Kevin Humphreys (Balmain), Peter Moore (Canterbury) and Frank Facer (Saints) if I was to sign Fulton. The fact was, however, that we were always the front runners. The news about him had not widely filtered through in Sydney—although anyone in Wollongong with half a brain who had seen him play knew they had seen a star in the making. He had one quality in him that attracted me more than anything else—a tremendous desire and determination to succeed. Even then, in those very early days, I had him tabbed as a future Manly captain. There was no doubt even way back then that he was a born leader. And I wanted him for Manly.

The crunch came when the blond-haired teenager got his opportunity in the Country Seconds side to play Sydney in 1965. In that side were a couple of other players who were to go on and make their mark in football up to international level—Terry Pannowitz and Gary Banks. Fulton was named at five eighth. He was 18, and 12 stone eight lbs (90kg). I well remember going along to that match with my fingers firmly crossed, hoping that he wouldn't attract too much attention. Well, he didn't. As can be the way of things in those games in which players find themselves alongside blokes they have probably never even met before, the young man who was to become one of the greatest of all Australian footballers didn't make too much of a splash.

But even that afternoon, anyone who had been watching

closely could have seen just by the way he positioned himself, by the way he passed the ball, by the sure way he made his tackles, that here was a player who knew what he was about. I didn't hesitate. I spoke to him after the game and made an arrangement for him to come to my office at Manly. It was there the next week that the deed was done; Fulton signed a modest contract. We shook hands, and Manly had a new footballer.

He really was just a fresh-faced kid when he came up to Sydney to join us in 1966. He had an uncle who lived at Frenchs Forest and I asked him how he felt about staying there.

'Oh, that'd be fine,' said Bob. 'He's a good old guy.'

At the time I was 37 and the uncle was about the same age. I thought, 'Gee, the kid probably sees me as an old bloke too.' Anyway, he arrived full of youthful spirit and enthusiasm for the 1966 season, walked straight into Manly's first grade team—and stayed there forever. He was an absolutely exceptional talent from day one and that never changed through the seasons of his long career.

I'll talk more about Fulton later. I'll just say now that his impact on the Sydney competition 30 years ago was like a bombshell. If ever there was an instant first grader, he was it. And I reckon the decision to leave him out of the 1967 Kangaroo tour, even though he was still only a kid, was a travesty of justice. It seemed that he had been groomed for the campaign in England and France.

Remarkably, in 1967 at 20 years of age he was chosen as captain-*coach* of City in the final Kangaroo tour trial against Country. They were obviously getting him ready—but they still managed to leave him out.

This is something that I've never said publicly before, but I suspect it was Bill Buckley's influence that knocked Fulton out of the tour. For some reason Buckley wasn't overkeen on him as a player at that stage—although Bill's opinion changed in the seasons that followed. The selectors did not cover themselves with glory on that particular occasion. In leaving out both Bob Fulton and Bob McCarthy (Souths) they ignored two of the greatest talents of modern football. Later events proved them sadly, badly wrong.

8

PESKY
RABBITS!

Football changed profoundly and forever in 1967. The arrival of the four-tackle rule, brainchild of the urbane English official Bill Fallowfield, meant that rugby league would never be the same again. In a small way, I'd like to think that I had something to do with the change . . .

There is a game that sticks in my mind from long ago. 1959 it was, the premiership final of that year between Wests and Manly. Wests, then in their 'millionaires' phase, had an all-star lineup; man by man we looked a bunch of moderates by comparison. Throwing away just about everything I believed about football, I changed tactics that day. As I have written, as a coach my football religion was that of fast, free movement of the ball, of adventure and attacking play. But on this day I figured there was little, if any, chance of us winning if we took on Wests in an open game. So we decided that if we lost the toss and ran into the breeze that we would do no more than lock the ball up. My final words to the team before they went out were these: 'Remember, if we've got the ball, they can't score.' They were the days, of course, of the unlimited tackle rule when teams could hang on to the ball for as long as they were able.

So, the boys from Manly headed out onto one of the most famous football grounds in the world and proceeded to play probably the most boring 40 minutes on record. We barely gave

Wests a sniff of the ball. A couple of times when it came their way they scored tries—but against the breeze we were able to hold them to 10–8 at halftime. For the second half I eased the reins just a little, and we came from behind to beat them 14–13 and thus qualify for the grand final. Straight after the match, Wests' secretary Lou Moses came out and declared: 'They might have won today, but the way they played they've got no chance of beating St George.'

My response to the media was direct: 'We've got more chance than Wests—at least we'll be playing.' Both of us were right.

Manly's performance that day seemed to stick in rugby league's collective mind. The possibilities of absolute conservatism under the 'unlimited' rule had been glaringly exposed—of a team bash-and-barging for 40 minutes, barely throwing a pass. I'm sure the 1959 game was still there in the memories of the men charged with the job of making the decisions when Fallowfield's radical four-tackle plan came along in 1967.

The fact that it was an Englishman who was the creator of the new rule guns down a popular Australian theory. There has been a growing school of thought over the years that the rule was brought in specifically to stop St George who at that point had won 11 straight premierships. Coincidence has added to the theory. In 1967, the first year of the four-tackle rule, St George's winning run came to an end. But it was just that: a chance event—the four-tackle rule was *not* brought in to stop a particular club. It was brought in for reasons not unconnected with the game Manly played against Wests in 1959—and with the growing theory that rugby league had become too predictable, and was bogged down in a bash 'n' barge style that was allowable under the old rule. The arrival of the limited tackle rule removed completely the temptation for teams to play the sort of stodgy win-at-all-costs football that had been possible under the old rule.

I supported the change to limited tackles—even though I quickly joined the growing band of league observers who reckoned four tackles were not enough. The push to increase the number of tackles had become a roaring torrent by the start of

the 1970s, and in 1971 the rule was stretched to a more acceptable six tackles.

Four or six—it was still the most dramatic and important
change that had been made to rugby league's rules since the
game was first devised in England's north in 1895. The diehards
opposed the new rule, of course. Rugby league has always had
a tendency towards the conservative; sometimes over the years
it has been slow to change when change was needed. I have no
doubt that even today there are those who would like to see the
game go back to unlimited tackles. I remember a few years back
there was a game or two played under the old unlimited rule.
League was in a different era by then—and you can't believe
how bloody boring the old game looked.

The beginning of rugby league's modern era can be traced to
1967 when the game itself changed. New teams came in to the
premiership that year (Penrith and Cronulla), the first real push
'outwards' to what the game was eventually to become. But
some things, it seemed, never changed. One of those was my
annual tussle with the Brookvale Show Society. For years the
Society had been staging their annual show on Brookvale, generally a week or two before the football season kicked off. Over
the seasons it became a hardy annual—Manly and me versus
the show people. The problem was that they just about wrecked
the bloody ground every year, particularly if there happened to
be a drop of rain around. In the show-jumping event the horses
would tear up great lumps of the beautiful green turf that had
been laid. In 1969, after we had spent $50,000 re-turfing the
ground, there was a tremendous stink when the show mob
wanted to hold a rodeo at Brookie—in March! Every year I
almost cried at the end of it when I looked out over the damage
and the divots. There'd be lumps of steel lying around and the
place would be just a mess. Milling around would be the members of a football team with whom we were hoping to win a
premiership. The next day I'd be blowing up in whatever newspaper wanted to talk to me. Anyhow, I battled them for years—
the Council and the Show Society—even taking it to the floor
of State Parliament at one stage. I really said some shocking
things about them, never stopped blasting away until I think

they simply got sick of me. It was said that at Manly Warringah Council a photograph of Ken Arthurson was pinned on the dartboard. Finally, sanity prevailed. The show moved elsewhere and we got on with the business of trying to be a professional football club.

And as we headed in that direction, standing between us and our ambitions was none other than Manly's nemesis of the early 1950s—South Sydney. Our continued progress towards the inevitability of a premiership was checked by the unfortunate fact that we happened to run into another great South Sydney era—of which there have been a few down rugby league's years. Souths were coming good in 1965, when they ran Saints desperately close under the coaching of Bernie Purcell, *came* good when they won the premiership in 1967 and stayed the testing material for everyone into the 1970s.

During those years of Souths' domination (checked only by the shock loss to Balmain in 1969) we were frustratingly close at all times. Consider Manly's record in the 'Souths Years', 1967–71.

  1967—fifth on 26 premiership points.
  1968—second on 31 points. Beaten in grand final.
  1969—fourth on 28 points. Finished third.
  1970—second on 33 points. Beaten in grand final.
  1971—first on 38 points. Finished third.

You can't get much more competitive than that. There were days in those seasons of such bright promise and ultimate disappointment that I would sit in my office at Manly and wonder if we were *ever* going to win the competition. We became (in)famous for what became known as the 'Manly Slump'. It happened in 1967 when we lost six games in a row to just miss the semis. In some circles we were known as the 'Swallows' or the 'Ruptured Ducks'. 'We need to win a premiership to start building a real tradition,' I told the *Sun* one day in 1968.

Boy, we had our chances. In '68 the grand final against Souths was a real touch-and-go affair. They led us 13–2 but we fought back to 13–9 with 14 minutes to go and pushed them all the way to the line. It was a match that I always thought we should have won. We gave them a 'gift' five points when Michael Cleary swooped on a pass meant for our winger Les Hanigan and ran 80 yards (73 metres) to score. That try made all the difference; at the end we were running all over them. In 1969, just when we looked set for a grand final showdown against Souths, Balmain's George Ruebner pulled out a 78th minute try to beat us 15–14.

The 1970 grand final in which Souths again had the better of us (23–12) is famous for the immense courage shown by Rabbitohs' captain John Sattler. To play a grand final with your jaw broken and hanging slack is an extraordinary achievement.

I can throw no real light on whether the attack on Sattler was premeditated, whether it was a pregame tactic to get the inspirational Rabbitoh skipper out of the game. Manly's front rower John Bucknell was the man who injured Sattler, catching him in an off-the-ball incident guaranteed to make you wince when viewed again on film. Filmmaker Graham McNeice included it in his three-hour video *That's Rugby League* in 1996.

If it was a tactic, it didn't work . . . even though it probably *should* have. When most players would have been off the field and out of the match, Sattler, raw courage personified, stayed on and inspired Souths to their 23–12 win. Bucknell, targeted by the tough Rabbitohs pack after the incident, was knocked out of the game in the first half with a shoulder injury.

The thing I *can* tell you is that Manly's coach that year, Ron Willey, was a very tough, shrewd operator. A lovely man, Ron, affable and caring. But the mild exterior masked a *very* tough football coach. He had a hard edge all right; could be absolutely ruthless at times. Ron Willey is so much part of the Manly story—the bloke who took us in 1972 and '73 to the premierships for which we had waited so long.

Ron loved nothing better than having a commanding no-nonsense forward pack at his disposal—blokes who could handle both the hard stuff and the skills side of the game. In 1970 we didn't quite have it—although the pack was a lively and talented one: Cameron, Morgan, Drake, Bucknell, Jones, Hamilton. Later, we did.

Arko

Ronny Willey was, and is, a very special Sea Eagle, Seagull or whatever you want to call it. A Kangaroo (from Canterbury) in 1952, a tour on which he pressured the great Clive Churchill, so strong was his form, he played seven seasons with Manly (1956–62) and scored almost 1,000 points. He was a brilliant goalkicker and a fine, rock-solid fullback. However it was as a coach (1970–74) that he carved his deepest mark.

Physical dominance was a big part of the Willey philosophy and anyone he thought couldn't stand up to the pressure when the tough stuff was on wouldn't be there. Simple as that. Ron wanted hard men, tough men. And if they brought him skill too—well, all the better.

The realisation that Ron Willey's health is failing has been a cause of some sadness in the Manly district in recent times. Ron is having problems with his memory. He sports a beard these days and lives in a place not far from the beach. Now and then I pop in, and we talk football. And if it happens that Ron forgets some of the great days and the great achievements, the rest of us won't. His contribution to the Manly success that we had all waited so long for was a grand one—and Ron Willey's place in Manly club's pantheon of high achievement is safe forever.

9

THE MATCH
FROM HELL

In 1970 I took away a team which unbeknownst to any of us was bound for one of the most murderous matches in rugby league history. If there has ever been a more savage football game played than the World Cup final of that year, Australia v England, I am not aware of it. The brutality of what took place on the afternoon of Saturday 7 November at famous Headingley, Leeds shook us all—and shook the game of rugby league to its very foundations. The next day as we licked our wounds and celebrated a truly remarkable achievement, the British press railed, in huge headlines, against the savagery of the match.

It was quite a tour . . . quite a story. Along with Queenslander Bert Quinn, an affable and capable travelling companion, I was chosen to manage the 1970 World Cup side. The man known as the 'old fox', Harry Bath, was the coach and Ron Coote the skipper after injury had knocked Graeme Langlands out of the running. We flew out of Sydney more in hope than high expectation—well realising the enormity of the job at hand. Earlier that season Frank Myler's touring Great Britain side had rebounded from a bad loss in the first Test to decisively win the Ashes on Australian soil. On home territory in November's deepening gloom we knew they were going to be fearfully hard to beat.

Arko

We set up camp in Bradford, in the Midlands Hotel, and got to work. We started perfectly, giving the New Zealanders a real towelling on a crisp, clear night at Castleford—with the footballing priest Father John Cootes getting two tries in the 47–11 win. But three days later we fell to the Englishmen at Leeds 11–4, and then lost again—17–15 against the unpredictable Frenchmen at Odsal Stadium. In England there was a great deal of harumphing about the fact that a final should be played at all. After all the Poms had won their three qualifying games; the other three teams had won one game each. But rules are rules— a final was written into the World Cup programme, so one had to be played.

There had been an 'edge' in the Australian camp from fairly early on. Under the tour rules, teams were to be selected by the coach and the two managers, and before the game against France, Harry and I had a significant disagreement which put poor old Bert Quinn right on the spot. Harry wanted a different front row to the one that I favoured. He was keen to play both hookers (Elwyn Walters and Ron Turner) but I was adamant that our reserve prop, Barry McTaggart, should be in the game.

'I'm going to play Walters and Turner,' said Bath.

'Jeezus, as far as I'm concerned you're not,' I said.

We argued back and forth without reaching agreement, and finally I said to him, 'OK, get Bert Quinn to adjudicate.'

Well, it was about the last thing Bert wanted. He was business manager for the tour, and a darned good one—a charming easy going bloke. From Queensland, he was fairly remote from the finer points of the Sydney form, happy to leave things pretty much to Harry and me. But on this morning he was right on the spot.

'Bert, we've got a disagreement,' I told him. 'Harry and I have argued the toss and we can't work it out. It's up to you— you've got the casting vote.'

Bert's face fell. 'Geez, isn't there *any* way you two can work it out?' he pleaded.

There wasn't. So Bert gritted his teeth . . . and sided with me. Maybe he figured that if he was going to be offside with anyone, he rather it wasn't me at that time.

The team had the benefit of outstanding player leadership on that tour in Ron Coote and his vice captain Billy Smith. Now Billy is a bloke who has done some things in his life that he shouldn't have and who has found a spot of bother here and there. But on that trip he was just outstanding—on and off the field. In fact he was a classic example of how well someone can respond when they are handed responsibility. Bill was proud to be vice captain of the Australian team, and took his responsibilities seriously. I remember one night when the skipper Coote had a media obligation with a local radio station and Bert, Harry and I had an engagement somewhere else, Billy was left in charge back at the Midlands. During the tour we had a rule that if you were going to eat dinner in the hotel's main dining room, then you had to wear a jacket and tie. Anyhow, on this particular night one of the players turned up smartly dressed in his blazer, and a roll-neck skivvy. At the door he was stopped by Smith.

'Where are you going?' asked Billy.

'I'm going to have a meal,' said the player.

'Not dressed like that you're not,' said Bill. 'You know the rules . . . Arko says you've got to have a tie on, and that's that.' Billy was going to fight him rather than let him in. If we ever had anyone running late for the bus Billy would be out like a flash to round up the recalcitrant. I couldn't have asked for any more from him.

After the early selection spat, roping Bert Quinn into the hot seat, things settled down, although Harry and I had our moments. We roomed together, and there were some lively debates between 'H' and I about how things should be done as the team made progress towards its goal. But by the time the final came around we were all on the same course.

Now and then there was an uneasy moment, though. In the lead-up to the final we put the team on an early curfew, and ruled there would be no nights out—apart from one evening when we went out together as a team to the movies.

Each morning we chased them out of their beds early and went running in the dawn light through the streets of Bradford. We trained bloody hard, and apart from that we never left the hotel. By the end of the week there was tension in the air. We were all sick and tired of looking at each other. As coach, Harry did a great job in that tough, tense week, building the team towards the job they had to do.

On the Friday night before the final, curfew was set at 9.30 pm. Right on curfew time Harry came running up to me in the lobby.

'Where's Ron Costello (our second rower)?' he shouted. 'I can't find Costello . . . as far as I'm concerned he's out of the team.'

'Hang on a minute,' I said, trying to calm him down. 'We'll try and get to the bottom of it.'

Just at that moment the front doors of the hotel swung open . . . and in walked Costello. 'Where have you been?' I asked.

'Oh, I just went next door to buy a book to read in bed,' said Ron, heading for the lifts. Phew! I think coach Harry was as much on edge as any of his players.

The final, played on a grey autumn afternoon, has been much talked about. A brilliant-quality colour film of the full match has recently been unearthed and shown in Australia. The film reveals an outstanding football match but it doesn't tell *half* the story, owing to the fact that it focused on the actual *play* and failed to pick up many of the countless off-the-ball incidents.

The match has become infamously known as 'The Battle of Leeds'. And it was just that. For sheer brutality I have never seen anything like it on the football field. At times there were groups of players fighting 50 metres away from where the ball happened to be. In those days the Poms only used one ball in matches, so if it got booted into the crowd the match had to pause until someone threw it back. I remember at one stage in the Battle of Leeds that the ball was somewhere up in the crowd. Meanwhile, on the paddock the action continued unabated as the players brawled. The story is told of a brawny English miner bellowing: 'Bugger the ball . . . let's get on with the game!'

It was desperate, dangerous, dastardly stuff—and the Aussies reached deep inside themselves to produce a magnificent performance and upset the favourites 11–7. We turned the table on the English that day: this time we kidded *them* into fighting and they fell for it. Over the years it had always been the other way around. Afterwards, England's fair-minded manager Jack Harding apologised for his team's performance. That was appreciated—but I've got to say in fairness to the English that it takes two to tango and that we thoroughly accommodated them in the rough stuff.

The game was intensely fought, and never safe; even near the end the Poms nearly pulled it out of the fire. What a win it was, under the circumstances, and afterwards I told the press I believed it had been 'Australian rugby league's proudest moment', which I did.

The atmosphere in the game had grown increasingly menacing in the final minutes. Referee Fred Lindop finally took a belated stand and sent two players from the field near the end—Billy Smith and England centre Syd Hynes. The crowd was chanting 'Go home you ——s' to our team; as the minutes ticked away it seemed certain that the Cup was gone. The match was like a time bomb and when Lindop finally whistled fulltime, it was to the relief of all. Australian fullback Eric Simms offered a handshake to England winger John Atkinson—at which Atkinson punched Simms on the jaw. Then, it was on again. Boy, it was good to get back into the dressing room—a place from which we had been cleared before the game incidentally, owing to a bomb scare. But in the room you could almost *feel* the hostility seeping in from outside. But they could go to blazes. We had what we had come for—the World Cup.

Well, we had it for a while, anyway. It is with some embarrassment that I confess to being the only Australian manager to come home *without* a major trophy after it had been hard won on foreign fields. We took the Cup back to the Midlands on the night of the final, and set it up on display in the foyer. The next day, I was heading down to London and when I walked through the lobby, I noticed the Cup wasn't there.

'Where have you put the Cup?' I asked the bloke on the desk.

'Jeez, I don't know,' he said, and promised he would investigate.

Arko

I didn't worry too much just then—I thought that very likely one of our blokes had it. But it soon became very apparent that the bloody thing had been nicked. It wasn't until 20 years or so later that it was found . . . on a rubbish dump in Leeds. I guess an irate fan was the culprit—someone still stewing over the events of that explosive afternoon had come to the hotel on Cup night and somehow sneaked the trophy away.

So it was that we came home Cupless . . . but triumphant. I came home with something else too—the very real opportunity to sign the most feared player in the world at that time.

10

MALCOLM AND THE WOMBAT

On the 1970 World Cup campaign in England the bloke our players talked about most was Malcolm Reilly, England's lock forward. It seemed that he was constantly a topic for conversation, and especially so in the lead-up to the final. I had the sense too that even the Poms themselves were a bit toey about him. At 21 he was the most feared man in football—an explosive package of talent and physical ferocity.

I made up my mind. *Here* was the bloke we needed for Manly, the player who could be our X factor in getting the premiership we so much wanted. So I began the chase, commencing negotiations with Reilly direct and also kicking off talks with his club Castleford via their respected official, later chairman, Phil Brunt. It was a long haul, featuring a great deal of toing and froing. Castleford obviously didn't want to let him go. We wanted him desperately. Our offer was a beauty, and Malcolm wanted to come.

In the end I brought it to a head, advising Reilly to hop on a plane and come to Australia. 'I'll fight it out with them then . . . and get the release,' I told him. And that's how it happened. He made the big decision to migrate to Australia and, safely landed, with a world record $42,000 transfer fee on his head, I continued the long negotiating process with Brunt. Phil was a tough bloke, but an honourable one. My dealings with him were much in the 'old style'. I levelled with Brunt and he with me and it was always that way in dealings we had concerning players over the years. There were nights I barely got to bed at all as the negotiations swung back and forth across 20,000 kilometres.

By mid-February 1971, Malcolm Reilly was a Manly Sea Eagle. I think that was the first time that a high-profile solicitor was involved in the negotiating process involving a rugby league player. Ex-World War II Battle of Britain fighter pilot and star Sydney University rugby league player Jim Comans had been involved with Reilly on the 1970 Great Britain tour here—acting for the Great Britain forward when Reilly struck some bother resulting from an incident outside South Sydney Leagues Club. Now Jim was the middleman in the negotiating process between Manly and Castleford. Later Jim Comans was to emerge as a significant figure in rugby league—as chairman of the League's Judiciary during a period in the 1980s in which we set out to 'clean up' the game.

St George had a crack at Reilly too, but we were always the front runners. When the plane bringing him to Australia touched down I was the only club official at the airport. We were in front then . . . and we stayed in front. In the end we paid Castleford $30,000 for Malcolm, and signed him for five years. He was a beautiful buy for the club.

What a player he was—and turned out to be for Manly. One right out of the box. I don't believe that Manly has ever had finer players than Malcolm and Bob Fulton, with Graham Eadie right up there making it a photo finish.

Reilly, quiet and methodical in getting ready for football, was pretty close to the toughest player I ever saw play the game. His consummate skill in looking after himself on the paddock (and some would say in 'looking after' his opponents) at times bordered on the cruel and brutal. And what a rare and brilliant talent he was as an attacking force in our side. Setting aside his legendary toughness, I rank him also as one of the most skilful footballers of all time. He was masterly with the short kick, and masterly at setting up support players with the right pass.

I remember a single moment in a game he played against Western Suburbs one afternoon. He really gave the Magpies hell that day—and they were a tough lot. Then right near the end of the game a Manly teammate threw him one of those balls that is known in the trade as a 'hospital pass'. And it was a true classic. It arrived in Reilly's arms at almost exactly the same time as a cluster of Wests forwards, each one of them hell bent on revenge. They didn't miss either, hitting the Manly lock with everything but the pickets from the boundary fence, and I'm not sure those mightn't have been involved either. I can still picture the dust rising and a cluster of black-jumpered bodies. Then from the midst of it all came a Manly arm, grasping the ball. With a flick of the wrist the pill was on its way—and our five eighth Ian Martin was under the posts. The Wests blokes couldn't believe it; they were still in there roughing up Reilly . . . and the referee was whistling 'try' and pointing to the spot. The Magpie forwards just shook their heads in disbelief. I doubt there's ever been anyone who could get the ball away better than Malcolm.

The big advantage he gave Manly was that he worried the hell out of anyone we happened to be facing. He was almost clinical in the way he could hand out punishment on the field. Anyone lined up against him needed to be wary. Not surprisingly Malcolm was a great favourite of Derek 'Rocky' Turner—one of the toughest men to ever pull on a boot. I'm sure Turner saw a fair bit of himself in Malcolm. He reckoned all the rest of the forwards around were big girls compared to Reilly.

By the year of his arrival in Australia, 1971, my dream of winning a premiership with Manly had become an obsession. 'Our object is to build an unbeatable team,' I told the *Daily Telegraph*'s George Crawford one day. I had played in a losing grand final, I had coached two teams which had lost grand finals, I had been club secretary during an era in which we had constantly threatened—and twice got as far as the big day, only to run second. The rot had to stop! The dating of my absolute determination for the club to win a premiership can be traced to that season, 1971.

We bought Malcolm Reilly, we bought the great winger Ken Irvine from North Sydney, the tough forward Bob Moses from Souths and we conscripted a chunky young fullback from Woy

Arko

Woy, Graham Eadie. We were out there in the market place. But the story of the purchase of Ken Irvine goes a fair way in its own right towards refuting the unfair and fundamentally untrue theory that grew up in the years of the 1970s and '80s—of Manly the ruthless pillager of clubs and players, so driven by blind ambition as to be completely uncaring of what the after-effects might be.

Make what you wish of that perception—but the image painted is grossly unfair. We were ambitious, sure. And we bought successfully from other clubs at times. No argument about that. It's the way of the world in rugby league. But we never brought across players to Manly without them being *absolutely* convinced that it was what they wanted it to do. Irvine, a player of legendary status by the time we got to him, was an outstanding example of that. I remember so clearly the conversation I had with him before he joined us.

'Ken, do you *really* think you should leave Norths?' I asked him. 'You're a legend there, you're a life member there . . . you're going to be giving up such a lot. I want you to think long and hard about what you're contemplating.'

Irvine was unhesitating. 'I've burnt my bridges at Norths,' he told me. 'The position is that I'm ready to go . . . I *have* to.' He was so emphatic.

'Ken, we'll be very, very happy to have you here,' I told him. 'But if we are to sign you . . . I only ask one thing, that *you* must be sure it's what you want.'

He was.

We were strongly in the market place, and we began copping the sort of flak that would become commonplace in the years ahead. In mid-season, with newspapers linking us to just about any player likely to be off contract in the next two years, we were publicly charged with 'trying to buy a premiership'.

I hit back: 'If filling gaps in our team with new players is attempting to buy a premiership, then Manly is guilty,' I told the press. 'My club is always interested in good players who come on the market and our policy will remain the same next year (1972). But we don't spend money recklessly.'

The signing of Graham Eadie, at 17, was especially satisfying for me. We bought him because he seemed a tremendous prospect, but effectively the signing represented a nice little 'get square' with St George too . . . an example of the truism that what goes around comes around and that things generally balance out over a period of time. It's a little known story in rugby league, but a fact, that we (Manly) were desperately close to signing the great Graeme Langlands back in 1962. I was club treasurer then and was involved in negotiations that went to the very brink before 'Changa' took Fearless Facer's bait—and went to St George.

In 1971, it was the same story, different punchline. In signing Eadie we pipped none other than . . . the Saints. I had had consistently good reports on Eadie from the Central Coast and we sent Jim Peebles from our Retention Committee up there to have a look at him in 1970. Jim came back with a glowing reference. Then I went up and had a look. It was pretty apparent that he was special. I remember, too, that when we signed him and he first came down, I looked at him at training that first night—the bulky frame and the solid legs—and I said to myself, 'Gee, I hope this bloke can run.' Well, he could—like a deer and with the power of a runaway bullock.

'Wombat' Eadie went on to become one of the greatest of all fullbacks. I will offer the opinion that in my view there's very little between Churchill, Langlands and Eadie at the top of that particular tree. Oh yes, I remember him so well. England 1973—he was 19 then, and just about unstoppable. That Kangaroo tour was both a difficulty and a triumph for him. His form was tremendous, yet Graeme Langlands was captain-coach of the team, and the fullback incumbent. In the early weeks of the tour the pressure grew on Langlands—and indirectly on the young Eadie who admired his captain enormously. Back home the media was saying that Langlands should step aside and let the young bull in. Eadie could say nothing, just keep playing the way he was. Then fate intervened. In a match against Leigh, skipper Langlands badly smashed a knuckle on his left hand. His tour was over, and teenager Graham Eadie was Australia's new fullback.

As the 1971 season unfolded with Manly firming to premiership favourites as the club stirred and shook, ready for something great, we added one more top player. Englishman Graham Williams, a tough, resourceful halfback originally from

Arko

Swinton and rated second only in the competition to Cronulla's Tommy Bishop. He joined us just before the 30 June deadline, on an $8,000 transfer fee from North Sydney.

It was in mid 1971, as we headed towards what many people believed would be an historic first Manly premiership (it wasn't to be), that I reached boiling point over the campaign being directed at my club. In an article hugely headlined in *Rugby League Week* magazine I growled out my disgust at what was happening in the game. In a statement that caused quite a stir I accused senior officials of the NSWRL of staging a 'hate campaign' against Manly, telling the paper's editor Geoff Prenter:

> I sat in the committee room at the SCG and heard prominent officials who I am prepared to name ride Manly into the ground (during a match against St George). It has been going on for some time but on Saturday it came to a head. I'm now convinced their attitude is rubbing off on referees and we are not getting a fair deal. The snide remarks passed during and after the game sickened me. What the hell have they got against us! The animosity directed against my club is bewildering for me and my committee. Isn't winning the premiership the name of the game? All Manly are trying to do is promote rugby league. League is thriving in Manly today. Are other clubs jealous of the way we run our football club? Are they jealous that we have no scandal in our football club?

And so it went on—a really decent 'spray', but one that honestly reflected the way I felt at that time. Manly have lived with plenty of the same ever since. The club has learned to live with antagonism, even to turn it to its own advantage. As late as March 1997, 26 years on, Manly's then chief executive Frank Stanton was still spelling it out on behalf of the club, claiming in *Rugby League Week* that the club had been 'unfairly targeted by continuing, persistent innuendo—virtually none of it factually based'. Stanton continued:

> I'll tell you one thing—we have become good over the years at turning things to positive advantage . . .
>
> It is sometimes said that many fans have two favourite

teams—their own and whoever happens to be playing Manly. Well, we can live with that—we are looking for no more than an honest coverage of what we do.

At Manly, it was ever thus.

I honestly believed during the early 1970s that rugby league's hierarchy was against Manly—and that referees didn't care too much if they gave our blokes a 'serve' in matches, because they knew there wouldn't be too much of a rebuke coming from Phillip Street. I was ropable.

But one night the wily old bird from Balmain, Norman 'Latchem' Robinson, pulled me over and offered a few words of advice. 'Son, I know how you feel,' he said.

> But in rugby league it's just the way of things that sometimes things will go your way and other times they will go against you. It seems to be you're getting a bit of a complex about all this. Just take it easy—in the long run it will even itself out.

I pondered Latchem's words and after that I was calmer. In many ways, of course, he was right.

The old Manly stalwart, Rupert Hudson snr, helped steer me at that time too. He was the heart and soul of Manly, old 'Reub', an enormous contributor to the club over many years. He was one of my greatest old mates—one of those blokes without much formal education, but with a terrific understanding of how things work. He always used to say that his knowledge was gained in the university of life. He was a shrewd bloke who knew how to handle people. And he was wonderfully loyal—when that over-worked word used to really mean something. Over at Manly there was a standing joke about Reub: he was a club selector and they reckoned he was the only selector who never *ever* dropped a player.

In later years, almost to the end, he used to look after the Manly door on match days. He would guard the sacred territory of the dressing room with his life, if necessary. It would be no greatly unusual thing to see old Reub at 80 or so grappling with some uppity interloper at the door, resolutely barring the way.

Street-smart blokes like Latchem and Reub and some others

have been tremendous contributors to the game of rugby league. Jack Gibson is certainly one of that ilk—a wise and knowledgeable bloke even if the wisdom and knowledge is not so much of the 'formal' kind. Gibson changed rugby league coaching profoundly, no doubt about that. From the late '60s through to the '80s he brought a new dimension to the game. He was the most innovative coach the game has seen—and just about every coach ever to wrestle with a clipboard since has taken some sort of leaf out of the Gibson book. There is no doubt that he stands as a monumental figure in the game—someone who dictated ideas and trends for years and years after his own 'reign' finished.

For all the speculation about us 'buying premierships' in 1971, we didn't win. The season was absolutely crammed with promise; we won the minor premiership by a clear margin of four points, but then fell over in the finals, our campaign not helped by Malcolm Reilly dragging the knee injury that was to become a *cause célèbre* in rugby league before too long—so famous and much discussed in the newspapers that the *Telegraph*'s Mike Gibson once conducted an 'exclusive interview' with the knee. It spoke with a Yorkshire accent. I got to the stage where I thought if I heard one more thing about Malcolm Reilly's knee I would jump off The Gap. It was the most publicised injury in the history of the game. I'd go down to training and there would be this cluster of doctors and physios around Malcolm. And there'd be this knee sticking up in the air. At one stage, part of Malcolm's rehab programme to try and get him fully fit was for him to go running . . . with me.

There was no happy punchline for us in '71. Arch rivals Souths beat us 19–13 in the major semi in a very tough, tight game, and then Jack Gibson's St George bowled us over in the final, 15–12, with the old firm of Langlands–Smith performing miracles. Two strikes and we were out. At an official level we consoled ourselves with the statistics of a record season—gate receipts of $45,000 and total crowds of 471,427.

So, even if we were still a sandwich or two short of a picnic in the football sense, we were for all of it as close as we had ever been in our lives to the glittering prize. Season 1972 shone brightly with promise . . .

11

TEARS OF JOY

There were a couple of things to be done. The first was settled
on Christmas Eve morning 1971, when South Sydney's excellent
utility man Ray Branighan decided that he wanted to become
a Sea Eagle. Branighan signed for around $10,000 a year, for four
seasons. Twenty-five days later the final cog fell into place.
Rejecting a huge, late offer from Canterbury the roughest, toughest
prop in the game, John 'Lurch' O'Neill, also from Souths,
signed for the same money. O'Neill had been a giant in my mind
since his astonishing display of raw courage in the World Cup
final of 1970. The Poms had hit (and kicked!) him with everything
but the double-sided Headingley grandstand that day, and
the big bloke kept picking himself off the turf.

On the signing of the two Souths stars, with the stories dominating
the headlines, the *Daily Telegraph*'s Mike Gibson wrote
simply: 'Now, for Manly, there can be no more excuses.' He
was damned right. We had the team we wanted—and if we
couldn't win it this year . . . it was never going to happen.

I'd had plenty to do with both Branighan and O'Neill and I
rated them both sky high as *people*. My philosophy of buying
and building was never just one of rushing out and signing
blokes because they were available. Building a champion football
team is a great deal about *blending*. You've got to secure
players who will not only work in comfortably with the players

73

you already have, but players who will also blend in with the philosophy and beliefs of the club and the way you do things. O'Neill and Branighan—tough, strong no-nonsense players—fitted the bill perfectly. The signings were a dream—just a handshake in both cases. Once you have a handshake agreement with blokes like John O'Neill and Ray Branighan, you don't need any more. I clearly remember the reaction of Souths' secretary Charlie Gibson to the loss of Branighan. Charlie knew he was going, but he didn't know to which club.

'Branighan's definitely leaving us,' he told me. 'Do you know where to?'

'He's coming to Manly,' I told him.

There was a pause and then Gibson uttered just two words: 'Oh, Jeezus.'

Now we had the pack: Reilly, Randall, Thomson, O'Neill, Jones, Hamilton. Tough with a capital 'T'. Talent with a capital 'T'. And we had the team.

That Alan Thomson was something. A real tough bastard. We had signed the second rower back in 1969 on the strength of his efforts in a match in New Zealand. I had flown over to watch the form on a tour the NSW Country team were making. In Auckland I saw Thomson pull on just about the entire opposing pack on his own. He was a demon tackler, a perfect foil for the super-athlete and home grown product who played alongside him in the Manly second row in 1972, Terry 'Igor' Randall.

You know, when I look back on the buying we did in 1971–72 it was pretty single-minded, ruthless stuff. There is no doubt that for a time I was driven by the emotion of anger coupled with the determination that I had always had for Manly to succeed. I was so obsessed, so annoyed with what I perceived to be the 'official' attitude directed at Manly. After 25 years . . . quarter of a bloody century . . . we were still the interlopers, still the blow-ins . . . still resented by the power base of the traditional clubs—Balmain, Newtown, Souths and so on. There was no way I was going to sit back and let Manly get pushed aside by crusty tradition. I'd sit there and think, 'We're not here just to make up the numbers . . . we're in it to *win* it!' I'd be sitting there at a match or a meeting with all this hostility around me and I'd be thinking, 'OK, if they're all going to be against us ... I'm going to get into them.' Resentment can be a strong motivating force.

You all know the punchline to this chapter. Yes, Manly had a marvellous, exhilarating year of football—and won the premiership after 25 years of doing our darndest. The game was of six tackles now and it suited our free-flowing style nicely; we were a team who liked to have the ball in our hands and the extra couple of tackles meant teams had more chances to work moves, more chances to run the ball. We set the pace all season, nudging out our major rivals Eastern Suburbs by two points to take the minor premiership.

September ran perfectly. We smashed Easts 32–8 in the major semi and on that night of 2 September stood just a fortnight away from the near certainty of the premiership we had waited so long for. I remember how the days dragged through those two weeks. I have never been as nervous in my life. I was confident because we had a great football team, but, oh boy, I was nervous. I can remember the North Sydney coach Roy Francis advising me one day, 'Look, the one thing you musn't do is let them see you're nervous. Because if you do, it's going to get through to the players.' Roy was right, and I assumed a cucumber-cool calm. But on the inside I was a bundle of nerves. Progressively, day by day, the pressure built, although coach Ron Willey and skipper Freddy Jones (more of 'Freddo' anon) kept things firmly in hand. At the halfway point in our long wait Easts showed their spirit when they bounced back to win the final over St George—8–6 in a tough, tryless game.

On 16 September before 54,357 fans, we faced them again. Punctuated by some controversy, the grand final was nothing like the points-scoring romp we had enjoyed in the semi final. We slipped behind 4–0 early, but were back to 4–all by halftime. Gradually, we edged away from them, to 8–4 and then 13–4 after our skipper Jones scored the most controversial of tries. Easts reckoned that Jones bounced the ball as he burrowed for the line. But a brilliant quality colour film of the match, rediscovered in the 1990s, leaves no doubt at all that it was a fair try—just as Fred has claimed down the years. With referee Keith Page under pressure via some tough decisions (a disallowed try to Easts' Ron Coote and one given to Ray Branighan in which there was a touch-and-go pass) we cleared away to 19–4. Easts' late flurry—tries in the 72nd and 79th minutes—brought respectability to the scoreboard for our opponents and thrills for some supporters . . . but the premiership was ours. On the scoreboard, it was 19–14. After 25 years we were the champions of the league.

I was sitting in the old SCG Members' Stand, out the front of our dressing room. It was just amazing. There were blokes crying, blokes with their arms around each other. All the anticipation and emotion of our quarter-of-a-century wait just spilled over. The atmosphere was one of unbelievable elation. We had been bridesmaids for so long. Now on one afternoon, after 80 minutes of football on a spring afternoon, the monkey was off our backs.

It was one of the great days of my life. The trip back across the Bridge to Manly on the team bus was a wonderful experience. Travelling with us was the J.J. Giltinan Shield, symbol of supremacy in the game of rugby league. The reception that awaited the team was little short of amazing, and the night that followed, long and liquid . . . the specific memories of it hazy now. I was still at the Leagues Club at 6 a.m. on the Sunday morning.

Victory was so sweet, and I wanted more of it. Almost before the dust had settled I was out in the market place, this time in negotiation with Souths' international backrower Gary Stevens. When I look back now I realise how driven I was then, driven by wanting to make up for all that lost time at Manly, all those losing years. But it was a popular pastime in the press then to link us with any top players who happened to be anywhere near finishing contracts. Bob McCarthy and Ron Coote were two specific cases in point. If you'd read the papers you would have had no doubt at all that both were ready to board the bus to Brookie. Those stories were greatly played up—and the fact of it is that we didn't make specific overtures to either. I was a great admirer of both players and I made no secret of the fact that if there had been the slightest chance of either

McCarthy or Coote coming across I would have been at their front doors within ten seconds.

Gary Stevens was a different story. We were very, very keen to get him. I admired the bloke greatly—one of the truly great defensive players in rugby league. He got very close to joining us. In fact he agreed to terms, but at just the time the NSWRL, in a desperate bid to curb inflation, introduced the short-lived $2,000 sign on and $200 match money ceiling payment system.

That was the first attempt by the League to impose some sort of restriction on payments to players which were bordering on out-of-control at that stage. For probably the first (and only) time everybody decided to stick to it. I certainly did—to the letter . . . until Easts broke it on us. I had a phone call in late 1973 with the news that Jack Gibson on behalf of Easts had offered John 'Monkey' Mayes $9,000 to leave us. I had told Mayes that I couldn't go above the $2,000–$200 arrangement. But they busted the arrangement and signed Mayes . . . and then we busted. I went straight across the Bridge and signed Kevin Junee, Easts' half back and a prolific try scorer who had two excellent years with us. Peter Moore was the next to break the $2,000–$200 limit, signing the talented Englishman Brian Lockwood, and by then it was a goner. It was a nice ideal in the interests of the 'greater good of the game'. Sadly, such things rarely work.

I can reveal that Mark Harris (Easts) was very close to becoming a Sea Eagle at one stage, too. Mark had been part of my team that won the World Cup in 1970 and had been a damned good tourist. I liked him as a bloke and admired him greatly as a player. Mark was different and people sometimes got the wrong impression about him because of his considered manner. The fact was that he was an extremely thoughtful bloke who gave due consideration to things before offering an opinion. He was a formidable footballer, big and fast—and he could kick the ball a country mile.

Mark was something of a pioneer, too. In 1973 he trialled for a gridiron contract with the Philadelphia Eagles then joined the Montreal Alouettes in Canada as a kicking specialist. I remember him telling me one day of his frustration at the role he played—which was just to kick the ball, then get off the field. One day, running out of patience, he punted the ball high downfield—and chased! Seventy or 80 metres down the paddock, Harris flattened the bloke who had caught the pill. 'I don't want you to *ever* do that again,' his coach snapped at him later.

With or without Stevens–McCarthy . . . or whoever, we were clearly the best team in rugby league at the end of '72 and we came back and won again in 1973. But only just. Cronulla-Sutherland under the dynamic leadership of Tommy Bishop had nagged away at us all year—and we had pipped them by just a single point for the minor premiership. We had lost a key player, our half back Dennis Ward (to Wests–Newcastle) and gained one, Johnny Mayes (from Easts). This was the first year of the five-team semi final set-up and it seemed a long haul getting to showdown day—especially when St George and Newtown had to replay their semi final after drawing 12–all after 100 tense minutes. We leapfrogged straight through to the grand final by beating Cronulla 14–4 in the major semi—a match made special by a simply dazzling Bob Fulton solo try.

For the grand final on 15 September we were red hot favourites—but we very nearly fell into the trap which had ensnared Great Britain in the World Cup final of 1970. Cronulla produced an old fashioned tactic that almost won them the game: they put the biff on. In a simply ferocious first half we were sucked in, as referee Keith Page just let it run. We were a 20-points better side than Cronulla and Bishop more than anyone knew it. So the tactics he employed were both desperate . . . and very smart indeed. The first half of that infamous grand final has been described as 'unrestrained mayhem'. It was just that—a violent collision of two teams the likes of which we will never see again. At that time there was the theory that grand finals were different from normal football matches in their nature and that it was perfectably acceptable for referees to give the teams half a match or so to sort themselves out. That certainly seemed to be Keith Page's philosophy on grand final day 1973, although twice in that shocking half of football he called in all 26 players on the field and issued mass cautions.

The Cronulla tactics jolted us, no doubt about that.

Malcolm Reilly, one of our trumps, was crunched by Cronulla's Ron Turner in an off-the-ball incident—a square up for something that happened in a previous meeting between the pair—and was forced out of the game with a badly damaged hip. But on that afternoon of brawls and bruises it was pure, dazzling football that won the day, via the twinkling feet of Bob Fulton. Fulton scored two marvellous tries, one in each half, in one of the great performances of his career—and got us home 10–7. As Bishop acknowledged later, he was the difference that day. I doubt there has ever been a more dominant individual display in a grand final.

That day Bozo Fulton was 'The Man'. And once again we were the champions. I can tell you . . . I was getting to like the feeling. It's a funny thing about that match. Do you know that I've never seen it again on tape? I am aware that there are copies around, but it was not a game of which the League was proud in any way, even though the selected highlights, featuring the Fulton tries, are about as good as football can get. For years afterwards it was pretty much the 'missing' grand final—the film of it tucked away on a dusty shelf somewhere, and those at Phillip Street happy to leave it there. Out of sight, and out of mind.

12

FREDDO

Because he captained us to our first (and second) premiership, Fred Jones will always have a special place in the Manly Hall of Fame. But Freddy will be remembered for a whole lot more than just *that*. If I put together a team of the greatest characters I have met in half a century in rugby league, Fred would be the captain, probably coach and certainly social secretary, too. In his years with the club (1961–63 and 1965–75) I would conservatively estimate that he caused me more trouble than any other dozen players put together. But for all of it, I loved Freddy. He was a gutsy, loyal, tough bastard trouble prone to an extraordinary extent off the paddock, but hugely likeable all the same. Fred spent many, many hours in my office as we tried to sort out this scrape or that he had managed to get himself in to. We had screaming arguments in which Fred would almost break down, then swear it would *never* happen again. A week later, he'd be back on the carpet.

While he was at Manly I think Freddy had more jobs than he packed into scrums. I helped organise more than a few of them. But then Fred would be gone, and we'd start all over again. Finally Tom Bellew (later to be president of the NSWRL), who was with the Stevedoring Association, helped get Fred a start on the wharves. There, Fred found his niche. He's been down there on the wharves ever since and has progressed to such an extent that he's one of the trumps these days.

Arko

I have always said that after Freddy retired at the end of 1975, my workload was immediately cut in half. I missed him and used to wander around the office thinking, 'Jeezus, I've got nothing to do.'

Fred was very special to Manly—a great footballer in his own right, and a magnificent captain. Safely tucked beneath that rough exterior of the ageing hooker were wonderful qualities of leadership. Fred had the knack of bringing things down to basics with his knockabout, commonsense approach.

I'll never forget the Thursday night before the 1972 grand final. After the last training session of the year, with the grand final looming, we gathered as a team and as a club and went down to the Brookie pub for a final yarn and a drink together. Nervous butterflies were rampant in the camp by that late stage of the week. I remember all the younger players ordering their drinks—lime and sodas, orange juices, and nothing stronger. Then captain Fred bowled in.

'What'll it be, Fred?' asked the barmaid.

'Ah, give us a schooner of Old and a packet of Rothmans, luv,' barked our beloved leader. Fred went out on the Saturday, played the house down—and helped bring home our first premiership.

Another of my favourite Fred Jones stories is also linked to a grand final—that between Manly and Cronulla in 1978. Malcolm Fraser was at the grand final that day, as Prime Ministers often are. To my knowledge Malcolm had never been to a rugby league game before. But I suppose he figured he'd better do some mixing with the common herd. Anyway, the big bloke was there this day and I had him under my wing for a time. I introduced the PM to Manly officials and players in our room, then marched him through the Members' Bar to the Cronulla room. On the way back we ran into Fred, long since retired as a player by then, who was having a drink with Labor's Mick Young. Young called us over, and after I had introduced the Prime Minister to our former captain the conversation went something like this:

Malcolm: 'Oh, how do you do?'

Fred: 'G'day.'

Malcolm: 'And what do you do for a living, Fred?'

Fred: 'I'm a wharfie.'

Malcolm: 'Oh . . . actually I've got quite a few friends on the wharves.'

Fred: 'Well, I don't fucking know any.'

Malcolm (Fumbling): 'Um . . . ah . . . well, no . . . they're mainly down in Melbourne.'

Fred: 'I never get down to the fucking mulga!'

By this time there were people everywhere, gesticulating and mouthing . . . 'Get him away from Fred!' I felt a bit sorry for the PM. I mean, how unlucky could you be? To go to the rugby league once in your life and to run into Freddo in the Members' Bar. I don't think Malcolm Fraser ever went to another rugby league match.

As a footballer, Fred Jones was one of the toughest men to ever strap on a boot. He wasn't a dirty player, but he was as tough as they come. I remember one time when he was working on a road gang and he got caught in a cave-in. One of his hands was horribly crushed, really mangled. Fred turned up at training that night, anyway. I think he missed one match. Another time he had all his teeth smashed when he copped one in a match. He was an awful sight. Back at the club after the game Freddo couldn't get a glass to his lips, so damaged were his mouth and gums. But he was there anyway. Drinking beer through a straw.

During the period of Fred's 'reign' as Manly hooker and captain, another notable No. 12 waited patiently in Seconds. Max Krilich was very special too—equalling Fred Jones in the qualities of club loyalty, toughness and ability. Max played on, and on, with us—his career spanning the years 1970–83. When a neck injury finally forced him to call it quits he had played a record 334 games for the club. After his long wait for recognition and fame, Max went even further than Fred (even though Jones played for Australia). In 1982 Krilich was named captain of the Kangaroos—the team which went on to immortality as 'The Invincibles' after they went through England and France undefeated. They were the finest outfit of my experience—a champion team, and a team of champions. That their leader was a home-grown, much-loved Manly man was a great source of pride for everyone at the club.

13

'THE CARTEL'

The death of W.G. Bill Buckley in 1973 inevitably changed things in rugby league—as the loss of a commanding leader does in any walk of life. 'Buck' had been the League's president and strongman for 13 years. He would be missed as a great friend of both the game and those in it and he would not be easy to replace in challenging times. When he died in Concord Repatriation Hospital, I told the press: 'I do not know how he will be replaced. His main attributes were his strength of character and his courage.'

His successor was Kevin Emery Humphreys, a strong, forthright bloke from Balmain, and a brilliant debater. On the floor of the NSW League Humphreys had long since been known as the 'boy orator' for his dazzling gifts as a forceful off-the-cuff speaker. There were certainly parallels in our careers. As secretary of Balmain he had come to Phillip Street a year or two after me in the mid 1960s. He was a bloke I took to from the moment I first met him. We became friends almost immediately. I liked his honest, straightforward style and I came to realise that in many things relating to league he and I were much on the same wavelength.

Kevin had been a front rower, a good strong no-nonsense forward with Balmain, starting a year or two after my own career had finished. Like me, he had gone on committee, then begun his climb up the ladder by being elected club secretary. In May '73 he was elected unopposed as President of the NSWRL, sparking talk of a 'revolution' in the game. *Rugby League Week* really grabbed the angle in a big way. Their major headline read 'YOUTH REVOLUTION' and the story below began: 'The "young bloods" headed by the dynamic Kevin Humphreys swept into office in NSW this week and launched a campaign which will see rugby league spiral to dizzy heights.' Among the 'young bloods' listed as being part of the 'Humphreys Revolution' were Charlie Gibson (Souths), Peter Moore (Canterbury), Bob Abbott (Cronulla) . . . and yours truly.

And so began an exciting rollercoaster of a decade in which a great deal of good and valuable work was done in preparing rugby league for a changing world in which it had become part of the highly competitive entertainment business. The timing was just right for the game to have new, vibrant leadership . . . and Humphreys was the man for the occasion. I know that he fell from grace because of events that took place in 1983, and I will address that later. But none of that changes my belief that Humphreys was one of the finest administrators the game of rugby league has ever had.

With him, alongside Queensland senator Ron McAuliffe, rests the responsibility for the birth of State of Origin football in 1980—the jewel in the crown of the modern game. It became a popular sport in the years after 1983 to knock Kevin Humphreys. But you'll get none of that from me. To me he was an achiever, and one with a genuine 'vision' for the game (that word which became so sadly devalued during the Super League struggle).

In so many areas we held shared beliefs as to the direction the game should head. We were friends and compatible workmates in the game we loved with equal passion. But an area in which we didn't share the same passion was that of gambling—and it was 'the punt' of course that eventually led to Kevin's downfall in '83. In that era there were some keen punters in the game, blokes like the *Daily Mirror*'s Bill Mordey who left newspapers to become the NSWRL's media director and Souths' secretary Charlie Gibson—both of whom shared Kevin's love of the track.

Over the years there has been speculation linking me to gambling—one theory being that I was an SP bookie. It was bull——. Gambling has never been of interest to me; football has provided more than enough of a sporting interest. The real truth is that I wouldn't even know how to box a trifecta!

In 1978 Humphreys and I were seriously defamed in Sydney's newspapers—the pair of us accused of running a two-up school at Brookvale. I took the strongest possible action against the three papers involved—suing the *Sun, Daily Mirror* and *Manly Daily*—and received a handsome settlement in each case—$25,000 from one of them—and an apology before the matter got to court. It was somehow representative of a life that has had some ill-fortune that Kevin Humphreys did not get a similar result via the court action that he took. That was cruel— he was as innocent as I was, but he took some ill-judged advice and chose not to go into the witness box when his case reached the courts. Unfortunately, it looked as though Kevin had something to hide over the matter—which he didn't. I was the opposite: I couldn't wait to get into the box when my cases neared—although it never got that far, out-of-court settling being reached in each case. The apologies made satisfying reading: '*The Sun*'s report in no way intended to mean that Mr Humphreys or Mr Arthurson were associated with organised crime or with the underworld . . . '

I'll tell you the story of how that scurrilous rumour began. There was by then a group of like-minded blokes in the game— mainly those named in *RLW*'s 'Youth Revolution' story—who used to knock around together. Now and then we'd have a night out, have a few drinks, then, because there were punters in the ranks, occasionally go to some place like the two-up school at Brookvale. Bill 'Break Even' Mordey knew 'em all.

I remember when the story about the Humphreys– Arthurson 'school' blew up in the papers Mordey rang me. He recalled a night at Brookvale when we'd all lost our money except him. We were all flat broke, including me, and Mordey had lent me $50. 'That was a funny two-up joint you "owned",' said Bill. 'You had to bite *me*.'

Through the years of Kevin Humphreys' presidency at

Phillip Street (1973–83) mention was often made of a 'power group' who 'ran the game'. That power group was generally identified as Humphreys, Peter Moore, Charlie Gibson, Bob Abbott and Ken Arthurson. The media picked up the nickname they gave us down at Phillip Street and in the press we became known as 'The Cartel'. I won't deny that in the ten years, this was the group in rugby league that got things done. I'm sure league has always had a core group such as we were—like-minds who join together and who collectively wield some power.

But through the years of the 1970s and into the '80s we were not driven by any pact or by blind faith. We were mates, sure, and we shared many views about the direction the game should be taking. But there were fierce differences of opinions at times. I can say without fear of contradiction that through-out that whole time, I was always my own man. And over-hanging everything, anyway, was a 48-man NSWRL general committee, an unwieldy, often-changing body which had the final say on all decisions. Incorporation in 1983, bringing in a streamlined nine-man board to run the game, was the best thing that could have happened to league. I remember those nights of the 48-man committee. A suggestion would come up for a motion to change and they'd all be sitting there thinking: 'Jeezus . . . how is this going to affect *my* club?'

There is no challenging the fact that 'The Cartel' was friend-ship-based. We were the best of pals, united in a common inter-est. The social life was part of it and if it happened that one of our teams won the competition, we would all join in the cele-brations. There'd be a day out on which we'd endeavour to restrict our drinks to only those that happened to be in the colours of the winning club. Souths (red and green) presented some difficulties. When Manly won it was easy: pink and white champagne.

There is a story that Bill Mordey tells about one of those days, when I had parked my car at North Sydney, then joined the others for a long lunch at a restaurant at The Spit, which kicked on late. Then *very* late. Finally, I'd had enough, and I left them to it and caught a taxi back to North Sydney, to pick up

Arko the club secretary—shrewd, determined, successful. He built an empire at Manly.

Left: Class 1C, Bondi Beach Public in the mid-1930s. Looking back through the mists of time, Ken reckons he *might* be the little bloke in the lighter coloured jersey on the far right of the second back row.

Above: Freshwater C Grade, 1947. Ken, third from right in the middle row.

Right: Ken's mum, Mrs Mary Arthurson with grandson Mark and great granddaughter Rebecca (Susan's daughter).

Above: Against all the odds the tenderfoot Manly team of 1951 made the grand final. They will forever hold a special place in the story of the Sea Eagles.

Right: Off to New Zealand with Manly in 1958. Coach Ken is third in the line on the left, behind him lifelong friend and Manly stalwart, the great front rower Roy Bull. Two outstanding Manly administrators flank the front row—Arnold Stehr (far left) and Reub Hudson snr (far right).

Right: Arko the footballer, featured on a plaque struck in his honour in the early 1990s.

One of Leagues great administrators
Ken R. Arthurson A.M.
Received an A.M. in the 1988 Bicentennial
Australia Day list of Honours.
Life Member Manly Warringah Leagues and
Football Club NSWRL & Leagues Club
Papua New Guinea and Australian RL
Director General International RL Board and
Executive Chairman Australian RL
Chairman NSWRL President Manly
Warringah Leagues Club SCG Trustee
Manly player 1950-52 Coach 1954-61

Sports Heritage

Bob Fulton the younger *(above)* and the coach *(below)*. To both roles—
player and coach, Fulton brought extraordinary abilities and a burning
desire to be 'the best'. In Arthurson's view he is Manly's supreme
champion.

Ken's years in rugby league brought him into contact with an extraordinary and diverse range of people. *(Left)* He shares a magnum of champagne with radio personality and keen Manly fan Bob 'Hidey Hodie' Rogers. *(Below)* With John Quayle (left) he joins supermodel Elle MacPherson at a League promotion in the 1990s, and *(bottom)* Quayle and Arthurson flank the NSWRL Writers' Association player of the year, Parramatta's Peter Sterling, in the early 1980s.

Prime Minister Malcolm Fraser *(above left)* was unlucky enough to run into Manly hooker, captain and grand character Fred 'Freddo' Jones *(above right)* at the Sydney Cricket Ground one afternoon.

Below: Referee Greg 'Hollywood' Hartley, rugby league's man in the hot seat in the 1970s, was flashy, flamboyant and prone to falling over . . . but fair, says Ken Arthurson

Above: The four Immortals—
(left to right), Bob Fulton,
John Raper, Clive Churchill,
Reg Gasnier. The number
should have been five, says
Arko. He would have added
Graeme Langlands.

Right: Action man Arko
after a morning's
snorkelling.

Queensland's Ron McAuliffe mightn't have been a dictator (despite the photo evidence)—but he was a strong leader and a great friend and supporter to Ken Arthurson.

my car. It wasn't the smartest thing in the world to do, but these were pre-breathalyser days and blokes sometimes did dumb things. The cab driver sure was a wake-up to me. When we got to the car I fumbled around and couldn't find any change. Eventually the cabbie said to me, 'Look, I don't want your money . . . just do me a favour and give me five minutes' start, will you?'

There were attempts to paint 'The Cartel' as something sinister. As often happens in life, people read far too much into the power we had, and what we might do with it. The bottom line to it all was that *none* of us was in the business of trying to push anything through that we honestly didn't believe was in the best interest of the game. We were fans . . . we loved the bloody thing and wanted to see it work as well as it possibly could.

It's a point worth emphasising, that we were driven collectively by our passion for the game and nothing else. There's a yarn that sticks in my mind about the group, which echoes the religious bias that was once a fact of life in sections of the game. The religion thing has *never* been a factor for me in any shape or form in my life in rugby league. But it was certainly true that over the years the game had its divisions along Catholic–Masons lines, and particularly among the referees. By coincidence the so-called 'Cartel' was largely a Catholic group— president Humphreys, Peter Moore, Bob Abbott, Charlie Gibson. There was obviously a presumption abroad that, working closely with those blokes, I was a Catholic too (which I'm not), and I remember a day when a member of the general committee came to me urging support for a certain candidate in an upcoming ballot. 'After all, he's one of us,' the bloke said to me. 'We can't let those bloody Masons get in for a takeover.' Or words to that effect. I was quite startled . . . I didn't have the heart to tell him the news.

My personal knowledge of an event long ago leads me to believe that the theory that NSW captain Len Smith was left out of the Kangaroo tour of 1948 for religious reasons is wrong. I have my own suspicions, revolving around the very shrewd and political Norman 'Latchem' Robinson who was a strong player at the game's top administrative level at that time. I am led to believe that Latchem was chasing the coaching job on that tour—and that the machinations involving his ambitions were the major factor in the injustice done to Len Smith.

To me, religion has never been a factor in the game, nor should ever be. Since 1908 rugby league has opened its doors to everyone, from the garbo to the brain surgeon. Colour, creed, belief—and these days sexual persuasion—don't mean a damned thing in the selection of footballers and football teams. Nor should they. Really, there's only one question in town: 'Can he play?'

14

BOZO

M y two favourite footballers in half a century of watching
rugby league have been Johnny Raper and Bob Fulton.
But how does anyone ever really pick with any certainty an
absolute *best*? I mean how could I say for sure that those two
were any better than Churchill or Gasnier or Langlands . . . or
some of today's champions? 'Chook' Raper and 'Bozo' Fulton
just happen to be my personal favourites.

And if I live to 110 Fulton will always be *very* special in my
memory. I have been close to him from the time he was a
teenager and the football he played in the years that followed
gave me enormous pleasure. His will to win was extraordinary
and I know that I contributed to that. Because I wanted to win
just as badly, too.

Bob's great strength as a player, among many, was his ability to turn a game in the twinkling of an eye. The 1973 grand
final was a great example of it—the first try off a Fred Jones
pass, with nothing on . . . but Fulton suddenly bursting
through, and streaking away. Then the second, an amazing pass
from Graham Eadie then Fulton off down the touchline in an
extraordinary sprint, beating defender after defender.

Oh yes, he was something out of the box, Bob Fulton. As I
have written, I believe his 1973 contribution to Manly's victory
was the greatest of all individual grand final performances. In

Arko

my memory only Dick Dunn's virtuoso display for Easts back in 1945 gets anywhere near it. And that was in a final, there being no system of automatic grand finals at that time.

There are many words you can attribute to Fulton the footballer. Ruthless, fast, aggressive, an unbelievable will to win, are a few thoughts that come to mind. And the other thing about him was that he played *all the time*. He was always fit and on the field. Whenever he suffered an injury in a game you could be quite sure you wouldn't see him back at the club drinking beer. He'd be home, the injury packed in ice . . . getting ready for the next week. The treatment would begin the instant the match finished. By the Tuesday night he would invariably be right. He was a professional from the top of his head to the tips of his toes.

For 30 years or more Bob Fulton has been part of my family. Some people seem to go out of their way to denigrate that. They'll say: 'Oh, he's Arko's son,' and, 'He gets special treatment off Arko.' Well, the truth of it is that Fulton *did* get special treatment off Arko . . . because he deserved it. Anyone else who had put in the same effort and done the things on behalf of the club that he did (and does)—they'd have got 'special' treatment too.

Defending my relationship with Fulton has never been a problem for me. And it's something I've found myself doing more than once over the years. When Bozo was named coach of Australia in 1989 I was asked if our mateship was a factor. Having shot that down, I told the inquirers, the *Sydney Morning Herald*:

> It's true that I've got a very close friendship with Fulton. I probably understand him better than anyone else in the world I would think—except his family. You see, Bob Fulton's a bloke who can easily get offside with people. But underneath all that he's a very kind and decent bloke. Apart from being the best footballer I've ever seen, he's an extremely competent coach. If you sit down and talk football with him you'll be astounded at his knowledge of the game and the way he plans to win a game.

Over the years, and especially when I reached a position of some influence in the game, I have been accused of favouring people (e.g. Bob Fulton) or clubs (e.g. Manly) in decisions I have been part of. I tell you something—I have *never* lobbied for anyone that I didn't think was worth it. Sure, I lobbied for Bob Fulton to be captain of Australia, and sure I lobbied for Max Krilich to be captain of Australia—but I did it because I *genuinely* believed they were the best men for the job. Their achievements in those roles backed my judgement. I can think of no occasion when I lobbied for something or urged something at executive decision level which was *not* for the overall good of the game, or for Australia's rugby league team. Yes, I've been loyal to Manly and to my friends there—but never blindly so. Yes, I would barrack for them at a game—after all they have been my team for almost half a century. People sweated on that as something sinister. On grand final day 1996 the *Daily Telegraph* got me with a long lens from 100 metres or so away as I leapt in excitement at a Manly try . . . and they no doubt delighted in the picture they ran the next day.

People who say I favoured Manly conveniently forget things. Like the time in 1984 I voted for Ray Price in the Australian team at the expense of Paul Vautin. Fatty Vautin was and is a close friend of mine and I believe him to be one of the best footballers we've ever had at Manly. Ray Price was a bloke who I had publicly, at least once, accused of being a whinger and who I had never been close to. But I admired him enormously as a footballer. At that time he was one of the greatest players in the game and when I had to give a casting vote, as ARL chairman, at a particularly stormy meeting, Price got it. In my role as chairman I didn't care whether a player came from Manly, Kalgoorlie or Upper Tanganyika. If he was the best player, capable of doing the best job for Australia, he'd get the nod. That season of '84, with the British here, was a contentious one on selections. I was called on to give another casting vote—Frank Stanton (NSW) v Arthur Beetson (Queensland)—with emotions and publicity high. I went for Frank Stanton for all the above reasons, believing him to be the best man for the job, despite having the utmost respect for

Beetson. The task of having to give a casting vote is an onerous one: the bloke you pick doesn't give you a wrap because he reckons he's entitled to the job anyway; the bloke you don't pick is crooked on you for life.

It would be a strange person indeed after long years with a club who *didn't* hold some sense of loyalty. I never tried to kid that I didn't support the Manly club. But I can honestly say that as chairman I never gave Manly any privilege they weren't entitled to. Not only wouldn't I do it—they wouldn't expect me to. In fact there was a theory about Manly that sometimes I made things tougher on them, not easier, in endeavouring to play a straight bat. That wasn't true either. I didn't want to give them an advantage—and I didn't want to disadvantage them.

It was ever thus. Kevin Humphreys, my predecessor as president of the League, was (and is) a Balmain man through and through. Bill Buckley before him was steeped in the traditions and the ways of Newtown club. Jersey Flegg was a foundation Easts player and official. The fact is that everyone comes from somewhere in the rugby league sense. Warren Lockwood, the NSWRL's new chairman, will confront the same situation. Warren is a passionate and loyal St George man—but that doesn't mean he won't do a wonderfully even-handed job for rugby league in toto. I totally reject the contention that 'Manly ran the game' during the period of my tenure or that Fulton, in particular, was given an especially cosy run. The bloke just happened to be tremendously talented—a front runner off the field in rugby league as he had been on it.

The qualities that made him a great player are those that have made him a great coach in the last decade. He is meticulous and never less than hugely enthusiastic about the job at hand. Fulton leaves no stone unturned in his search for perfection. Day after day, hour after hour through the season, he'll be checking the videos—pinpointing a weakness here, a strength there—searching always for the 'edge' as he did relentlessly through a long and distinguished playing career.

Significantly, Fulton and the great lock forward Raper were two of the four 'Immortals' named by *Rugby League Week* magazine in the early '80s. A distinguished judging panel had the task of picking the four outstanding players of the post-war years. After a long night's deliberation they named Clive Churchill, Reg Gasnier, Johnny Raper and Bob Fulton. I have always regretted the fact that the rules weren't bent a little that night—and an extra Immortal added. In my book that man would have been Graeme 'Changa' Langlands. I mean, how could you leave Langlands out of anything when you're talking about greatness in football? Frank Hyde (one of the judges) has always argued quite reasonably: 'Well, who would you leave out (of the four chosen)?' It's a very fair point. I'm just saying that Langlands should have been there. There should have been *five* Immortals.

Manly football has been peppered with great characters and outstanding players over the years. We had a great deal of success with English players—with Malcolm Reilly clearly the best of them. But when you talk of the likes of Phil Lowe, Steve 'Knocker' Norton, Gary Stephens, John Gray and 1987's one-season success, Kevin Ward, you talk about absolutely top-drawer footballers, all of them notable contributors to the 'cause'. The New Zealander Mark Broadhurst was another. 'Raging Bull' shouted the *RLW* poster when Broadhurst came to join us. He was a tough player and a very thoughtful and decent bloke, and is remembered in part for the terrible one-on-one fight he had with Newtown's Steve Bowden in the semi final of 1981, one of the worst big-match brawls I've ever seen.

Broadhurst was an interesting bloke, very deep, and a thoroughly decent human being. Being a prop forward he also wasn't a particularly good sort. They always used to reckon I brought him to Manly specifically so I could stand alongside him in photo shoots.

Then there were the locals. Ian Martin, our five eighth during years of success (he was at the club 1969–74 and 1976–78) was a real tough nut. Martin was a powerhouse in defence and a real hard guy. The only thing he wasn't real keen on was training. I remember the day when he came over to my office, limping noticeably, with the news that his ankle was crook and he wouldn't be able to train that night. The pained expression on his face was something to see. He delivered the news, and dragged himself agonisingly on his way. At that time I had those mirror windows in my office—I could see out, but people outside couldn't see in. I glanced out soon after he had gone, and there was Martin in full stride, not the slightest hint of a limp.

I threw open the window: 'Caught you!' I shouted.

Martin knew he was gone . . . 'Yeah, you've got me,' he said with a slightly embarrassed grin.

John 'Lurch' O'Neill was one of the bravest players I have ever seen. O'Neill played every game in the manner of a runaway express train, putting his body fearlessly on the line week after week, and never shirking an issue, never taking a backward step. And the thing about Lurch was that he never complained. He dealt it out, and he copped plenty back . . . and he saw no need to discuss it further.

Ray Branighan who came across from Souths at the same time as O'Neill was one of the best utility players I have seen. A man for all positions. He'd play anywhere and do it justice, a grand footballer who loved the game, enjoyed a schooner and just . . . fitted in.

Terry Randall was very special for a couple of reasons. For one thing he was one of 'ours'—a home grown product who worked his way through the grades. For another he was dynamic—a raw-boned destroyer in the second row. I credit Randall with the two hardest tackles I have ever seen. One was in a World Cup match in Wales in the '70s when he almost snapped Jim Mills in two. Mills played his football at around 17–18 stone. The other was on Bob 'The Bear' O'Reilly at Sydney Sports Ground. Randall hit O'Reilly just beneath the short ribs, driving in with his shoulder. The ball flew out of O'Reilly's arms as if it had been fired from a gun.

Our two Thom(p)sons were special too—the classy five eighth Alan Thompson, a simply wonderful club man, and the second rower Allan Thomson who turned out to be a fine club man too after some early reservations on our part. Thomson had a reputation when he came to us for being pretty wild off the paddock. We had word that he had been barred from a club or two.

On the day that he signed with us, I said to him, 'Allan, if you misbehave, you and I are going to fall out. And if you don't agree with what I'm saying, we might as well rip this contract up now.' I challenged him by offering him the contract which lay on the desk before me.

Thomson just looked at me with his firm gaze. 'You won't have to worry,' he said. 'I'll do what I have to do.'

And he did. He never put a foot wrong.

Alan Thompson, the five eighth, who graced the club for such a long time—a record 260 first grade games in 12 seasons—was a model footballer, one of the all-time favourites at Manly. Alan was a local boy who played his football with scrupulous fairness and great skill. There was nothing showy about him, but the crowd just loved him. I have always felt that the sort of qualities Alan Thompson showed—loyalty, sportsmanship, skill with the ball in his hand, great courage in defence—were the sort of things that rugby league was built on.

Big Phil Lowe, a tall and powerful English second rower, was a considerable coup for me when I signed him in 1973. Lowe was on $40 a win and $18 a loss with his club Hull Kingston Rovers when the Kangaroos were campaigning in England that year. In the first Test at Wembley, Lowe simply slaughtered the 'Roos with his power-running. He was a wide runner, just about unstoppable. He was *exactly* what we needed at Manly. I flew to England a day or two after Easts signed Johnny Mayes for $9,000, effectively killing the $2000–$200 scheme. Lowe was now the man in my sights, and it was open slather in the wake of Easts' action on Mayes. If that hadn't happened we would not have moved on Lowe. In a car outside Headingley football ground after the second Test, I convinced him that Manly needed him . . . and he needed Manly. He signed in London the next day, for three years with a further two year option clause.

In a newspaper report of the event was the following revelation: 'Mr Arthurson said Lowe had been signed on the regulation $2000 down and $200 a match. The sceptics will have a picnic with that.'

Yes, dear readers, I had thrown a dummy in the interests of diplomacy. Phil in fact was getting a *little* more than that.

Arko

Then began the usual tussle before we got him on the paddock at Brookvale—arguments over the transfer fee to be paid ($22,500 in the end), threats of legal action, and threats to play Lowe without a clearance. A good deal of huffing and puffing, you might say. But in the end we got him onto the paddock and he turned out to be a terrific buy for us in the three seasons he played 1974, 75, 76. I think he was pretty close to the best free-running forward I have ever seen. Absolute dynamite.

Unfortunately the ending to Lowe's career with Manly was not a happy one. After helping us win the premiership of 1976 big Phil went home—to Hull Kingston Rovers. He left quickly and quietly, to sort out some problem with the tax department, I think. I had talked to him here, and advised him not to go back.

'We won't release you,' I said. But he went, anyway. He was still on contract with us, but once he got there the messages were flooding out of England that he wouldn't be back. Then after weeks of drama, my phone rang late one night.

'Mate, it's Phil,' he said. 'Everything's OK. I'm coming back, I'm coming back.'

But by then I had had enough—and the decision had been made. 'I'm sorry, Phil,' I said. 'It's all over.'

The caravan had moved on, but the squabble of late 1976 has not dulled our friendship. Twenty years on Phil Lowe and I are still great pals.

15

THE ONE
THAT GOT
AWAY

Bob Fulton's decision to leave Manly in 1977 was the biggest kick in the guts I took in all my years with the club. It was like a death in the family. And the bloke I was fighting then for the services of Manly's champion was none other than loyal Easts' fan Kerry Packer—the Australian Rugby League's ally in 1995–96 in the battle against the Murdoch empire. Make no mistake, it was Packer who induced Fulton to leave Manly and go to Eastern Suburbs.

All these years on I can reveal what went on in those traumatic weeks and how close Fulton was to staying a Sea Eagle. In the face of Easts' huge offer we had put together a package to keep him. And although it was considerably less than Packer had offered him, Fulton was ready to stay. The final decision came down to the last minute of the last day, and it hinged on a sponsorship package which collapsed, just when it looked as though everything was right.

As the struggle between the two clubs raged back and forth, all of it lovingly detailed in the media, a sponsor had stepped forward with an offer worth an extra $5,000 a year to Fulton. That completed our package, and to his everlasting credit Fulton was prepared to take the substantially lower offer and stick with the club that had given him his chance. But right at the end the bloke rang and said he couldn't come up with the money, after all.

Arko

The morning I delivered that news to Bozo in my office, he cried. And so did I.

There is no doubt I could have found the extra five grand. Easy. But the money involved in the whole thing had been well-aired publicly, and for me to have done it would have been to create problems with the other players. The Fulton offer was up to a certain level and even to have quietly slipped him the 'missing' $5,000 wouldn't have been acceptable. No-one would have believed that he had stayed for the money that he apparently had. I could never have sold that story. In the end I had no alternative but to let him go. And the day that happened was the toughest of them all in my life at Manly. Conversely, on the day he came 'home' to Manly after his seasons with Easts (1977–79) it was among the happiest days of my life. At the club that day they were all saying: 'Arko's son is back.'

I suppose Packer was always going to win that tussle for Fulton in 1977. The Packers and Murdochs of the world will just about always keep beating you with money. I had known Packer for a while by that stage, and over the years we became very good mates. From my point of view the events of 1996 changed that to a large extent, as I will explain later.

Tackling Packer at that time was very much a case of stepping into the big league—a quantum leap, I suppose, from the unwritten code to which I had adhered in my years as Manly secretary. Look, I know I was a great chaser of players and always did the best for Manly, but in the background if I was mates with the opposing club secretary and had respect for him, I would *never* poach a player without reaching some amicable and reasonable agreement first. Canterbury's Peter Moore and I had an arrangement for years, on nothing more than a handshake, that neither of us would poach a player from the other club.

Bob Fulton went out a winner with us in '76, although he's always been that, whatever the scoreboard might have said on this day or that. Our hopes of a St George-style extended winning run after the triumphs of 1972–73 had been dashed by the emergence of a dazzling Eastern Suburbs side under the coaching of Jack Gibson in 1974–75. We were Easts' main challengers both years—runners up in the minor premiership on both occasions, although eight points behind in 1974 and ten behind in 1975. Canterbury then Western Suburbs snuffed us out in two hits in the semis of 1974, and in '75 Easts were too good for us in the final (28–13) before destroying St George in the grand final (38–nil).

In 1976, under the coaching of Frank Stanton, it was a different story. Minor premiers, we survived a semi final loss (23–17 to Parramatta), then won a tense premiership final against the Bulldogs (15–12) to qualify for a grand final showdown with the Eels. This match, played on 18 September, ranks as one of the great grand finals—desperate stuff at a time the Manly–Parramatta rivalry was beginning to rise to boiling point. Trailing 11–10 with seven minutes to go, Parramatta had their chance to win the match, but right winger Neville Glover dropped a pass near the corner on one of the more dramatic moments in grand final history. But would he have scored? I'm not so sure. I've always had the thought that Glover had an eye on our Steve 'Knocker' Norton who was flying across field, looking very determined. We steadied, Graham Eadie booted a late goal, and we won the day 13–10. The match, such a triumph for coach Stanton and skipper Fulton—his first premiership win as a captain—spawned a wonderful photograph of the two of them shedding tears of relief as they embraced after the fulltime hooter had sounded. It was a grand game and a great win. Unbeknownst to all of us it was also the end of an era—Bob Fulton's 219th and last game for the club.

That grand final of '76 featured one of the great coaching moments. When Parramatta tried a 'Flying Wedge' at a critical moment, their entire forward pack propelling hooker Ron Hilditch towards the line, it was an absolutely inspired piece of coaching by the Eels' Terry Fearnley. We held them out by a fraction, with Graham Eadie prominent in that. I helped too, from the grandstand . . . just about pulling a hamstring in the excitement of it all.

It was a real touch 'n' go grand final, and probably the game that sparked the animosity between Manly and Parramatta which became such a feature of football in the late 1970s and

Arko

1980s. In a way the two clubs were soul brothers. We had come into the competition together in 1947 and the race had been on from that point to see which of us would first win a premiership. By fulltime in '76 we'd won three, and that very likely narked Parramatta more than a little. Parramatta fans telling the story of the 1976 grand final will always begin, 'If Neville Glover had held that pass we would have won.' To that I would just reply that if my aunt had balls, she would be my uncle . . .

As it turned out Parramatta moved away from us with their achievements in 1977. They were runaway minor premiers, with our Bob Fulton-less team scraping into the semis fifth, ten points behind them. We departed swiftly, well beaten by a Balmain side inspired by the quicksilver Englishman David Topliss. The Eels then went on to lose the premiership after two controversial and historic weeks and 180 minutes of football. The first-ever drawn grand final, between Parramatta and St George (9–all) brought the two teams back the next week, a day on which St George's furious assault overwhelmed the Eels, and Saints won 22–nil.

It seemed doubtful that rugby league at the business end of the season could get any more dramatic than that. In 1978, it did. And for those that thought Bob Fulton would be simply irreplaceable at Manly, well, they probably learned the lesson that the cemeteries are full of 'irreplaceable' people. We missed Bozo badly for sure. But in 1978 we won without him.

16
1978

In 1978 for reasons that are complex and still not fully explained all these years later, the game of rugby league turned feral. The season started with a horror of a match in Melbourne in which lay the beginning of the infamous Manly–Wests, Silvertails–Fibros feud. And it ended with Frank Stanton's Sea Eagles bringing off one of the most heroic victories in the history of football—only to have it devalued by speculation about a referee nicknamed 'Hollywood' and a controversy that wouldn't die. The team of '78 have never got due credit for what they achieved—and that's one of the cruellest things I know of in 50 years in football.

The season had the whiff of something sensational about it almost from the start. At the invitation of Fitzroy club Manly went to Melbourne in 1978, along with Western Suburbs, to play an 'exhibition' match at an innovative Festival of Football staged at Junction Oval. Some exhibition! Before the game Wests coach Roy Masters gave a talk to his players that turned the air blue. People in the near proximity walked away shaking their heads in disbelief. Roy really stirred things up, to the extent that he told his Magpies that the Manly players didn't want to have anything to do with them—didn't even want to travel on the same bus. Nothing could have been further from the truth. The match that followed before small groupings of bemused spectators was about as vicious as rugby league can get . . . a real nasty one. There were brawls and blues and biff—call it whatever you like—and we beat 'em, only making things worse from Wests' point of view.

To complicate the equation we all had to travel back to Sydney on the same plane. League folklore has players from the two teams grouped at opposite ends of the terminal at Tullamarine, glaring at each other. It wasn't really like that. Roy had his Wests boys glaring at *us*, sure . . . largely because he had told them that we felt superior to them and wanted nothing to do with them.

Right there was the beginning of the Fibros v Silvertails feud which provided huge headlines for years to come. Masters was really something as a motivator—the greatest in my time in rugby league. He was terrific at it, and ruthless. Wests players appeared on national TV slapping each others faces, they reportedly head-butted lockers, punched their way through wooden partitions and generally got *very* steamed up whenever a football match was nearing, and especially if it happened to be one against Manly. It certainly worked. Wests players would give 110 per cent every time they took the field.

At the heart of it all was this Fibros and Silvertails myth. They (Wests) were poor downtrodden battling working class people living in modest houses . . . people we didn't even want to speak to. Meanwhile we were over on the peninsula, swimming in our beautiful blue pools, swanning about under swaying palm trees and sipping our coloured drinks on the pool deck. It was all absolute crap, of course . . . but it had the desired effect. Wests v Manly games became akin to World War III every time they were scheduled, and especially at Lidcombe Oval.

It was all tremendous bullshit, but pretty inspired coaching. At the time the Wests' club president was driving a Mercedes Benz, from memory. And the Magpies' club doctor went one better, he would arrive in his Rolls Royce. We used to laugh about that. Anyhow, we were the 'Silvers' and they were the 'Fibros', and that was that.

The fact of it is, of course, that Manly is just like any other club—made up of flesh and blood people, almost all of whom are fine human beings. Our signings in the '80s of Wests players Les Boyd, John Dorahy and Ray Brown (all bush blokes that Wests had bought, incidentally, not home grown) really stirred up the Magpies, building on this 'hate' thing aimed at Manly. We were one of about ten clubs chasing those blokes; the certainty was they were going *somewhere*—away from Wests. There has always been a good deal of hypocrisy in the Manly-as-villains myth. The fact is that Wests—rugby league's first 'millionaires'—have done very nicely indeed over the years out of talented Manly players such as Dennis Meaney, Doug Walkaden, Steve Knight, Robbie Parker and Tony Antunac. Never has it been one-way traffic. Manly players have come . . . and gone, enticed elsewhere, over the years. Fulton, the Blake brothers Phil and Michael, Wayne Chisholm and plenty of others. The crux of it is this: As tall poppies of the game of rugby league since the early '70s Manly have paid the price that achievers inevitably pay in Australia . . .

Some of those Manly–Wests games of the period bordered on the shocking in their intensity. I remember one at Lidcombe in which Wests deadset went out to put on a blue. Right at the start when Terry Randall ran the ball up, John 'Dallas' Donnelly just belted him . . . then kept belting him with upper cuts in the tackle. Randall, who was no shrinking violet, just threw the ball away . . . and it was on. And that's the way it generally was at that time.

With Parramatta too there was always an edge from Manly's point of view. I remember even as a player back in earlier days there was a sense of apprehension about going to Cumberland Oval. The reception there was nothing if not consistent. Hostile. You'd be getting changed in the old dressing rooms under the grandstand and you'd hear the sound of a thousand feet drumming on the wooden floor above. It was enough to send a chill down your spine. In the late '70s, in the era of referee Greg Hartley, it got a fair bit worse.

Readers may be surprised to know that Parramatta is a club for which I have always had high regard. I think some of the Parramatta–Manly games of that golden, if explosive, period were some of rugby league's greatest and most dramatic ever. And I have always said that when Parramatta were going well, then rugby league was in good shape. And I admire the Parramatta fans too—they're stickers. Loyalty in its traditional sense is a big thing with me and the folk who follow Parramatta have always had that quality in abundance. And what sensational players they had then and later—Ray Price, Brett Kenny, Peter Sterling, Steve Ella, Mick Cronin, Eric Grothe. Just fabulous.

But in the declining relationships of the '70s, things got very tense and tough indeed. As far as Parramatta and Manly were concerned they did sink to an all-time low. If you had anything to do with Manly you'd be guaranteed to cop abuse as you walked in to a game at Cumberland. I was always pretty wary about taking my car up there. There'd be no maroon and white ribbons within a bull's roar of it, and certainly not a Manly sticker to be seen. Some days they really got up my nose. One Monday I really blew up, telling the papers that one group of Parramatta supporters watching a battle at Cumberland the previous day were 'nothing but a bunch of louts and hooligans'. That day there were fights and swearing and filthy language. A member of Channel Seven's camera crew was struck with a ball-bearing and pandemonium reigned. It didn't get any better. After the 1978 semi final replay in which we finally got over the top of Parra—and they then protested on the grounds of Greg Hartley's refereeing errors in the match—I'd had enough. 'They whinged after last year's grand final, they whinged after our first semi—and they're still at it,' I stormed.

Hartley, a former capable footballer who reached first grade standard, then chose the refereeing path when serious injury ended his playing days, was inevitably pretty close to the heart of any drama in those days. Mention Hartley in any pub, even today, and you'll start an argument. My own view is this: that he was a very good rugby league referee, with the necessary confidence and strength to control any match, no matter how tough. He was *not* a cheat. A lot of people were against him because he was showy, a demonstrative performer accused of taking the spotlight away from the players. I don't agree with that. I think he was a great crowd pleaser at just about the time people in rugby league were starting to realise it was part of the entertainment business. I've seen him trip over in matches (which he did fairly regularly), do a forward roll then bounce up as if nothing had happened. He was about the most colourful referee we've ever had. A show pony? Well, it's probably not an unreasonable description. Boy oh boy, he was controversial though, and some commentators sailed close to wind in barking out their views on him. Ron Casey, for example, who fell squarely into the anti-Hartley camp declared at the start of the 1980 season: 'If Manly and Hartley go out on the paddock together there's no doubt in my mind that the Sea Eagles will be the 1980 premiers.'

In August that year Casey overstepped the mark as far as Manly and I were concerned. We placed a ban on Channel Nine as a result of some outrageous comments made by 'The Case'— a bloke with whom I have been on good terms for most of my years in football. In a column Casey wrote for the *Daily Mirror*, he went too far again. I responded:

> Casey has suggested that I am in collusion with Greg Hartley. I am not a saint, but I have never in my life offered anyone a bribe. I have given my entire life to this game and I don't want to be labelled a cheat. There have been numerous times when I have defended him (Casey) to Manly people, assuring them he was only riling us because it was part of his image. This time I've had a gutful.

As I write this book Casey's penchant for lashing out, occasionally overstepping the mark, has again got him into strife. Ironically, his 1997 problems again concerned rugby league— his tangle of words in identifying the new sponsors of the game's premier award (the Nokia . . . ex Rothmans Medal) as Japanese, rather than Finnish. Casey's comments then and later cost him his job on radio 2GB. In my view it was a 'nothing' statement, and if it was just that that cost him his job . . . then the decision was a joke. The Case and I remain good mates. I have always liked the guy because I know that underneath that bluster and bravado is a decent human being. He's done some terrific things for people during his life. And I've enjoyed the differences I have had with him over the years.

Referee Greg Hartley over whom Casey and I had one of our 'tiffs' had his problems, sure. It has often been said of him that he wasn't the greatest technical ref the game has seen. That's true enough. And his temperament was excitable—now and then he'd get carried away. But he had plenty of ability and excellent control on the paddock, because he was so confident and so much in charge. And the thing I liked about his approach to refereeing was that every time he went out there he went out to try and make a good spectacle for the fans.

Season 1978 was the one in which it all blew up around Hartley, masking, as I said, a truly heroic Manly premiership victory. There are no doubt still many people in the game who believe that Hartley cheated that season to get Manly home. Yes, he *did* referee Manly in eight second round games, and we *did* win them all. But good teams can do that—and we're talking about a champion outfit. I have heard all the whispered stories—that his 'payoff' was a block of land on the northside; that he was promised a trip to England with the Kangaroos if he did the 'right thing' and so on. All of it is absolute hogwash—and among the most vicious and scurrilous mischief-making I have heard in my years in the game. I will deny until the day that I die that there was any wrong-doing that year.

The rumours even took the form of poetry! On grand final eve that year I received one long, anonymous offering which began:

I'll tell you a tale of Manly-Warringah
The team with the League wrapped around their finger
In the grand final they wanted to be
So Ken went and brought them a referee

Humphreys and Arthurson threw a small party
There was only one guest, his name Greg Hartley
Kev told him the plot, all with a grin
Greg thought, then replied: 'OK, count me in.'

And so on. There was scurrilous material abroad, and all of it cruelly unfair to the referees and to the football teams which fought out that exciting series.

Yes, Greg Hartley *did* have a chequered and controversial run through the most explosive finals series the game has ever witnessed. Yes, he *did* make mistakes as referees do, with tackle counts. And yes, he did accompany the Kangaroos on part of their campaign in England and France . . . and I'll tell you why right now. Long before the finals, the English League had asked us to send our best referee as a working guest on the tour. Hartley, the top referee through the finals, was the logical choice for that honour. Nothing sinister there.

Hartley's critics from '78 fall back on selective memory when they try to justify the claims that the referee was 'hot' that year. They'll tell you of:

- Tackle miscounts in the semi final replay (Parramatta v Manly), six of which went in Manly's favour.
- The fact that he sent off Parramatta's Ray Price for punching in the first half of that match. Price was subsequently exonerated.
- Wests claiming Hartley had robbed them of a try in the final (v Manly).
- Cronulla's complaints that Hartley had turned a blind eye to Manly foul play in the grand final (v Manly).

But you can be sure they won't mention such things as:

- In the preliminary semi final the supposedly anti-Parramatta Hartley awarded the Eels the penalties 13–4.
- In the Manly–Parramatta semi final replay Hartley sent off Manly's John Gray—with Parramatta leading 11–2.
- In the drawn grand final Hartley awarded Cronulla a questionable 71st minute scrum penalty from which the Sharks (via Steve Rogers) goaled for 11–all. Late in the day both Rogers and our Steve Martin missed with field goal snaps that could have won a premiership.

Hartley was flawed now and then in that volcanic month of football. But I think any referee would have been, considering the enormous dramas and pressures that existed. The fact of that goal kicked by Rogers in the grand final is one of rugby league's great forgotten moments. It never gets a mention when the Hartley era is being discussed. But I can still picture the referee scurrying around a scrum to award Cronulla their penalty—and the drama as Rogers potted the goal from a wide angle, tying the match-up, just as had happened exactly 12 months before when Parramatta and St George made history by playing the first-ever drawn grand final.

I'll just say that the awarding of that dubious scrum penalty (most scrum penalties were pretty dubious, scrums being what they were) was a bloody strange action by a referee who 'favoured Manly'. It set up the opportunity for Cronulla to win the match. They couldn't do it, neither could we . . . and then the Manly boys came back and smashed them in the replay 16–nil the following Tuesday afternoon.

I'll tell you what it was about, Hartley and '78. A lot of people didn't like him, and that was a fact. There was a bit of the mug lair in him, and that was also a fact. But I reckon what they *really* didn't like was that Manly were winning again, for the fourth time in the decade. We were not a popular club with many fans, and people looked desperately for excuses, reasons to suggest that we were being 'favoured'.

I can say with absolute honesty that never in my years in league have I known of a referee to cheat, or to take a bribe. I have heard rumours, yes, and I have already recounted the story of Darcy Lawler and the semi final of 1961. I wouldn't be human if I didn't have suspicions there. I am aware that there are people who believed Lawler was a punter and a cheat, and that George Bishop before him was questionable, too. I have no first hand knowledge of any of that. The rumours about Hartley were pretty much confined to the overseas trip being some sort of 'payback'. They are untrue and unfair. But the lies and the rumours flew thick and fast in that season of 1978. I remember blowing up at one stage when stories reached my ears that some liar in the Referees' Association claimed to have heard me say eight weeks or so out from the semi finals that Greg Hartley *would* get the grand final. Bullshit!

Eric Cox, the referees' director at that time and the man responsible for appointing Hartley, tells a wry story against himself. On a blazing hot day in the summer of 1978–79 as the dust gradually settled on the dramas of the season, Cox was painting his house at Revesby. Sweating furiously in blazing temperatures and covered in paint, he finally gave up. Slumped in a chair inside Eric said to his wife: 'Colleen, tell me what am I doing painting the bloody house in 110 degree (42 degrees Celsius) temperatures . . . when we're supposed to have got $50,000 out of the Hartley business!'

On reflection, all of it is very sad. A very great, gutsy football team won the competition in 1978, surviving six finals matches, five of them sudden death, and two replays in 24 days. It was one of the finest achievements by a team in the game's history. You'd walk into the dressing room after a game and there would be blokes smothered in ice and bandages . . . and blood. How they got back on the field game after game, week after week, I'll never know. It was a magnificent and heroic achievement and a wonderful tribute to Frank Stanton's strength and leadership qualities as coach.

Strangely enough, I think all the drama surrounding Hartley, Parramatta's fury at what allegedly was going on (which included a protest seeking to have the semi final replayed for a *second* time) and the persistent air of high drama fuelled the team. The Manly players reached the stage where they were so incensed with the innuendo and the criticism that they became an irresistible force every time they took the field. The controversy became a mighty motivating tool—and we used it as shrewdly as we could. Probably I overplayed it. I had the team believing the whole *world* was against us . . . 'So let's get out there and give it to them.'

Twenty years down the track I've got used to the criticism of Hartley and to what some people believe went on in '78. Those people are wrong. But I'm still angry to think that a great team in history is overlooked to a large extent considering its momentous achievement. In more than one game in those tumultuous weeks the Manly boys looked done to a dinner, only to somehow drag themselves off the canvas. I'll certainly never forget them—skipper Max Krilich, such an inspiration, Graham Eadie, Alan Thompson, 'Wombat' Eadie, hardman John Harvey, Johnny Gibbs with his head in the air and his socks around his ankles and all the rest . . .

From all the drama and turmoil a wonderful Manly year was constructed—one of the best. Frank Stanton, so thorough, knowledgeable and expert at what he did, had a marvellous season—taking over as Australian coach, and eventually guiding the Kangaroos to an Ashes victory in England. 'Biscuits' Stanton has always been a very special Sea Eagle and a very special rugby league man. He was a near-champion player (128 games for Manly, 1963 Kangaroo tourist) and he became a champion, ground-breaking coach. Manly's grand final heroes provided a strong foundation for his touring team of '78.

Stanton's selection as Sydney, NSW, then Australian coach was preceded by one of most intense lobbying tussles that Phillip Street has ever seen. With the Country League throwing their weight behind the popular Don Furner, the appointments went right down to the wire. I was accused of lobbying hard for Stanton. Well, I make no secret of that, I did it because I thought he deserved the job—and that was intended as no reflection on Furner, who went on to coach the 1986 Kangaroo 'Unbeatables' and who became the best selector I have ever worked with. In '78 I reckoned Stanton, such a firm displinarian and hard-edged professional coach, was just the man to take Australia's representative teams into a new era. He did it brilliantly, laying the foundation with the '78 Roos—although they made the mistake of dropping the intensity in France—then bringing it home majestically with the performances of the peerless team of 1982, the 'Invincibles'. So, if I played politics in '78, made some phone calls, lobbied some people, I make no apologies. In the end, 'Biscuits' Stanton bolted in 28–13 in the State coaching ballot. I was happy. We had got the best man for the job—and really, isn't that what it's all about?

I did some lobbying in my time—but I'll tell you that I never lobbied for anyone who wasn't worth it. In 1978 I lobbied for Fulton to be captain of the Kangaroos because he was the standout candidate. Ditto for Max Krilich and the '82 Kangaroos, with Krilich coming home from that campaign rated one of the finest and most inspirational captains Australia had ever had. I had influence in the game but it was never used unless the bottom-line outcome was for the benefit of the game. People who know me, know how fiercely loyal I am to Australia and Australians, would understand very deeply that I would never do anything to the detriment of an Aussie sporting team. Player responsibility to the game and its traditions, in turn, are very much part of that equation . . .

17

HILL
CLIMBS THE
MOUNTAIN

On a morning in late September 1994 I sat in my office on the fifth floor of the NSW Leagues Club, Phillip Street. Across the desk from me sat Terry Hill, the hulking Manly, NSW and Australian centre. Tears streamed down Terry's cheeks. I had called Hill into my office that day with every intention of pulling him out of the Kangaroo team for England. Hill was in the news at that time, in the worst possible way. An incident outside the Woollahra Hotel had caterpaulted Hill into court on assault charges and into the newspapers, in huge, ugly headlines. There was a rising clamour of opinion that Hill should not be allowed to tour with the Kangaroos—a campaign for which he was a certainty on the strength of the form he had shown that year.

His immediate future lay in my hands that morning. Opposite me sat a remorseful young man, full of regret for what he had done . . . and regret for what damage his actions might have done to both his career, and the game. The tears flowing freely, he said to me: 'If you believe I should withdraw from the team—then I'll withdraw right now.' I will admit frankly that his demeanour, his attitude, his obviously heartfelt regret touched me a great deal. I paused, and considered . . .

The silence was a long one. Then, I made my decision. 'I'll tell you what I'm going to do,' I told him. 'I'm going to let you go with the team, but I want an assurance from you that what happened in this business will *never* happen again. Give me that assurance—and I'll accept it from you. But if there is a moment's trouble on the tour you'll be on the first plane home.'

And so Terry Hill went to England and France with the 'Roos when perhaps many people thought he shouldn't have. And I'm proud to say that on tour, he was an absolute model player—a fine representative of his country. The pressure was right on him and he never put a foot out of line. I was very, very proud of him. He had responded like a man; I felt that his behaviour, his contribution to the tour and his form vindicated my decision to let him go.

I had to laugh one day in '97 when I bumped into Terry, down at Manly training. By chance I was at the ground at a time that Terry was in the news over a driving charge which had ended with him in court . . . and in the headlines. As I walked into the dressing room, Hill was there with one of the Manly trainers, Brian Hollis, a considerable character known as 'The Sheriff'. Hill had his back to me and couldn't see me, although the Sheriff could. They had obviously been talking about Hill's problem with the law and on spotting me the Sheriff said loudly: 'I'll bet if Ken Arthurson was here now you'd be pretty red in the face about it all.' Next moment I was alongside Hill— and I don't think I've *ever* seen a bloke go redder in the face than he did as he stuttered and stammered trying to explain what had gone on. In fact, I wasn't down there to see Hill at all. I had come to see the doc about a bung knee.

The subject of the off-field behaviour of footballers is too often in the news—more so these last couple of years. It almost seems in the aftermath of the destructive Super League raid on the game as if there has been a decline in manners and responsible behaviour. It saddens me to contemplate the various incidents of boorish and unacceptable behaviour hitting both the headlines and the courts.

Some of it comes back to individuals, and some to a lack of firm guidelines. No-one expects absolute perfection in behaviour from groups of young footballers; there will inevitably be noise and chiacking and some fun and games. But out in the public arena people are thoroughly entitled to reasonable behaviour, respect and consideration. I am pleased to say that the teams which came under my direction over the years remained well within the bounds. It was to do with control; I was never out to win popularity polls with the players I managed. A lot of people confuse popularity with respect. Players in my teams knew that if they did the right thing by me, I would do the right thing by them, and go out of my way to help them in any way that I could.

We have had our problems now and then on tours. The 'Bowler Hat' tour of 1967 is the most infamous of all, featuring a sad old run-down hotel in Ilkley, some homesick footballers and behaviour that at times went over the top, leading to two leading players who were never named being fined when they got back from England and plenty of juicy headlines. The enduring legend is of an Aussie player parading through the streets of Ilkley in a bowler hat—and nothing more. It never happened.

The Australian Rugby League also had cause to impose fines after the Kangaroo campaign of 1990. That was a highly successful campaign, featuring a simply breathtaking second Test at Old Trafford in which Mal Meninga's last gasp try got the 'Roos home and safely on their way to the Ashes.

Yes, there were some problems with that team. The 'Cricket Club Incident' received great play in the media back home in the wake of the tour—concerning a fight that broke out at a club outside Manchester as celebrations raged in the wake of the second Test win. I was still in England after the third Test when the phone rang one night, with team manager Keith Barnes on the line from Paris. Keith asked me to have a word with the team leaders Bob Fulton (coach) and Mal Meninga (captain). He could see signs of a team going off the rails, and wanted to nip it in the bud. I spoke to them both, and made some strong points which needed to be passed on to the team including the reminder that the Kangaroos were ambassadors for Australia, and should never forget that. In the fortnight following, the French leg was negotiated successfully. But when the team came home we took due account of the reports of the managers Barnes and Les Stokes, and imposed across-the-board fines totalling around $10,000 to cover damage done to hotels on tour. In almost all ways it had been a tremendously successful tour, but we felt we had to take a strong stand to reinforce the point about expectations of behaviour for teams which wear the green and gold.

Managing football teams is no easy job. It's a great challenge, but a stressful one. Keith Barnes, such a fine, admirable bloke, probably did it tough in 1990. Very likely the tour aged him—although he's not the first sporting team manager to suffer from that phenomenon. Keith was probably too nice a bloke to be looking after 28 young footballers among who there was an element of potential trouble here and there. I'm sad to say that there were blokes on the 1990 tour who exploited Keith Barnes to an extent because he was too decent, too gentlemanly. That disappointed me. It's at times like that players see the other side of me. There is a line of reasonable behaviour drawn and if they step over it, my attitude was always, f— 'em. If blokes overstepped the line, did the wrong thing by teammates and managers, I had no element of sympathy for them. If it happened on a national team tour that was even worse . . . they were letting their country down. I have always said to tour managers. 'Look, they can't do anything to you, but you can do plenty to them. If you feel you have to—send them home.'

There are other ways of dealing with the troublemakers, too. I'll be frank—there have been players over the years whose behaviour has virtually disqualified them from tours. There have been blokes that I just wouldn't tolerate. I'm not going to name names . . . they know who they are. They disqualify themselves. All it needs is a quiet word to selectors . . . 'Don't even mention his bloody name to me'.

I have sympathy for what leading sportspeople have to put up with in public in a world in which they are such recognisable figures, thanks to television. Take the North Sydney players for example, and what has now become their *infamous* appearance at the Pakistan–Australia one-day cricket match in Sydney on New Year's Day, 1997. There is no doubt they were copping some verbal flak from people around them. But high profile sportspeople have to learn to live with that. The fact of life for today's footballers is this: they can't expect to walk around getting the huge money they're getting, the adulation, the publicity ... and not be prepared to sacrifice something. And one of those sacrifices is that when they're out in public they have to be *ten times* as aware of behaving reasonably and responsibly than most people. They owe that to themselves as public figures, and in many cases role models, to the clubs they play for, and especially to the game that has given them their chance. The game must never tolerate loutish behaviour as the norm.

I always made that very clear to the teams I was involved with on tours. I didn't care how much they enjoyed themselves—in fact I wanted them to do exactly that. I didn't expect them to stand around like toy soldiers. But enjoying yourself in my book doesn't extend to kicking down doors, or using bad language in front of women or generally acting like a lout. Anything that intrudes on the comfort or safety of other people is out of bounds in my view. I always said to my blokes: 'The more you do the right thing by people, the better time you will have because they will go out of their way to look after you.'

Whenever I bought a footballer for Manly I considered several things. Of course he had to be the *player* we wanted—the right position, the talent. But of vital importance was that he had to be the type of bloke who would fit into the community at Manly, and fit in with the club and the other players. I didn't care if blokes were a bit wild and woolly, but the main thing was when they were representing the club, they had to behave themselves. These days players have to accept that because of their enormously high profiles, they are representing their clubs at all times. The Manly players knew that if they did the right thing I would treat them as my sons. If they didn't— I'd chop their heads off; wouldn't think twice about it.

I believe that the 1970 World Cup tour, which I had the pleasure of managing, was a pretty fair example of the way it should work. It wasn't perfect—and you don't expect that with 24 or so young, healthy, energetic blokes. But it was pretty close to trouble free. I'm sure the players from that tour would tell you that they had a terrific time. I remember when we first arrived at our hotel in Bradford, the hotel manager approached me with a list of strict rules: they can't do this, they can't do that. I interrupted him. 'Listen,' I said, 'I'll give you my personal assurance that there will be no misbehaviour in the hotel, but there has to be some give and take.' So we talked about such things as players having guests in their rooms (which was against hotel rules) and some other areas which demanded flexibility—and reached a basis for agreement. We shook hands and made a deal on that first day. I told the players the rules, and they never put a foot wrong. In fact the hotel went out of its way to fit the presence of a football team into its general day-to-day running. They provided us with a special room and a juke box—and that became the place where we had post-game parties and celebrations.

There's a good yarn from that tour involving the footballing priest Father John Cootes and Billy Smith who roomed together. The story goes that Father John said to Smith one day: 'Billy, if you follow me and behave yourself, I'll see that you're put through the Pearly Gates.'

Billy, never short of an answer, replied: 'Father, if you follow me on the football field . . . I'll put you through under the posts.'

Rugby league's wonderful mix of colours and creeds and shapes and sizes and good guys and bad guys has always been one of the big things that has drawn me to the game. League has always been a large and troublesome beast, with drama never far from the surface. But I loved, and still do, the fact that it was a game with the common touch—a game for everyone, no matter what race, belief or persuasion.

For most of its life league has been a game of opportunity, equally for black and for white. The racist sledging incident of 1997 involving North Sydney's Chris Caruana and the young Newcastle Aboriginal Owen Craigie was, I hope, an aberration. Placed in the public arena it certainly brought a swift and firm response from Phillip Street. Certainly there has been chiacking and talking and what is now known as 'sledging' on the football field ever since the game began. You don't expect ambitious, determined players to be deathly silent over 80 minutes of a match.

But I'd like to think that racial prejudice is not part of our game . . . and must never be. Maybe I'm a little naive about that. Evidence of it, as in the highly publicised Caruana–Craigie incident, is certainly not acceptable to me. I'll tell you my philosophy: I didn't give a bugger what colour they were, where they came from, what religion they were—if they could play . . . they were in! And that's exactly what I like about the game—that in the main those questions aren't even asked. Whether a bloke's a garbo or a brain surgeon, Catholic or Callithumpian, snow white or coal black—he's going to make my side if he can play football. My own way has always been to treat the bloke who picks up the garbage the same as I'd treat the Prime Minister. They are all men. And rugby league is like that too.

Occasionally over the years I have heard remarks that could come into the category of 'racist'. There used to be a theory, long since discounted, that Aboriginal players tended to be unreliable or perhaps lacking in the necessary courage to play league at a sustained high level. In the flood of wonderfully talented and courageous Aboriginal players who have graced the game, that theory has long since sunk without trace. Now the Pacific Islanders are making their spectacular contribution. And years ago I heard a club official of my acquaintance offer the opinion—more in jest than seriously, I must say: 'If you've got four darkies in your team you can win the comp . . . if you've got five or more, you're in trouble.' It is a tired and unacceptable theory long since despatched to the rubbish heap. As I've said, it's not the colour or the creed of football players that wins matches. It's the ability.

18

THE
DOWNFALL OF
A PRESIDENT

The tenth anniversary of anything is supposed to be a celebration. For Kevin Humphreys, seventh president of the
NSWRL, it was a tragedy worthy of Shakespeare. In fact
Humphreys never quite made the ten years, falling a week short
in the most dramatic circumstances imaginable in the autumn
of 1983—his reign as the President and kingpin of rugby league
over. It had been a rollercoaster ride, with all of us in the game's
elite administrative group hanging on tight in changing times.
Club sponsorship had arrived as a factor in the game, television
was looking more and more like the shaper of sport's future,
Australian supremacy had been established on the world stage.
We had introduced new teams (Canberra and Illawarra in
1982). Manly had won some premierships (1973, 76, 78) and
magnificent teams had emerged at Easts (1974–75) and
Parramatta (1981–82 . . . and with '83 still to come). We'd had
some fun, made some mistakes . . . and kicked some goals. The
best of them all was the decision in 1980 to begin the 'State of
Origin' concept—with Senator Ron McAuliffe throwing up the
idea and Humphreys, to his credit, embracing it with cautious
enthusiasm. Those of us in the group which pretty much pulled
the strings in the game perhaps felt that the good times would
go on forever . . .

But, of course, things never do. In May '83 rugby league's

house came tumbling down with the immense drama surrounding the ABC's *Four Corners* episode, 'The Big League', which claimed Humphreys as its victim—even though the programme's sights were more specifically set on even higher targets. The 'Big League' claim was about corruption in high places in NSW. The NSWRL president just happened to be caught in the middle of it, a pawn in a much bigger game.

The four day period before and after the programme went to air was unbelievably dramatic. Through that week, the tension and the anticipation had been building, and little else was talked of in rugby league. It was like a huge storm brewing in the south—everyone was uneasy, knowing that it was coming. On the Friday (with the programme going to air on the Saturday night) the members of the Australian Rugby League met in Brisbane, at Lenon's Hotel. It was a knife-edge meeting. The NSW delegates Gibson, Bellew, O'Toole and myself were still supportive of the president, but it was clear that the Queenslanders McAuliffe, Hunter, Stafford, Gallagher and Livermore had their doubts. They met privately at one stage, and clearly were no longer supportive of the president. The forthcoming programme and its implications were far and away the major factor—although there were dark rumours of Queensland discontent at other aspects of Humphreys' performance, relating to the Kangaroo tour of 1982. Now and then in ARL circles there had been rumblings of discontent about Kevin's gambling habits. Finally that day Humphreys got to his feet and with characteristic strength delivered the words: 'In view of the split that is very apparent here, I have decided that I don't want to do anything further to bring discredit on the game. I hereby submit my resignation.' Humphreys told the meeting he did not want to see any further shadow cast over a game that he loved. The resignation was accepted with sadness and regret—and Ron McAuliffe appointed caretaker president of the ARL.

The *Four Corners*' 'Big League' episode when it hit the next night was a stunner. It focused on the circumstances which had led to Humphreys' acquittal in August 1977 on nine counts of misappropriating $52,519 from Balmain Leagues Club. In its implications the programme was to lead to NSW Premier Neville Wran stepping aside temporarily from office, to a Royal Commission—and eventually to the gaoling of the former NSW chief stipendiary magistrate, Murray Farquhar. Kevin Humphreys, however, was its first victim.

Late in the afternoon of Monday 2 May 1983, Humphreys read a prepared statement to an assembled media army in the board room at NSW Leagues Club, and resigned from his positions as president and executive director of the NSWRL. I was an arm's length away, sitting to his left. It was a sad, sad day, a great shame really and my face in the now-famous photo taken by John Elliott of the moment of resignation, truly reflects how I felt.

Later, I took him to the downstairs bar of the Leagues Club for a beer. I was to spend a lot of time with him in that painful period in his life. He was very, very down—at the lowest ebb I have ever seen him. I remember him saying to me: 'You know, I feel bloody awful about the problems I've caused my family and obviously about the damage I've done to myself . . . but the worst thing is that I've been an instrument of causing discredit to the game . . . and that's the last thing I would ever have wanted to do.' Jeez, I felt for him. In fact not until the events of 1995–96 did I ever again feel that sense of depression about my association with rugby league.

Back in 1977 Kevin Humphreys had hit a hurdle, brought temporarily to his knees by what was probably the single weak spot in his make-up—his love of gambling. It was to repay gambling debts that he had taken the money from Balmain Leagues Club. Significantly, Humphreys paid back every single cent of that money—unlike some of the Australian 'folk heroes' of later years . . . those bastards who stole millions and never looked like paying anything back.

People reading this may perhaps consider that my views on Kevin Humphreys are coloured by my friendship for him, a friendship, incidentally, that has endured strongly to today. But I think that any close study of the Humphreys era would arrive at the conclusion that from 1973 to 83 the game had a leader of strength and high ability, who engineered changes which readied rugby league for the challenges it faced in becoming part of the wider entertainment industry. I believe that Humphreys has been unfairly maligned over the years. He made a mistake—yes—but he paid for that tenfold, his reputation shredded by sections of the media who seemed hell-bent to 'get' him.

Many people would contend that Kevin Humphreys had his faults. He could be abrasive and difficult—and there is no doubt he made some enemies. He was an unforgiving person— when he fell out with someone . . . well, that was that. If the person involved happened to be in the media, that sometimes made it a bit tougher still. I have always felt in Sydney particularly that there are sections of the media who are not *really* rugby league-friendly. They tolerate the game, sure, but deep down they don't *really* approve. Give them a chance to sink the slipper—and they'll do it. As Kevin found out.

In my own dealings with people I have worked hard over the years to try and be patient and reasonable and understanding, and have genuinely tried to accept the truism that other people have other views, and that that should be accepted. I have rarely closed doors on people. Things happen sometimes and people get offside with each other, but however serious it all may seem at the time . . . life goes on. I have (almost) always been prepared to forgive and forget. I guess Kevin and I differed markedly in that regard. I'm happy to say that my relationship with the media over the years has been pretty good. I don't agree with them all the time, and they don't agree with me . . . but both sides have a job to do, and accepting that makes life easier. Generally, I have been treated fairly, quoted accurately, and have enjoyed the cut and thrust that regular dealings with the media provides. Now and then I've said something dumb and been quoted. At those times I can honestly say I never went for the old fallback, 'I was misquoted'—I've been far happier to admit that I made a blue. People can live with that. I count many friends among the members of the 'fourth estate' over the years, and some others with whom I have now and then been on collision course. But it would be a boring old world if we all agreed on everything, wouldn't it?

Kevin's lines of communication weren't good. Answering letters was not a strong point, and there was a perception of him in the early 1980s of being increasingly remote from 'ordinary' league people. This was reflected in a 1983 poll of 2,500 people undertaken by *Rugby League Week* magazine which revealed serious reservations about aspects of the way the game was being run. The problem with Kevin in the main was that he took on too much of the work load himself, failing to delegate. The basic sadness that I felt for Kevin in the aftermath of his downfall was that he was painted in some places as a bad or evil person. Nothing could be further from the truth. He is essentially a bloody decent person, with a lovely family, and a bloke who cares a great, great deal about the game of rugby league.

On 3 May 1983 the NSW and Australian Rugby Leagues had to begin coming to terms with the fact that an era had ended. In the wake of Humphreys' departure the game was in a state of shock. I think 'turmoil' and 'chaos' would be reasonable words to describe its condition. It was as if all the bad stuff—real and imagined—was spewing out in some sort of cleansing process. There were rumours of games being fixed, of gross mismanagement, of dishonest behaviour and backroom deals, and jobs for the boys. We were in seriously bad odour through the country districts in 1983 on the basis of the decision to take (live) Saturday league away from the ABC, and hand it to Channel Nine. In retrospect, the decision was calamitous. Our belief was that the commercial network would reach all the areas covered by the ABC. They didn't, and the howls of protest continued, week after week. It was a short-sighted and poor decision, but we were big enough to change it as quickly as we could. Most of the rumours doing the rounds were untrue, but the fact was undisputable: that the game was at the lowest ebb of my experience—to that time.

Tom Bellew, with a fine working background in the Australian stevedoring industry and the public service, was elected president of the NSWRL, and late in May on the persistent urging of Senator Ron McAuliffe, I became chairman of the Australian Rugby League. McAuliffe really worked hard on me. He was concerned that we were missing the boat nationally with the promotion of our game . . . and he was right. I was then in my 21st year as secretary of Manly.

Arko

With Tom Bellew it was very much a case of the right man for the right job at the right time. Rugby league sorely needed a steady hand to steer the ship in the aftermath of Kevin Humphreys' dramatic departure—and Tom was perfect. A precise, thorough man with a fine eye for detail, he was the supreme expert on the game's constitution. Much had to be written and rewritten, and he was the man to do it. He was a tower of strength as we headed towards incorporation (December 1983), with the running of the game to be taken over by a streamlined nine-man board. Tom Bellew stayed at the helm as president for three years or so, always declaring that when I wanted to take over the NSW presidency, he would step down. He did a wonderful job, rebuilding the game's reputation and building, technically, the structure needed to carry it on towards 2000. Credibility is a big word with Tom Bellew, and in the period of his presidency he did a lot towards helping the game of rugby league win back its own. He stayed as president until the annual meeting of 1986 when he stepped aside in my favour—having made a priceless contribution.

Regrettably Tom did not get on with his Queensland counterpart McAuliffe. The pair were so different: Tom the conservative, thorough career administrator; McAuliffe, the ex-politician hardened in the rough-housing of Federal Parliament. Chalk and cheese. Sadly Ron McAuliffe never looked on Tom Bellew as a genuine 'rugby league bloke'. Being a knockabout himself Ron was more on the wavelength of those sort of blokes, blokes who had played the game, liked a beer and an argument. Scrappers. If they happened by chance to have a slight larrikin streak, that was no problem at all.

The pair of them were good mates of mine and I tried desperately to get them to work comfortably together. I never really succeeded. More than once I had to prevail on McAuliffe to apologise to Tom after he had gone over the top with some statement or other. It was a bloody shame—they were two terrific rugby league men and at 75, Tom Bellew is still soldiering away in the cause.

I miss old Ron McAuliffe a lot. He died in 1988 and a jazz band played at his wake at the QRL's State of Origin Bar. He was a great bloke with a tough, pragmatic way of looking at things. He had a saying for most occasions. When the State of Origin machine was in full flight at Lang Park, the locals used to give me hell. I remember Ron saying to me one particularly noisy night: 'Look, you never want to worry about it. It's nice to get a cheer and it's not quite as nice to get a boo. But, either way, it's a helluva lot better than being ignored!'

Ron always reckoned I was a bit too easy-going with people, too inclined to stop and listen to every Tom, Dick and Harry. He once quoted me something an old Queensland parliamentarian used to say, 'If you're on your way to Parliament House to a meeting and you stop to attend to every stray dog that barks at you—you'll never get there. Just heel them off, and keep walking.'

Things moved with amazing speed in rugby league in the momentous year of 1983. When I reflect on the period it seems to me akin to the early days of the Whitlam Labor government in 1972 with its succession of exciting announcements and initiatives. Almost every week for us in '83 it seemed as if some giant step was being taken towards the new deal that had to happen. The basic building block for the game's great revival was a two-day forum, held at Sydney's Regent Hotel. It remains in my memory as one of the most interesting events associated with rugby league I have ever attended, full of plain speaking. Speaker after speaker from the game's broad community—players, coaches, media, the public, referees, marketers—got up and explained their thoughts on the game, its faults, and the direction in which it should be heading. Sometimes the debate sizzled: Referees Director Eric Cox copped plenty of flak from colleagues like Don McDonald and Laurie Bruyeres, some of it relating to the Hartley years. But being of thick skin 'Ecca' was a bloke quite capable of hitting back . . . hard.

In July came the big one—the appointment of John Quayle in the newly created position of general manager of the NSW Rugby League. Quayle these days has his place in league history, rightly regarded as a major contributor and guiding hand in one of the greatest eras the game has ever experienced. But there is a little known story I can now tell about an early fumble that almost cost him the job at Phillip Street. I have always been a believer that the key jobs in the game should be held by people who have come from *within* the game. I think such people have a passion for the game, a real feeling for it. When I heard back in '83 that Quayle, an ex-international forward, was to be an applicant for the job, I was pleased. I had had some dealings with him in his role at Easts Leagues Club where he was assistant manager, and I had been impressed.

But when John came to his first interview down at Phillip Street he went horribly close to blowing it. I don't know whether he was stage struck or just got himself into a tangle, but he didn't handle it well at all. At one stage it reached the point where I thought: 'Jeezus, what's he talking about?' In answering questions he kept going off on different tangents and when he left there were some glances across the table, and around the room. It is fair to say that the board, collectively, was not too impressed. He had gone from odds-on to a somewhat longer quote.

That night he rang me and asked me what I thought. I told him straight. 'John, you didn't go too well. You seemed to be trying to act and talk like someone else.' I reminded him of a simple truth—that he had got to where he was in the game by being John Quayle. 'Just be yourself next time . . . be your own man,' I advised. (I recently gave the same advice to Warren Lockwood when he stepped in as the new chairman of the NSWRL after my retirement.) A few days later Quayle was back in for his second interview—and this time he blitzed them, handling it tremendously well.

Fourteen years down the track I can say that I had some influence in his appointment back in '83. And I say it with pride, for John Quayle turned out to be an administrator of exceptional ability. He did a marvellous job for the League and a great deal of the achievement of wonderfully successful years can be attributed to his initiative and hard work.

During the bad times of the ARL–Super League war he was absolutely rock solid. The quality of his unswerving loyalty to the game, and to myself as chairman, was just terrific. He was under continual fire—and he never wilted.

Quayle developed enemies; I am aware of that. He was a
bloke who was never afraid to speak his mind, to say what he
honestly believed. In some quarters that trait brought him
unjust criticism. Some people judged him brusque, arrogant,
and hard to get on with. And he is none of those things.
Throughout the years of his tenure he was guided only by his
determination to the best for the game of rugby league—and if
it happened that he stood on some toes on the way through,
then so be it.

With Quayle on board, and the ship steadying, the League
began the long haul back. Incorporation brought a new central
core of officials to guide the game; the historic first board of the
NSWRL, comprising nine men. They were: Tom Bellew, John
Quayle, Alex Mackie, John O'Toole, businessmen Alan David
and Graham Lovett and club representatives Denis Fitzgerald
(Parramatta) and Monty Porter (Cronulla) plus me. A good
board, a well balanced board in my view. For the first time in
its history rugby league had a central voting body in which the
parochial thinking of individual clubs would not be a factor.

Initially there was some unease about the two clubs specifically represented on the board. But the cynics overlooked the
overall balance of the board. We were there to do a good job
for *rugby league,* not to do sweetheart deals for this club or
that. Later, the club representatives on the board changed—
with Peter Moore (Canterbury) and Terry Parker (Souths)
replacing Fitzgerald and Porter.

I thought Porter and Fitzgerald did the job pretty well on
that first board. But Fitzgerald at that stage didn't have the
maturity that he has now. I'll say it quite openly that over the
years I haven't always seen eye to eye with Denis. Particularly
during the Hartley business I found him vindictive to an extent,
certainly dogmatic, and immature at times—a young official
still learning the ropes. As relationships between Parramatta
and Manly dipped to their lowest-ever levels in the late 1970s
and early '80s so too did my relationship with Fitzgerald. Back
then I made some scathing comments about him. He was so
abrasive and I have never been a bloke to keep turning the other
cheek. I always took the view that if there was going to be a

blue, well, let's get our coats off, roll up our sleeves and get into it. Fitzgerald and I had some ding-dong rows, in person and in print.

But over the years I've watched him grow in the job and in my opinion he has become a very good chief executive. These days he has my respect and my complete confidence, and I was very pleased to have him along for my farewell dinner at Phillip Street in early 1997 . . . something that certainly wouldn't have been a chance years ago. I think so much of him now that I am of the opinion that one day he will be president of the NSWRL. He is a man who obviously cares about the game, and one thing has never changed: my admiration for the loyalty he has shown Parramatta.

One day, as a man with a deep love for the club he serves, he may have to make the decision that I wrestled with in 1983 . . .

19

So Long, Sea Eagles

I grew sick of the sound of Ron McAuliffe's voice in the winter of 1983. It seemed that every second day Ron would be on the phone. The topic was almost always the same: his belief that I should leave Manly and take over as executive chairman of a newly established ARL secretariat in Sydney. Ron saw vast deficiencies in the way we were promoting (or not promoting) the game on the national stage, and he played on my conscience. 'You've done the job for Manly,' he would say. 'Rugby league is in trouble and if you are serious about its future, you must take the next step.'

I resisted his overtures for months. I had a job I loved, at a club I loved. Why would I move? But on long nights spent thinking about it I knew the senator was right. To that point we had only been toying with spreading the gospel of rugby league. With the Kevin Humphreys drama, the game had reached a watershed. It could either head on to greater things . . . or plod along forever as a sporting underachiever.

In August, I made the big decision. I would leave Manly and give it a go at the ARL. It was a huge wrench—a decision that came only after a great deal of agonising. I had been secretary of Manly for 20 years and the club had been in my blood for 35 or so. But the challenge of doing something bigger and perhaps better nagged at me. So I said yes and with a trusty lieutenant Bob

Abbott and my great friend/secretary/Girl Friday Pam Parker we became the ARL secretariat, taking block in an office in the old Legal & General building kindly provided for us by the Rothmans people, high above busy Bent Street, Sydney. If it hadn't been for Rothmans, the secretariat would never have got off the ground.

Pam and Bob have been wonderfully loyal allies to me over long years. When we became the seceretariat on the borrowed 100 grand I guess none of us really knew where our salaries would be coming from. Yet neither of them hesitated for an instant. And neither held back in the contribution they made. I think if we'd been paid on hours worked, the $100,000 would have gone in the first week. Pam, such a great partner over so many years—around 22, I think—is one of those meticulous people who provide the nuts and bolts back-up, via records, precise detail etc. so necessary in making a business function efficiently. I have been so lucky to have terrific people around me over the years—Alison McArthur my first secretary, Judy Lewis, a great friend and wonderfully efficient person, and Meryl Jones at Manly Leagues, always there to provide back-up support when needed and towers of strength. I think the joy of a productive working life is in the company of the people around you. I have been very lucky in that regard.

Bob Abbott left the Rugby League at the same time as I did, in early '97. Bob has had his detractors—people who say that he pushes his own barrow to hard. But when he left he did it quietly, the reason being that he didn't want to deflect any of the spotlight away from my own exit. His attitude then was indicative of the loyalty he showed me over the years. Bob worked bloody hard for the game over long seasons, and especially so in recent times in the Pacific Islands where he built a nice foundation for rugby league's successful future. I know he was shattered by the Super League incursions in 1995 which stole away most of what he had set up. That was one of the cruellest things I have ever seen.

The first thing that Bob and I had done back in early '84 was hop on a plane and head off on an all-stops fact-finding mission to the minor league states. The response was good, the news was bad. Just about all of them were on their knees. We got the message loud and clear that all of them were feeling very, very badly neglected by headquarters in Sydney. The fact was that no-one had had the time to get out and help. We listened, and tried to understand what was needed.

They were heady, challenging days. We kicked off with that borrowed $100,000—and within a few years had turned that into an $8 million credit rating for the ARL. Within three years we were spending $1 million-plus a year in the developing areas, planting seeds in previously foreign soils.

It's a funny feeling when I look back on that now. Because, you know, in what we did back then, from 1983 onwards, was sown the seeds of Super League. The greatest expansionary period the game had ever seen was the catalyst for News Ltd interest in the rugby league 'product' in 1994. League had gone from being a Sydney game to a national game. Corporate eyes lit up at the prospects it held. Ultimately, we were victims of our own success. I can tell you that it stung me deeply when some of those States which we had counselled and helped and developed grabbed the Super League cheques as soon as they were waved in front of them in 1995. Don't talk to me about loyalty.

There is a little known yarn I should tell about one of my last player sorties at Manly, a near miss just before I moved into town. Few people these days would have the slightest idea that Terry Lamb went within a whisker of becoming a Sea Eagle for 1984. It's really a lovely story that says a lot about Terry Lamb. At the time he was on the market, ending a contract with Wests and having shown enough to indicate that he was going to be a very special player. Canterbury were strongly in the market . . . and so were Manly. The tussle for his services went right down to the wire . . .

With Terry's decision due, I sensed he was having real difficulties and at our final meeting I said to him. 'Look son, you seem quite worried about coming over to Manly . . . is there something you want to tell me?'

There was a pause and then Lamb said, 'Mate, to tell you the truth I don't think Mum will ever speak to me again if I join Manly.'

Arko

He was half-joking . . . but only half, and I knew it. What he told me had the ring of sincerity about it, and I knew he had a genuine problem. If he *hadn't* said it I would have bumped up our offer—and very likely we would have got him. But I sat pat, and Terry Lamb went to Canterbury.

I have thought about it now and again in the years since. At that time he was *potentially* a great player—and he went on to become just that. He would have looked great in a Manly jumper, and he would have been a champion club man . . . as he became at Canterbury. But I could see that deep down on that morning he was wrestling with something that meant a fair bit more to him than he could really put into words. To *not* sign Terry Lamb that day was in line with my personal beliefs about doing business. Never in my 20 years as Manly secretary did I sign a player who had genuine reservations about coming to the club.

At Phillip Street there were tough and difficult days and nights as we wrestled with the future direction of the game. The toughest came in September 1983, when the decision was taken not to invite Newtown and Western Suburbs into the 1984 competition. They were difficult and painful calls, certainly not made without a great deal of anguish and soul-searching. The fact with Newtown—the old 'Bluebags' (later 'Jets')—was that they simply went broke. They had no money, couldn't pay their players, and the bulk of their supporters had moved away from the district in line with the changing nature of inner-city suburbs in Sydney. They were, and are, a club which had produced magnificent players and built unbreakable traditions. To show them the door hurt everyone of us at the general committee meeting that Monday night. The great thing is that Newtown have stayed alive as members of the League. Active and successful participants in the Metropolitan Cup, their players still proudly wearing the old royal blue jumper.

Wests, of course, stuck like glue, and simply refused to accept the sentence that had been imposed on them. Using every possible device available to them and heading resolutely through the courts, Wests kept alive. After they had won only one of 24 matches in 1983, the decision was *again* taken by the

NSWRL to exclude them from the competition. But they were the club that refused to die, driven tirelessly by blokes like their secretary Rick Wade. Jeez, he fought hard for Wests. Along the way he said some outrageous and cutting things . . . but it never worried me. I'd look at him and think, 'I'd be doing exactly the same if it was Manly in the gun.'

Wests were suspicious of everything Phillip Street did, suspecting the League's motives on even the simplest things. Wade, in fact was responsible for one of the funniest things I ever struck in my years as chairman. In the '80s we introduced a system under which the chief executives of clubs were required to write a report on the performance of the referee in their weekend match. One Sunday Wests played St George and got pipped at the post in a game which was highly controversial. When the reports of the match came in the one from St George read something along the lines of: 'Good control, observed the five metres well, a fair performance.' Then we opened Rick Wade's report. It read simply: 'MISSION ACCOMPLISHED.' Fair dinkum, I nearly fell off my chair laughing. I thought it was one of the funniest things I had ever heard, and yet I related to Wade: he truly believed that every possible thing was slanted against Wests.

Finally, in December 1985, we received High Court backing on our *right* to exclude clubs from the competition. But by then, anticipating a considerably later decision, we had voted to include Wests in the 1986 premiership. And so they stayed, progressively building their professionalism, eventually shifting to Campbelltown in line with demographic trends and enduring as a tough, viable part of the competition—as they had been since 1908. I've had my problems with Wests over the years, but the people from that club are salt of the earth rugby league folk, and I admire them a great deal. What's more, my wife Barbara is an old Ashfield girl. Her second team is Wests. In fact I think deep down they might be her *first* team . . . it's just that she's not game to say it.

At Phillip Street in those early years of the '80s what we had going was pretty much akin to a revolution. 1983 in particular was a very dark year. People had lost faith, crowds were dwindling and the game was suffering from a crisis of confidence. At one stage I broke away for a few days, heading to Fiji with Peter Moore to recharge the batteries. Flying in, the pilot told us that a big storm was on the way—a cyclone.

'You might be lucky—it might miss the island,' he said.

It didn't. But thanks to the calming effects of several bottles of champagne taken with and after dinner, the Bullfrog and I managed to completely miss one of the worst storms to ever hit the place. While we slept peacefully through at The Fijian, the cyclone just about wrecked Fiji. I awoke next morning in The Fijian to a bathroom that had crumbled in, and to devastation everywhere. I can only think that it must have been very good champagne. It turned out to be a very eventful few days. Earlier, on the day of the storm, I had 'rescued' Peter from a tricky predicament. We had crossed a tidal inlet on a run and when I had headed on, Peter had turned around. The easy crossing had deepened with quick-flowing water and Peter got only about halfway across before latching onto a large log sticking up out of the water, and staying there. When I got back, there he was, still hanging on for dear life in the current. I steered him back in.

'I wasn't going anywhere until you came back,' he said.

What a headline that would have been: 'BULLFROG SWEPT OUT TO SEA!'

So much seemed to be going on in my world in that momentous period of 1983 and beyond. Along with wrestling with the changing scene in town, I did my best to keep a tight grip on my duties at Manly Leagues Club, where I had been president since March 1974 and a member of the board since 1967. In August 1983 we announced a gross profit of $959,000 at a time when a number of leagues clubs were struggling in the tough economic climate that prevailed.

That place has been so much part of my life, starting in very humble beginnings indeed back in the 1950s. 'Headquarters' then was a little old stone house on the site in Pittwater Road where our fine Leagues Club now stands, owned by a Dr Boag. After matches on mid-winter days we would come back to the 'club' and stand around big drums in which fires had been set. Blokes like Reub Hudson and Jack Martin—the first secretary of the licensed club—did wonderful work in starting and sustaining the dream of Manly having its own licensed club. They formed a group of foundation members to get the club going. I was one of those pioneers and of that original 250, about 90 of us are still alive as I write these words.

The club has been a wonderful meeting place for people over the years, a real community centre. These days, in the club on Pittwater Road we have moved on a long way from the old stone house. Today there are around 35,000 members, and a huge array of 'clubs within the club'—catering for fishing, cricket, golf, dancing, pigeon fanciers, bridge, indoor sports . . . and just about any other leisure pursuit you can think of. In many ways the growth of the licensed club has given me as much pleasure as the football club which paralleled its growing professionalism and development. I am proud that both of them have made a worthwhile contribution to life in the Manly district. In turn, men such as Roy Bull and Gordon Willoughby have virtually given *their* lives to the two clubs. What great and loyal friends that they have been to me and to Manly football over the last 50 years.

League in the early '80s was blessed with the champion team it needed (Parramatta, premiers in 1981, '82, '83) and the extraordinary and shining jewel of the new State of Origin concept. Manly nagged away at Parra (beaten grand finalists in 1982 and '83) but were never quite good enough to knock them over on the big day. I've always reckoned we should have beaten them in 1982. We whipped them 20–nil in the major semi, and were looking great for the title. But that wonderful Parra backline: Sterling, Kenny, Grothe, Cronin, Ella, Hunt and Taylor fired on all cylinders in the grand final and they were too good for us, 21–8.

In 1987 when I was long gone from Manly club (although not emotionally, or from my role with the Leagues Club), Manly finally won again, beating Canberra in the last grand final played on the Sydney Cricket Ground. It was quite a day. Summer had arrived with a fiery burst, months early, and the players battled through heatwave conditions. In the sweltering centre of the SCG, the big pale-skinned Englishman Kevin Ward, not long off the plane, performed magnificently, running

Cliff Lyons close for Man of the Match. It was a grand and emotional day—marking Bob Fulton's first premiership as a coach. The monkey was off his back. And a triumph too for skipper Paul Vautin, one of the most popular of all Sea Eagles over the years.

Through the 1980s, the fingers-crossed Origin experiment soon became a guaranteed, explosive highlight of every season. It produced football of supersonic quality and immense drama under the lights of Lang Park or the SCG (later the Sydney Football Stadium and the MCG).

State of Origin quickly spawned its own heroes and villains and a referee named Barry Gomersall fell into both categories— depending on which side of the border you happened to live. Barry came from North Queensland and brought a trademark moustache, plenty of confidence and pretty fair ability to the job. He was a touch flamboyant—in the Hartley mould—but capable. Down south they called him 'The Grasshopper', and booed the joint down every time he got near a football field.

My feelings about Gomersall are that he was a very *loyal* bloke, influenced to a large extent by Ron McAuliffe. Some people called Gomersall a cheat. I wouldn't. Perhaps it would be fair comment to suggest that if there was a fine line decision to be made the loyalty factor might lead him in the direction of the Maroons. I thought that overall he was a good referee and certainly a very confident one who always seemed to have good control; in fact, one year we were even considering him for the (Sydney) grand final.

My favourite story about Gomersall concerns a mid-week Cup match between Manly and Brisbane, a semi final, for which Ron McAuliffe was hell-bent on appointing the North Queenslander. I told him no way, under no circumstances; we would play on their ground (Lang Park) but we weren't going to give them the bloody referee too! We had a tremendous blue over it. It got so loud we didn't really need the phones. Next day McAuliffe was back on the blower. 'Mate,' he said, 'how about this. What about if we give Gomersall the match and I tell him to referee fair dinkum?'

Oh yeah, he was an old politician and a wheeler dealer and

a fighter for Queensland, McAuliffe. But a genuine rugby league man too. He cared deeply about the game and when things looked like getting out of hand in Origin football so intense was the feeling in every match, it was with Ron McAuliffe, and then the ARL board, that I sat down to work out a code of conduct to keep what had become our classic showpiece match within acceptable bounds. The code, taken on board by players who were so proud to be part of *that* game provided the bit of balance, and helped kick the annual Origin contest on to becoming pretty close to *the* standout event on the Australian sporting calendar.

I'll never forget the night of 8 June 1994 in Melbourne with a crowd of 87,161 under a brilliant moon. I walked in with John Quayle and we just stood their, in awe. 'Jeezus, mate, you've done it with this!' said Quayle. We shook hands. League hit the heights that magic night when Origin football first went to Melbourne, although the match that Queensland and NSW turned on was not all people had hoped for, a hard, grim battle more suited to the league aficianados of many years, rather than the new breed who had come to the MCG to taste the thrill.

Rugby league stood on the peak of the mountain that night in June. Things had never looked better for the old game from the mills and mines of England's north. It's amazing to reflect now that within a single year it was shot down in flames, relegated to trench warfare which has done irreparable damage.

Sport in Australia in modern times has no sadder story.

20

THE YEAR OF
LIVING
DANGEROUSLY

Interstate relations between NSW and Queensland have never hit a lower point than they did in season 1985. At one stage things were so bad that it wouldn't have surprised me to see troops gathering on the border. Football and the politics and personalities within were the cause, and as ARL chairman I was at full stretch trying to keep the two sides from each other's throats.

We blundered at ARL level that year. It was a season of a full-scale Australia–New Zealand Test series, programmed to fall in the middle of the State of Origin battles. Unwisely we put one of the State coaches—NSW's Terry Fearnley—in charge of Australia, and that statement is no reflection on Fearnley, a coach of real ability. It was a season of seething passions and deep feelings. NSW, outstandingly coached by Fearnley and inspiringly captained by Steve Mortimer, won the first two Origin games in dramatic fashion, to give the Blues their first-ever series win.

Then right on top of that came the Test series . . .

So almost before the shouting and tumult had died after the fierce encounters of the first two Origin games, Fearnley was handed a mixed bunch of NSW and Queenslanders and charged with the job of shaping them into an harmonious 'team'. It was always going to be tough. I'm sure some of the Queenslanders did not feel too kindly towards a coach who had played his part in bringing them down from their Origin pedestal.

The situation was explosive almost from the start. The first Test in Brisbane featured one of the game's truly infamous moments when opposing props Kevin Tamati (New Zealand) and Greg Dowling (Australia) brawled on the sideline after being sent off. One hundred metres away in the grandstand I had the feeling there was going to be trouble the moment they were sent off. Tamati was a tough bloke who had done a bit of fighting and who could handle himself, and Dowling was no shrinking violet. Why the two camps didn't send someone out to lead them off, I don't know. But they didn't, and next thing the pair were 'into it', brawling wildly up against the perimeter fence. They closed on each other like two pythons in mortal combat. No-one won. The only loser in the whole bloody thing was the Australian Rugby League. We took disciplinary action against Dowling and the Kiwis did the same with Tamati, but the event was played over and over on television. It was vicious, ugly stuff and about as bad as I've seen on a football field . . . or just off it, actually.

The tour to New Zealand that followed didn't ease the tension. Within the Australian team there was building drama. The Aussies won both that first Test and then the second, in Auckland, with last-gasp tries to clinch the series. At Carlaw Park John Ribot's last second try for an Australian victory was greeted with deathly silence. This was not a happy Australian team; interstate passions and ill-feeling bubbled beneath the surface. Fearnley reportedly was scathing in his criticism of his team in the dressing room after the second Test.

A day or two later, apparently with the support of David Barnhill (NSW) and John Garrahy (Qld) the tour managers, Fearnley dropped four players from the third Test side, all Queenslanders: Dowling, Greg Conescu, Mark Murray and Chris Close. In fairness to Terry Fearnley he did exactly what he believed was right for the team.

I was over there, and Fearnley intimated to me before the third Test that he was going to make the changes, but he didn't mention Chris Close. I thought he erred in dropping Close, whose form had been solid. But changes in the team were justified, no doubt about that. I thought that he was thoroughly entitled to change the halfback and the hooker in particular.

One of the big difficulties on the tour was the gulf that developed between Fearnley, the coach, and Wally Lewis, the captain. Lewis wasn't close to Fearnley in any way and claimed he had not been paid the respect of being consulted before the players were dropped from the team. Fearnley worked more closely with the tour vice captain Wayne Pearce and it became apparent after the tour that that had got right up Lewis's nose, particularly on the publication of his 1987 book, *King Wally*.

The book caused an enormous storm. In *King Wally*, Lewis ripped into various people, including Frank Stanton and Fearnley, but the thing I took most exception to was his criticism of Pearce. Pearce didn't deserve it. I told Lewis that, castigated him for it publicly and raised the matter officially at ARL level. Lewis was severely chastised at the meeting and subsequently offered a public apology to those he had offended in the book.

Then Ron McAuliffe felt honour bound to stand up for the Queensland captain (and his favourite player). He had a big go at me, and I had a go back at him. I told him to go and get stuffed, and he told me to get stuffed. A fair while later, Ron came back to me and apologised. He told me that because I had come out publicly and criticised Lewis he had no choice but to hit back. Eventually we got back on to an even keel, but it took a while.

Well, after Australia lost the third Test 18–nil in New Zealand in '85 all hell broke loose. In Brisbane Ron McAuliffe, as president of the QRL, went off like a madman.

'What has been happening in Beirut (where war was raging at the time) is nothing compared with what happened to Queensland players in Auckland,' stormed McAuliffe. Adding that it was in his view the 'biggest mess since King Alfred burnt the cakes'.

I remonstrated strongly with McAuliffe about his outburst. I told him: 'Whether you're right or whether you're wrong, what you did was not the thing to do publicly.'

All these years later I can assure Fearnley that he got the *strongest* support from myself and NSW. It was done privately, sure, but, I mean we weren't going to make a big brawl of it in the bloody media. I wasn't about to go public and call McAuliffe a low bastard or something like that. About the last thing the ARL needed at that time was a public stand-up brawl between the chairman and vice chairman. Our brawl wasn't quite up to Tamati–Dowling standard, but it wasn't a bad one. I thought some of McAuliffe's comments were over-heated and pretty disgraceful. I told him so, and if Terry Fearnley believes that he got no back-up at that difficult time, he's wrong.

Things didn't get any better of course. Queensland won the third Origin game with feelings still running sky high, and Greg Dowling veered towards the NSW dug-out at one stage of the match to 'verbal' Fearnley. Fearnley hit back with his own strong views via the media. Later came Lewis's book, then Pearce's views. And so it went on—the claims and the squabbling and the arguing—adding up to an unfortunate episode in the game's recent history. As a direct result of it we changed ARL policy. In future we decided that whenever possible, a State coach would not coach an Australian team.

A prickly year, 1985, but the news wasn't all bad. In what was a singular honour for Australian rugby league and a source of some personal pride for myself, I was elected director general of the International Rugby League Board. England had virtually held sway on that body through its 40 or so years of life, so it was a nice 'kick' for Australia. I must say that I thought the title was a bit flash. I was actually put up as 'chairman' at the meeting which decided it, in France. It was the French who decided that 'director general' more befitted the position. That meeting was the beginning of some stirrings of activity internationally. I think all of us on the board had had the feeling for a while that although we met fairly regularly, nothing too much happened. In the wake of the meeting there seemed new enthusiasm in the air. Things started to happen: we got rugby league going in the South Pacific, with Bob Abbott a major contributor to that. A foothold was gained in South Africa. They were promising initiatives. Sadly, like just about everything else in the game they were crash-tackled by the arrival of Super League.

21

DRUGS, SMOKES AND A FEW BEERS

I reckon it would be a fair assessment to say that I have 'run for my life' for most of my years on this earth. Ever since I was a young bloke I have been a mad trainer. I was that way as a footballer, kept up the physical stuff as a coach, and then *especially* made sure I kept up an exercise regime when I became a desk-bound official. I think I was spurred along by visions of the old-time officials I used to mix with down at Phillip Street in my early years as a Manly delegate. There seemed to be droves of them—big hearty red-faced blokes who could sink schooners like they were going out of fashion, and work their way through mountains of food. I'd look at some of them down there on those Monday nights and it would seem to me they were getting bigger and redder each week. I pledged to myself back then: 'I'm not going to tumble into that.' It would have been so easy; rugby league is a social game, there's always a beer around, or a chance of a lunch or dinner . . . often a long one.

I was pretty obsessional about my running. Even after a big night out I'd be up and off first thing in the morning. Over the years I must have run thousands and thousands of kilometres. I reckon I probably ran around the world a couple of times. I did it because it made me feel good, and because I knew it was a big help in my working life. Some mornings I'd head off with a problem nagging away in my mind. I'd go down to Manly Dam

Arko

or through the bush somewhere, and by the time I got back, the problem would be solved. There was always a run on somewhere. With a bunch of blokes I used to run with, including my great mate Gordon Willoughby, we'd catch the hydrofoil into the city, then run back to Manly. I had various courses plotted through the bush on the North Shore and loved that best of all, getting away from it and into the peace and quiet of the bush.

I rarely missed a day, and ran some good races competitively, including a win one year in the Manly to Palm Beach run. To my (slight) regret I never ran a marathon . . . not that I couldn't have, I just never got around to it. The thing was I could never come to terms with *just* running one. If I had done it, I would have wanted to run a good time, and to do that you have to put in a vast amount of training. That was my problem; finding the time as rugby league became more and more demanding and professional, and life became busier and more complicated.

I have no doubt that my lifetime obsession with trying to keep fit has been an enormous help to me in my career. In more recent years I have walked, rather than run, but I haven't stopped at least trying to look after myself. I have no doubt the reservoir of fitness I had built up over the years helped me through the bad years of 1995–96. Even when I suffered bad chest pains during that period and went to hospital for tests, the doctor told me that the fact that I had been fit and kept myself healthy through the years had been much to my advantage.

I was a smoker once, but gave it up on a single day 30-odd years ago. It happened in Papua New Guinea. I'd smoked for a few years by that time, given it up now and then, but had always gone back. In 1966, on a tour with the Manly team, Freddy Jones and I were the only two blokes who smoked. No-one ever had a match, and I was becoming increasingly aware that smoking wasn't such a great idea anyway. So one day on that tour I just decided, 'Bugger this. I'm going to give it away.' I threw my fags away and have never smoked since that day.

The generous support given by tobacco company Rothmans for so many years to rugby league became increasingly contentious as the seasons passed and smoking became more of an issue in the community. I defended Rothmans' right to commercial involvement in the game to the last puff as it were, despite my own firmly held views about smoking. The fact is that I'm not a smoker, and I really detest the habit these days. I don't object to other people smoking, although I question their wisdom in doing so, but people make their own choices in life. The thing I was crooked on was the rank hypocrisy of the Federal Government. If the Government was sincere in its objection to cigarettes in the light of the health risks involved, then it was in their hands to do something about it. But the tobacco industry, of course, was a huge revenue producer for the Government. So while they were quite happy to put their hand out and keep taking the money, they tightened the screws on anyone else getting support from the industry. It was extreme hypocrisy, although governments are pretty good at that. The other angle of course was that we *were* dealing with a legal substance.

I could never really put into words just how deeply appreciative I was, and am, of the support Rothmans provided for rugby league. In many and varied ways they helped the game grow to what it had become at the time Murdoch's minions launched their Pearl Harbor raid in 1995.

When the controversy over sports sponsorship by tobacco companies was really gathering a head of steam, various sports associations concerned at the effect the ending of tobacco sponsorship would mean to them banded together and formed the Allied Sports Council. I was the Council's first chairman. One of our first initiatives was to distribute leaflets at many professional sporting venues asking people: (1) Whether they objected to their sport being sponsored by a tobacco company and (2) Did they believe cigarette sponsorship influenced people to smoke. The answers were overwhelmingly 'No!' And in huge numbers—the percentages being 94 per cent and 86 per cent respectively, from memory. There were so many responses we had to hire a truck to get them to the Government. At that time I also led a delegation to the Australian Broadcasting Tribunal to discuss the issue with the Tribunal chairman. I remember it well because one of our negotiating team was rugby union's representative Ken Elphick, who is currently spending some time in one of Her Majesty's prisons. As soon as the meeting opened Elphick ripped straight into the Tribunal bloke, as abrasive as you could imagine. 'Well, if that's going to be your attitude,' the bloke said, understandably getting his back up. I had to shut Elphick up and spend the next ten minutes trying to restore some harmony.

I am very proud of the stance rugby league took, via the Australian Sports Drug Agency, on *illegal* drugs in the early 1990s, and of my part in that. Rugby league led the way in Australian sport in the testing of players for illegal substances, the drawing up of a penalty structure, and the setting up of a rehabilitation process. I have always been particularly strong in my anti-drugs stance. It is something that touched my own family, as it does so many; my daughter Susan had a problem for a time, causing much heartache and drama. To her great credit she straightened herself out, and the change in her is remarkable and wonderful to see. I hold bitter and strong views about drugs because of those personal experiences. It's not something I want to hide—the reality of what happened in my family will help explain to people why I feel as strongly as I do about drugs.

I have nothing but contempt for people who peddle drugs, and especially to kids. The pushers represent to me just about the lowest form of life. My personal view is powerfully against the illegal drugs, soft or hard. The League copped some flak for including marijuana, a so-called 'soft' drug, in the range of drugs for which we originally tested when our scheme kicked off in 1990. People argued that marijuana was just a 'social' drug, not a 'performance enhancing' drug. Those pushing that line ignored the reality that it is potentially a performance *detracting* drug. Clubs paying blokes hundreds of thousands of dollars a year are entitled to have their players free of it for that reason alone. But there is more to it than that. I have always regarded marijuana as a 'stepping stone' drug—an introductory drug to heavier stuff. I am immovable in my opposition to it.

When the League's drug policy was in the news Jack Gibson and I went on ABC TV one Saturday to discuss the issue with the station's football caller, Warren Boland. We had a hell of a clash, with Boland taking a 'soft' line on marijuana. Jack backed me up very powerfully. Like me, his life has been touched by the horror of drugs; his son Luke died of a drug overdose several years ago. I think Boland was stunned by the fury of our attack that day.

Football, inevitably, has been touched by drug scandals in the last decade, the game being a microcosm of the wider society. There have been positive tests for marijuana, steroids and cocaine, with publicity and suspensions. And now and then there have been rumours of individuals, or even whole teams, slipping through the net before it was tightened.

Rumour and innuendo surrounded the performance of a premiership-winning team of a few years ago. There are those who will tell you that more than a few players in the side were pumped up on a steroid programme. I prefer to think not. When a team wins as well as this one did, I like to look for positives. Their effort in winning the premiership was a beauty, and I don't believe they deserved to be denigrated by a whispering campaign. But it's a fact that the stories have followed them down the seasons. Maybe it's just something peddled by a disgruntled opposition. All I can say is that I have never been confronted by any evidence that supported the rumours.

My own 'vice' is a beer now and then, although less and less as the years pass and I become more conscious of looking after myself. I've always liked a beer—no doubt about that. Occasionally, in a mellow mood because of it, I've done silly things . . . as most of us probably have. I remember a barbecue the League put on in the early '80s on Shark Island in Sydney Harbour. It was a day we put on for the media and we had a nice lunch, and plenty of beers. One of the group happened to be Des Renford—the 'King of the English Channel'.

It was as hot as buggery and as the afternoon drew on Des said to me: 'Feel like swim?'

I'd had half a dozen cans or so and was feeling pretty chipper. 'Yeah, I'll dive in with you,' I said.

Well, Des's idea of a 'bit of a swim' was a lap of the island, which is a fair lump of land. I would remind you too that the island in question is called Shark Island for reasons that do not take too much working out. Fortified by the beers, I went with him. I kept looking down through the water and seeing these huge deep crevices, expecting to see a large Grey Nurse appear at any moment. About half way around the effect of the beers was starting to wear off and I was thinking, 'God, what am I doing *here*?' But Kevin Humphreys had bet on me making it, so I stuck on Des's shoulder and he steered me safely and slowly around and back to terra firma, to the welcome sight of another cold can. I was happy to be back.

22

JUNIOR AND THE KING

I've had some tough days in football, the worst of them in recent times thanks to Rupert Murdoch and his henchmen. But a morning in early October 1986 sticks in my mind as one of the most painful I ever experienced, even though I wasn't directly involved. It was the day that Wayne Pearce was ruled out of the Kangaroo tour. The story is a well known one in football, of Pearce, the 'model' footballer and Australian vice captain, suffering a serious knee injury in a Test against New Zealand. And how, against all the odds, he worked eight to ten hours a day to reach the point where he was unexpectedly back in the running for the Kangaroo tour of that year.

Crunch day came at Redfern Oval on a warm spring morning a week or so before the team was due to leave. Under the gaze of the ARL medico Dr Bill Monaghan and the Australian selectors, Pearce went through a searching fitness test, which featured him being tackled by, and tackling, two of the hardest men in the game, front rowers Les Davidson and David Boyle. I can still picture the final moments of the trial—a length of the field sprint, and Pearce buckling at one stage before regathering momentum and finishing the run. After a brief deliberation, and while no doubt confronting some inner turmoil, Monaghan ruled 'Junior' Pearce out of the tour. Doc Monaghan has told me more than once in the years since that it was pretty close to the most upsetting decision he ever had to make in football. His dilemma was a shocker. Pearce was not only held in sky high regard as a footballer, he was special to the game because of the man he was—a wonderful role model to young footballers. He was also a proven success story in English conditions, turning in a wonderful contribution to the 'Invincibles' of 1982.

The subsequent Wally Lewis drama of 1990 was high voltage stuff, but it was 1986 that really bruised us all most deeply—I guess Wayne Pearce and Bill Monaghan more than anyone. At ARL board level we had virtually no choice; our doctor had ruled a player out on medical grounds. We weren't going to over-rule that. Bill Monaghan consoles himself for the difficult ruling he had made that day with the firmly held belief that in the long view the decision was a positive one for Pearce, enabling him to sustain his career longer than he may have if he had gone to England on a suspect knee.

It was a controversial and difficult time, and especially because Wayne Pearce was at the heart of it. Merv Cross, the doctor who had performed the operation on Pearce's knee and supervised his rehabilitation programme, went public with the opinion that Pearce would be ready to play in two weeks. It was a fearfully difficult call Doc Monaghan had to make and the pain on Pearce's face when the doctor gave him the news will live with me forever. I will say this about Wayne Pearce: there has been no player in the game in my time that has commanded more respect than him. And you can throw them all in. I can still see that last fateful run with Pearce going strongly . . . then the stumble . . . was it a pot-hole? . . . and then the silence that followed as Monaghan pondered his decision. A tough day. One of the toughest.

In the wake of it, Wayne Pearce characteristically didn't say too much, just bit his lip and declined the temptation to make a fuss, although he certainly set out his own beliefs strongly in his later book, *Local Hero*.

Conspiracy theorists tried to make something of the decision to rule out Pearce. The main claim seemed to be that Pearce was knocked out of the tour because a spot had been promised to Canterbury's Steve Folkes. That was absolute bullshit, and a cruel and unfair reflection on Bill Monaghan who as fan, doctor and official put a great deal of honest hard work and expertise into rugby league over the years. In this highly controversial time Parramatta's wing champion Eric Grothe was also ruled out owing to a knee which blew up like a balloon after matches.

The decision to exclude Wally Lewis from the 1990 Kangaroo tour, made emphatically by the then-ARL doctor Nathan Gibbs when he ruled that Lewis had not recovered sufficiently from a broken arm, created a similar storm to the Pearce case of four years earlier. But there was little similarity in my book. For all the sound and fury that followed Nathan Gibbs' announcement, Lewis was patently not fit. In Queensland it was billed as a monstrous southern conspiracy and Lewis himself fuelled the fire with some fairly outrageous statements, which I hope he may have regretted in the cooler light of day.

I was a great fan of Wally's during his career. So many times he was the difference (for Queensland) in State of Origin football. In sticking up for him over the years I got battered all over NSW, Wally being a real villain to anyone south of the border. I can tell you that Lewis would never have been Australian captain without me. He had his opponents, did Wally, and there were more than enough times that I gave him my casting vote. I have no idea whether he knows that or appreciates it. Often it would have been easier for me to go the other way; it sure would have got some Lewis critics off my back.

I remember once Joh Bjelke-Petersen said to me, 'I hope you're going to support Wally for captain again?'

I told him, 'Joh, I'll do what I always do—I'll go for the best man.'

Most often I reckoned Lewis was just that—notwithstanding the controversy that used to follow him around. He tested us plenty of times with things he said, and things he did. I remember fining him $5,000 after an Origin game in Melbourne in 1990 in which he gave referee Greg McCallum a real workover and swore at a touch judge. And I remember how resentful he was after that. The previous year he had been fined

Arko

$2,000 for spitting. On his pedestal in Queensland Wally had been used to getting his own way. To be very honest there were things that Lewis did at times that did not make him the ideal role model that we looked for in an Australian captain. But he was such a supreme footballer and natural leader that we chose to stick with him.

I think in some ways Ron McAuliffe contributed to what Wally Lewis became. Ron made him an idol, and at times it seemed as though Lewis was above the law in Ron's eyes as far as the game was concerned. But in the end, I know too that McAuliffe was disappointed and hurt by him. When Wally was at the Broncos he wrote an article for the Brisbane *Courier-Mail* which was critical of McAuliffe. Some time after that when the Australian team were in Sydney, readying for a Test, I had a conversation with Lewis.

'Wally, have you spoken to the old bloke (McAuliffe) lately?' I asked him.

'No I haven't,' said Wally. 'To tell you the truth I've been a bit reluctant to ring him. It's been a long time.'

I counselled Lewis to ring McAuliffe. 'He thinks the world of you . . . give him a call,' I said. I have no idea if he ever did.

But at this time after his exclusion from the Kangaroo tour in 1990 he really tested my patience. Nathan Gibbs still has the X-rays which prove the rightness of his decision on Lewis. There is absolutely no argument at all that he made the right decision. Absolutely none. And deep down, Wally knows that too. But at the time he made a huge fuss and there was an enormous hue and cry in Queensland with Lewis quite happy to fuel the theory that it was a southern plot, which was total bloody rot. I'll tell you how loud the noise was. At the height of the Kuwait crisis, Wally managed to put Saddam Hussein off the front pages! I had a shocking clash with him about it.

Wally pulled out all the tricks. He claimed in the media that Queensland specialists had cleared him, although we never saw the evidence of that. He told the Queensland media he was the victim of a 'set-up' aimed at keeping him out of the tour. Through it all Doc Gibbs, a good honourable bloke, kept his head and just ruled on what he knew to be right medically—

that it would be six to eight weeks before Lewis's arm was fully healed. It was crazy stuff: why would the Australian Rugby League be involved in any sort of plot to keep the best player out of the team? We wanted to go away and win (which we did) and I would have given anything for Wally Lewis to be fit and in the side. But he wasn't.

Controversy was Wally's constant travelling companion. He seemed always at the heart of any Origin drama—a reflection of his status as the 'King' (which he was) and his great ability to polarise the fans. Loved in Queensland, he was hated south of the border. I remember the Pansonic Cup final of 1989 in which the Broncos beat Illawarra 22–20 in a terrific game at Parramatta Stadium. Afterwards the crowd behaviour was disgraceful as fans booed and jeered Lewis and his winning Broncos. I expressed my embarrassment and disappointment to the Broncos at the time, and it was heartfelt. A fair bit of the crowd reaction, I suspect, had to do with the 'Lewis factor'.

People know how tough rugby league is on the paddock. Sometimes I've wondered if they have any idea at all how tough it can be away from the playing field.

23

AMERICAN
DREAMER

I crossed swords over the years a few times with a large
American named Mike Mayer. In the US in 1987, Mayer, self-
styled 'President of the (non-existent) US Rugby League' issued
the following threat to me: 'Listen, you'd better realise that I've
got some very powerful friends in Chicago. And people who
cross me can sometimes find themselves in a trunk somewhere
at Chicago Airport.'

I flew into him. 'Listen you great heap of —— don't you
threaten me,' I said.

We were 20 storeys up in a hotel room at the time, and I was
thinking, 'I'd better be careful here or he'll throw me and Barry
Rodgers (the St George official who was with me at the time)
out the window.' Little Barry was resolute that day, and resolute
and remarkably effective right throughout the fascinating
experiment we conducted in '87—trying to sell league to the
Yanks. With Mayer and me it was always pretty straightforward. He didn't like me and I didn't like him. He wasn't worth
two bob to rugby league as far as I was concerned.

The US Origin experiment of '87 has been called a 'folly' by
some people. I dispute the assessment. It was in fact a fair
dinkum genuine try to strike a spark for rugby league over
there. We sent over a forward scout in the capable and energetic
Rodgers and, later, a follow-up team of Roy Masters and Peter

Arko

Corcoran. We decided that if we were going to have a crack, the only way to be do it would be in a big way, via our showpiece product, State of Origin football. And so we took NSW and Queensland's finest to the Veterans' Stadium in Long Beach to give it a go.

The match in Long Beach turned out to be a pretty fair success, despite the many hiccups of the build-up. I can tell you though that five minutes before the game I was distraught. There was hardly a soul in the joint. But then someone said to me, 'Go and have a look outside.' I did, and was greeted by the amazing sight of queues snaking hundreds of metres. There had been some sort of hold-up on the freeway which leads to the ground and the mob had all arrived late. We put the kickoff back 20 minutes and finished up with a healthy gathering of 12,349. It was a darned good game too, a worthy example of top level rugby league.

Unfortunately though, we had made the decision to co-opt Mayer to 'help out' with the State of Origin promotion we took to Long Beach, California in '87. Mayer had been on the scene for years at that stage, failing totally to have achieved anything of note. But we figured that he at least knew the American scene and market, and we paid him $25,000 to offer us some expert local knowledge in our promotion. In fact he did his utmost to stop the game going ahead, at one stage threatening legal action if it proceeded.

'Do what you like . . . do your best,' I told him.

There are stories I could tell about Mayer and a credit card that belonged to Barry Rodgers, and about threats that were made to another co-opted worker, Bernie Gurr, now chief executive of Sydney City Roosters. After my earlier dealings with him I should have known better than to have him on board.

By the end of a promotion to which he had afforded more hindrance than help, he had changed his tune. Just about the last words he said to me were: 'You guys putting this game on here has done me and the American Rugby League the biggest favour of all time. By November this year I will have raised $5 million in sponsorship.'

'What if you can't?' I asked him.

Mayer replied, 'Well, if I can't—I'll take a hike.'

'You'll get out of rugby league?' I asked.

'Yes,' he said.

Of course, he didn't. That was 1987, and a decade later he's still somewhere on the scene, trying to muscle in.

One thing I'll say about Mike Mayer is that he's a survivor. It seems aeons ago that he first came to Australia scratching for cash to get the 'American Rugby League' up and running. The sum in question was $40,000, and I think Mayer was forever crooked on me (and will always be) because I would not accede to his request for the money. In 1987 he was just about as obstructionist as it is possible to be as we set about the tough job of trying to promote an 'unknown' sport on alien territory.

By that time Mayer had been dragging on for a dozen years or so with his bullshit plans to kick league off in America. Mayer was always a smooth talker. The Poms really fell for him in a big way, and I note that as late as 1997 he was still being trumpeted in the English magazine *Open Rugby* as some sort of rugby league folk hero. Garbage. He was just a big talker who could never deliver. He got a good lump of money out of the Poms over the years, though. Maurice Lindsay (boss of the English League) fell for his blarney and I remember a conversation at one stage in which I said to Lindsay: 'Maurice, I'm telling you. Don't be in it. It's a con and you'll do your money cold.'

Various sources in England subsequently forked out for a God-forsaken ill-fated 'promotion' that Mayer scraped together somewhere in the States. Lindsay has said to me more than once since: 'I wish to God I had taken notice of you at that time. Not only did it cost the English Rugby League a fortune, it cost me a lot of money too.' Private investors in England put in thousands of pounds. What they got for their cash was a debacle.

I have a personal wish that Mayer might find Super League one day soon. He'd be a sensation with them. No doubt he has a 'vision' for the game too. You might have got the drift by now that I just can't cop the bloke. I recall once when he was out here—the last time I think—and he asked to address the

Arko

International Board, which was meeting in Sydney. That request was knocked back, but I agreed to ask delegates to give him an informal half hour after the meeting had officially finished.

His opening gambit at that gathering was as follows: 'Gentlemen, I've come here to address you on the rugby league movement in the United States of America. I will not have any interruptions.'

It was at that point I broke in. 'Just a moment, Mr Mayer,' I said. 'I don't know if you're aware of it, but I'm chairman of this meeting—and as long as I'm chairman the meeting will run the way *I* say it's going to run . . . not the way *you* say it's going to run. You've got half an hour.'

So Mayer droned on for his half hour, and at the end of it the board members were just shaking their heads in amazement.

24

A WEDDING . . . AND SOME FUNERALS

1987 was an eventful and happy year in my life. It was the year that Barbara Barnes and I got married. I had met Barbara through rugby league—her brother Barry was a prominent first grade referee—and our friendship gradually blossomed into something more. The wedding was a quiet one, a morning trip to the Registry Office in Phillip Street, then lunch in a nice place I used to go to down the road, the Macquarie Inn. Barbara has given me very happy years, and been so supportive of me in my role in football. She was an absolute tower of strength in the tough years of 1995–96 and without her quiet, unfailing support I doubt that I would have got through. I was hardly ever home and when I was, I was on the phone. The 'troubles' now safely out of my hands—although I suppose never completely out of my mind—we are looking forward to many more happy and, hopefully, healthy years ahead.

When you get as far down the track as I have in life, the death of friends and loved ones is an occasional and bitter travelling companion. I seem to have had my share in more recent times. The years 1985 and 1986 were particularly painful for me. In June 1985 I was shattered by the death of my mum Mary, and by the circumstances of it. Mum was 82 then, living in a retirement place up at Allambie Heights. I used to contact her almost every day or she'd ring me, and when I hadn't heard from her one day I rang my sister. No, Jean hadn't heard from her either. So I went up to Mum's place and rang and rang at the front door. No answer. I went around the side and kicked the bathroom window in, climbing in with some dread and trepidation.

I found my poor old mum lying there. She had had a heart attack during the night, and died on the spot. It was the most devastating thing—she had been such a terrific person and a terrific mother to Jean and me. Thankfully it had been a swift departure, and her health had been pretty good up to that point. It was still a tremendous jolt in my life . . . as it is to everyone, always.

In 1986, my first wife Judy, who had been troubled by asthma through her life, died suddenly. The shock and pain of the loss of someone who had shared much of my life cast an immense shadow—as it does to everyone who goes through such an experience . . . which, in reality, is every one of us.

The death of loved ones and pals shakes you to your foundation, drives home the reality of your own mortality. I have had more than a little of it. The man who replaced me as secretary of Manly when I left, bound for the ARL in 1983, John Tenison, died suddenly in Vanuatu in 1985. John had been reserve grade secretary for years, a quiet, dedicated, wonderfully loyal bloke without an enemy in the world. He had been a player with Manly (110 matches in all grades), coming off the northern beaches where he was a sprint champion with greyhound speed. John was away on holidays with his wife Frances and one of our long-serving committeemen Jim Peebles and his wife when he died. The four of them were at dinner when John had this enormous heart attack, and just keeled over. The news devastated the club. He was such a sound administrator, and one of the most popular men we've ever had at the club. John's death came not long after that of tough, old Reub Hudson, founding member of both the football and Leagues clubs and such a worker through his life for the cause of rugby league in the Manly district.

The bloke who replaced John Tenison as Manly secretary, Doug Daley, was a very special pal. In 1994 I was to deliver the eulogy at Doug's funeral after his tragic, painful death. I remember Doug from way back, remember his first trial with the club in 1956—a chunky bloke in a red and black striped jumper, playing with great vigour.

I commented to my co-selectors, 'Who is this bloke? . . . he sure is having a go.' After the match I introduced myself to him. 'What's you name?' I asked.

'Oh,' said self-effacing Doug. 'You wouldn't know me. I'm Doug Daley, just a little battler from the bush.'

Doug duly signed with Manly, and went on to play 139 games with distinction in the maroon and white strip and prove himself to be one of the gamest footballers in the club's history. Doug, a second rower, played stones above his weight. Often he would take a terrific battering and I can remember saying to him a number of times at halftime in matches: 'Doug, are you OK?'

The answer would always be the same, 'Yeah . . . I'm as fit as a mallee bull!'

Being a city bloke I was never quite sure what a mallee bull was . . . but if they are anything like Doug Daley, then they are a brave beast indeed.

Doug became a great administrator with the club—as treasurer, then secretary (1985–92). We were the closest of friends and I still miss him badly. He went through a very traumatic period with the club in the late 1980s when Paul Vautin, such an immensely popular player, was in dispute, and coach Alan Thompson under huge pressure. Doug bore the brunt of most of the flak that was flying—and there was plenty of that. He was nature's gentleman Doug, and all the aggravation at that time sat heavily on him. He had been so proud a couple of years earlier when his son Phil won a place on the 1986 Kangaroos. Doug and his wife Gloria went to England and I was there too; I'll never forget the look of pride on their faces when Phil ran out for the first time in the green and gold.

When he contracted bowel cancer we watched Doug fade away before our eyes. It was so sad—he'd been such a fit, healthy, happy bloke. One of life's good fellows.

So it was with one of the greatest mates of my life, Geoff Gardiner, the kindest, most generous person I've ever met.

Geoff could have been a millionaire several times over but he was so intent on helping other people—sometimes to his own detriment—that he never bothered about that. Geoff had the dreadful misfortune to decline into Alzheimer's Disease in his early 60s. I visited him regularly and took him for walks and drives . . . and watched the man he had been slip away. That condition is so cruel. In his years of his good health, Geoff was a ball of style, always beautifully dressed. It used to break my heart to see him in the later days, unkempt and in stained clothes. If Geoff had only known, he would have been mortified. I had known Geoff for more than 30 years and what happened to him affected my very deeply. When he died, at 64, it was a relief—so far down had he gone.

The sad days in rugby league tend to draw the game together. The death of the great winger Ken Irvine in late 1990, at just 50 years of age, rocked everyone in the game. Ken played three seasons with us at Manly late in his career (1971, '72, '73), scored 41 tries in 58 matches, and won himself a couple of premierships. But he shaped up against a far tougher opponent than he had ever met before when he contracted leukaemia in his late 40s. He was ill for a long time before people knew it, but he never bothered anyone with his problems.

I don't know how many times I said to him, 'How are you, mate?'

Ken would always reply the same, 'I'm good, feeling terrific.'

He wasn't, of course. His courage and calmness throughout it all was extraordinary. At his funeral I said I believed he was the greatest winger to ever play the game. His record adds all the necessary weight to that theory. St George's brave five eighth Phil Hawthorne was to show the same sort of stoicism in the personal struggle he fought. Those men showed such dignity and strength and courage. Rugby league can nurture the legacy of those sort of qualities in those who play it.

So too the great Clive Churchill during the great battle of his life with cancer. The tribute dinner staged in Clive's honour at the AJC Centre, Randwick, in mid-1985 was one of the most emotional experiences of my life—and the same, I'm sure for everyone who was there. It was beautifully done, the highlight being the arrival of small, frail Clive with his wife Joyce and son Rodney to the thunderous reception. The little bloke hadn't lost any of his trademark wit or pluck, telling the gathering a joke about the 'Irish barber Kim O'Therapy' (chemotherapy) who was responsible for his baldness. Clive was full of cheek and fun and courage, reminding everyone of the qualities that made him the footballer he was. The night was a wonderful, wonderful tribute to a very great rugby league man. Maybe the greatest of them all. I remember sitting there, soaking in the tremendous feelings and emotions of that evening and thinking, 'This is what our game is about . . . and this is why I care about it.' Rugby league is about people sticking together, caring about each other in a common, loved cause. The night of Clive Churchill's tribute dinner captured it better than anything ever has.

And when they buried the great fullback a few months later, half of Sydney came out to say their goodbyes.

25

THE FIRST
LADY

The signing of Tina Turner as the sound and soul of rugby league in 1989 has been called many different things. 'Bizarre' and 'ridiculous' are two that come to mind from early on. I prefer to think of it as 'inspired', because that's exactly what it turned out to be. I think it is to the everlasting credit of the NSWRL board that when John Quayle and the Hertz Walpole people put forward the whacky idea for us to sign a 49-year-old black rock star who had never been within a bull's roar of a game of rugby league, the board barely hesitated, so persuasive was the approach. With barely a murmur of dissent Quayle was given the green light to 'go for it'.

What a success it turned out to be. Without doubt the most inspired piece of marketing ever introduced into Australian sport. Via Tina's 'What you get is what you see' and then 'Simply the best', rugby league's marketing drive became the envy of every other sport in Australia. The financial outlay was heavy, with Rothmans backing us enthusiastically as they always did. But whatever it cost was repaid countless times over as the images, the messages and the pounding beat of Tina's songs opened the door to a whole new army of fans.

She was a great and gracious lady for us, and the game will never forget her. She built a wonderful rapport with the leading players, and that shines through in the TV advertisements that went on to win world awards. I'm sure one of the secrets was that Tina's exuberance and vitality mirrored the qualities that the game itself possesses. I found her a delight to deal with, although I used to joke with John Quayle that no-one could get near her but him. She fitted so smoothly into the rugby league community. Tina Turner became the game's First Lady and her songs our anthems.

Tina opened unexpected new doors for us, bringing new fans flocking to games. The number of women coming to football matches increased dramatically. The game had a sexy, dynamic image by the late '80s. Much progress had been made. Expansion was underway with the new teams added (Brisbane, Newcastle and Gold Coast) and league was a cleaner, fresher product than it had ever been. The importance of the legacy left by 'Gentleman' Jim Comans to the Tina Turner era can never be underestimated. In hindsight it can be said that Comans' period as head of the NSW Judiciary (1980–86) got rugby league ready for its New Age. A stickler for clean and fair play, Comans held a deep understanding that in the time of vast colour TV coverage, rugby league could no longer carry a 'thug' tag if it was to thrive. His six years at the helm can be viewed as both a campaign to clean up the game and a continuing education for future generations of players. The hard men, whose style had spilled over from previous eras, found themselves up against a brick wall in Comans. Some of his suspensions were jolting crash-tackles, virtually ending the careers of men such as Bob Cooper (Wests), Steve Kneen (Cronulla) and Les Boyd (Manly). Comans made his point about what the game needed, and kept making it for six vital years.

It was up to we administrators to build the right structure for the game itself around the champions we had on the periphery, people like Tina Turner and Jim Comans. I believe that one of our greatest initiatives was the introduction of a fairly benevolent draft system in conjunction with a salary cap imposed on clubs. The draft—successfully used in other sports—was about checks and balances. It shared new and available talent fairly among the clubs. At its heart was our search for balance in the competition.

But almost from the start the draft had its opponents—the

two Ryans (Kevin, head of the Players' Association and Warren, coach and newspaper columnist) foremost in the fray. The announcement that we would be introducing the draft from the start of the 1991 season brought the following response from Kevin Ryan: 'The draft is totally unacceptable. It is an unreasonable restraint of trade.' The fight was on. Regrettably, it was a battle we were to lose within 12 months. In October 1991 the full bench of the Federal Court ruled against its legality, and with reluctance we dropped it . . . while other sports, such as the AFL, continued along happily with a draft system that was undoubtedly one of the major underpinnings of their success.

I remain convinced that it was a bad decision for rugby league. Kevin Ryan no doubt believed he was fighting for the 'right' of the players. And I can't be too critical of him—Kevin was a bloke I admired greatly as a footballer, but I have no doubt he was on the wrong tram here. Subsequent developments have proved him shortsighted in his view. Overlooked in the whole thing was the most important point of all: that the draft was about the *greater good of the game*. That being the case, it was also about the greater good of the players. It had been proved many, many years before that individual clubs were unable to impose their own levels of responsibility on the game. Parochial clubs were only interested in one thing—their own success—and had long before shown they would stretch and break rules in that quest. If it was to be done it was the *game* itself that had to impose reasonable conditions of fair play and a level playing field. And that's what we tried to do with the salary cap and the draft. I think the two of them together would have brought loyalty back into the game, and encouraged players to stay with clubs instead of roaming from club to club like mercenaries from the Middle Ages.

Warren Ryan was a very vocal critic of the draft, too. I used to smile about Warren, who many times sounded-off furiously about Manly's 'capture' of players over the years. Interestingly, when Ryan left Canterbury amidst a spate of bad feelings to go to Wests, he took some key Bulldogs with him. I think 'expediency' is the word. The old line about people in glass houses comes to mind too . . .

Arko

The Federal Court decision of 1991, like the astonishing turn-about on the Super League matter in 1996 (and more of *that* later), makes me wonder very deeply how the law works. The draft–salary cap balance was introduced for just one thing: the good of rugby league. And to me the overall health of the game is the essence of everything in a sport. If the sport is in good shape, then the people in it will be in fine shape too. That the learned legal gentlemen couldn't see that in '91 still bewilders me, and makes me wonder that if sometimes in their lofty deliberances they are way out of touch with the way things work in the real world. At the League, we accepted the principle that the draft was a 'restraint of trade' . . . but I would argue forever that it was a *reasonable* restraint of trade in the interests of the game of rugby league.

The salary cap remained in place as an imperfect, but useful brake on ridiculous spending—until the virtual collapse of everything in football following the Super League raids. People argue against the principle of the cap, claiming that it can't work because clubs will always cheat. Well, in my view that's absolute bullshit. If the penalties are made tough enough, it will work all right. I'm talking about things like huge fines ($500,000 or so), loss of premiership points, and disqualification or suspension of the officials involved. If the penalties are made tough enough I question just how many chief executives would put their livelihood on the line knowing that at any moment some player or loose-lips might give them up. Of course it can work, the League could do what the AFL does and appoint an expert whose sole job is to investigate any hint of salary cap breaches.

I would like to think that further down the track when and if rugby league is restored to sanity and health, that the draft and salary caps might again be part of the game. I'm sure it could happen—that players could accept the principles of both in the contracts they sign. I mean, here I'm talking about players accepting things that are good for the game. That shouldn't be a problem, considering the way players have sold their souls with the Super League contracts. Under our draft there were plenty of regulations to protect the rights of players, but under the Super League contracts the fact is that players can be sent over to play with Upper Tanganyika if it happens to suit News Ltd. In May

1997, a meeting of the ARL club captains in Sydney debated the pros and cons of the draft, and reached the conclusion that very likely it was good for the game. There was a signal at that meeting that the game was growing up and something like the draft, designed to help secure the game's long-term health, would be acceptable one day before long. The League hasn't been perfect in its dealings with players, but has never set out to create hardship for them. Quite the reverse in fact, and the introduction of the draft was always and entirely about the health of the game in the knowledge that a game in vibrant health is good for everyone—and especially the men who play it.

The death of the draft was not great news for rugby league, and nor was the revelation of Canberra's salary cap rorting in 1990 (when they won the premiership). Canberra, 'The Green Machine', were league's glamour team in a brief heady period. Their extra-time win over Balmain in the grand final of 1989 represented one of the truly glorious matches in the game's history. But in 1991 it was revealed that they had cheated on the salary cap in 1990, over-spending by more than $85,000. Furthermore, they were full-steam ahead to another blow-out in 1991, until we stepped in, at which point Canberra players had to take across-the-board 15 per cent salary cuts.

There is no doubt whatsoever that Canberra rorted the system. Yet ever since, there has been a seething resentment aimed at Phillip Street over the matter. There is no doubt the ongoing bad feelings led to Canberra's enthusiasm about jumping to Super League. Chief executive John McIntyre and president Jim Woodger both departed in the wake of the revelations. And you know, I'm sure old Les McIntyre, the Canberra club's father figure, has always blamed me for the demise of John his son. Nothing could be further from the truth—in fact I defended the bloke before the NSWRL board. I agreed with the fines slammed on the club (totalling some $185,000) but I told the board that I believed John McIntyre had done little different to what plenty of other people in the game had done, and that I believed he should not be dumped. The fact of it was that it was the Save The Raiders people—the committee set up to rescue the club—who wanted no further truck with John McIntyre.

Arko

The Canberra blow-up led to a very public row between Prime Minister Bob Hawke and me. I came out publicly and had a crack at the Raiders who were trying to plonk the money raised by the Save The Raiders committee *on top of* their salary cap. No way, I said. Hawke came out and accused me of trying to rattle the Canberra players before an important match against Manly the following Sunday. I suggested that Mr Hawke would be far better served trying to fix Australia's ills rather than involving himself in a rugby league administrative matter. Come Sunday, the PM was a special guest in the Manly box at Brookie. I was the host. I reckon every photographer and cameraman in the southern hemisphere turned up for the occasion. We had an army around us as we walked along talking. But if the media were hoping for a punch-up, they didn't get it. Hawke and I had been pretty good mates, and we were both used to a bit of scrapping. He'd hopped into me and I'd hopped back into him. And that was that. At Brookvale that Sunday we laughed about it, shook hands, and enjoyed an afternoon at the football. And bugger me if Canberra didn't get up and beat us on the bell!

In 1991, 15 of the 16 clubs were strongly behind the principle that we had the right to choose our own sponsor, i.e. Winfield. The noose was beginning to tighten on tobacco sponsorship in sport at that time. Winfield's wonderfully loyal support of rugby league deserved loyalty in return; we were not about to discard them. The dissenting club was North Sydney—largely through their outspoken president David Hill—and on one weekend there was a huge squabble about four *Quit for Life* banners placed around the ground before the match . . . then eventually moved on the NSWRL's insistence.

Hill did not believe Winfield should be sponsoring the League, and said so. He was thoroughly entitled to his opinion, one that was shared by plenty of people. But it was the *way* he went about things that got him offside with Phillip Street. Instead of making his views privately known within the League he went screaming to the media, creating a situation of discomfort and embarrassment for his club, and for the game itself. Hill wasn't my kind of bloke, and I didn't have all that much to do with him. But I rated him an intelligent and capable man. For all my disappointment with that, I reckon Hill did a good job in turning around his club North Sydney, transforming them into a modern, competitive football club ready for the challenges of the '90s. He would not, however, have won any popularity contests at Phillip Street.

Rugby league became a travelling show in the '90s. You'd never know where we might turn up—down a mine in Cobar . . . or on top of Uluru. I climbed that mighty rock, along with a bunch of travelling journos, one day. The reach of the game via television backed by enthusiastic and creative marketing was extraordinary, kick-started each year by the wide-ranging road show of the pre-season competition. And everywhere it seemed to me there was great enthusiasm for rugby league. For a heady period we were the envy of every game in Australia, with Tina Turner pumping out the anthem, and the annual State of Origin confrontations, in particular, producing sport of a breathtakingly high standard. The game was just flying, the momentum as never before. When I think back on that time now it is almost impossible for me to comprehend how the game has been brought to its knees just a few short years later.

An article I wrote for the *Sydney Morning Herald* in April 1992 summed up how I saw the state of the rugby league nation in those pre-Super League days. I wrote it in response to a savage, and I felt unfair, piece the *Herald* had run under the heading RUGBY LEAGUE'S MONEY MACHINE. My response read as follows:

> In 1992, rugby league is a very tall poppy indeed on the Australian sporting scene, its administrative structure and demonstrable success of the past decade are much admired by other games.
>
> We take some pride from a few historical facts.
>
> When the League became an incorporated body in 1983 (on the advice of an outside agency, the respected management firm W.D. Scott) eight of the NSWRL's 14 clubs were technically insolvent. Four could not pay their players. The decision was taken that for future survival, rugby league should be taken out of the clubs' hands and placed in the hands of a nine-man board of directors. The clubs effectively made that decision.

In 1982, the last year before incorporation, the League's payments of clubs totalled $1.365 million, including a grant to each club of $22,000 for administration.

Each club had to return 15 per cent of the payment by its major sponsor, averaging $7,000.

Last year, the total payments of clubs was $7.879 million—*not* $4.640 million as claimed.

The $7.879 million represented 91 per cent of the year's operating surplus (8.635 million). That's 91 per cent of the surplus returned to members; Fairfax shareholders would be happy with that. The claim that clubs received only $290,000 each was one of many substantial inaccuracies. The figure represented the base, across-the-board grant for administration purposes from the League's general funds which, of course, included the monies received from the Winfield sponsorship.

Supplemented by television, finals earnings and Challenge Cup figures, clubs received as much as $821,000 (Canberra), $865,000 (Penrith) and $628,000 (Norths)—all the way to Souths, the only team to receive no more than the base amount of $302,000.

North Sydney president David Hill claimed requests for access to the League's financial accounts had been denied him. Hill has not made such a request. For the past two years, Hill had his opportunity to probe as deeply as he would like and to ask any question he wishes regarding the League's finances by the simple act of coming to the League's annual general meeting. Both times Hill has failed to turn up. He seems to prefer to snipe from afar, and inaccurately, via the media.

The suggestion that clubs get a less than fair 'cut' is ridiculous. A sin of omission was the failure to record the support to Illawarra ($1 million loan), Gold Coast ($1 million), Canberra Raiders ($1 million), Newcastle ($500,000) and Cronulla ($500,000)—all at below market interest. The loans are either to do with the building of a new club (Illawarra) or for ground improvements.

Norths, so often critical via David Hill, in 1989 were provided with a letter of support from the League for presentation to their bankers in a successful application for a $400,000 overdraft facility. That support is still in place.

The article also didn't mention the substantial travel grants. This season the grants to Brisbane and Gold Coast will be up to $200,000 each.

The outstanding loans to clubs, which at the end of the last financial year totalled $3.89 million, are included in the League's reserves of $10.704 million.

It has been the League's stated aim from 1984, and with the clubs' full blessing, to build substantial reserves to plan ahead with confidence and to be sure that, in the event of major disaster, sufficient liquid funds are available to quickly overcome problems.

The League views with pride and the achievement of the goal. It is now self-sufficient, and in a position to provide funds for development and improvement of spectator facilities when required. It no longer requires clubs to pay any proportion of sponsorship monies. The board discarded that system in 1984. With the reserves objective now reached, the amount to be retained this year—from expected revenue of $18 million—won't be more than $750,000.

The League made a critical decision in 1985 that it would not prop up clubs which had got themselves into trouble through poor management or rash spending.

That year, the board knocked back requests for $250,000 in loans made by the two grand-finalists, Canterbury and Parramatta. It was made plain that clubs which overspent would no longer be bailed out.

Clubs had to become efficient, well-managed businesses.

The *Herald* and David Hill have consistently shown concern at the licensing side of our operations, looking, it seems, for something sinister. They will continue to be disappointed.

The division was established in 1978 as a partnership between the then 14 clubs and the League. It was conducted on behalf of the partnership by an outside agency. Returns to the League were minimal.

In 1982, the net return was $110; and in 1983, $6,273. The arrangement was a miserable failure. It was terminated in 1985 and in the course of television negotiations with Channel Ten, a new arrangement was reached with News Ltd, then owner of Channel Ten.

Through the expertise, marketing skills and endeavours of News Ltd, the division, something of a 'joke' in 1982–83, is now viable, netting $700,000 in 1991. That goes into total revenue.

John Ribot's belief—that the only way Brisbane could make any money from Broncos' gear and its logo was by setting up its own retail outlet—was well wide of the mark. The Broncos share in the annual revenue generated.

Some enterprising clubs have established their own retailing and are doing very nicely.

The Broncos' logo would be worth nothing without NSWRL membership.

The undisclosed Winfield sponsorship seems to stick in Hill's craw, but the NSWRL is following normal business practice.

Does Hill, as managing director of the ABC, disclose the television fee paid to the League for Saturday rights, or, as Norths president, the amount injected by major sponsors Citibank?

Norths' chief executive, Bob Saunders, at the last two annual conferences was told the full extent of the sponsorship, as were all other chief executives.

Perhaps Hill should contemplate the impact of Winfield's extra financial support—way above and beyond their formal sponsorship arrangement. This includes the Tina Turner (now Tina Turner and Jimmy Barnes) advertising campaigns, the grand-final buses with their colourful club logos, the flags that adorn the city at grand-final time and myriad other involvements.

Without Winfield's generosity and support, such financing would effectively come out of club funds. With the exception of Norths, clubs share annually in $1.2 million of Winfield investment in ground signs.

The clubs have not surrendered their power to control the game's destiny. The articles of association provide that ultimate power resides with League members. To say the board is virtually autonomous and has only limited accountability is a gross misstatement. The childish comment that the board would admit five, 50 or 500 members of its choosing is quite ridiculous.

The sarcastic comment that the League 'condescends' to invite clubs to participate is quite self-serving. While the competition could not exist without them, the reality is that clubs would not have a competition without the League. The League won't accept applications from clubs guilty of serious breaches of the guidelines—such as failure to pay players.

Clubs are given information as required by legislation and by the articles of association.

If they wish to change that, then the means are readily available—by submitting a resolution to the annual general meeting and having it passed.

Denis Fitzgerald claimed I had a major hand in him losing his seat on the board.

Has it ever occurred to Fitzgerald that his defeat might simply have been because general committee members—myself included—believed there were better candidates?

The NSWRL is as open and accountable on financial matters as any major corporation. At all annual general meetings, the financial accounts are presented in the presence of a senior partner of the highly respected firm of KPMG Peat Marwick, the League's auditor.

Rugby league has nothing to hide. Instead of seeking imagined dark demons in our workings, the *Herald* might contemplate the vast amounts of good news in rugby league's quiet revolution of the past decade.

In its 85 years, league has never been on a higher plane. Crowds, television and radio ratings, player payments and media coverage have never been higher.

The annual surplus has risen from $1.32 million in 1982 to $8.36 million in 1991. Club payments have gone from $1.36 million to $7.88 million in that period.

The game has spread its wings. Adelaide, Perth,

Melbourne, Auckland, Darwin and countless places in between have drawn bumper crowds.

The League now finances eight full-time development officers in NSW (there were none in 1983), the Academy at Narrabeen is going great guns, and the Country Rugby League is nowadays the recipient of a healthy annual grant where once it received nothing. The development budget this year is $1.6 million.

Much remains to be done but I believe we are entitled to feel some satisfaction at the achievements of the period 1983–92.

It was on the last day of November 1992 that we made one of the biggest decisions in the game's history and announced the addition of four new teams to the 1995 premiership—two from Queensland, one from Perth, one from Auckland. The *Herald* talked of the 'enormity of the League's expansionist step'. We knew it was a big call . . . the biggest!, but we knew too that it was time to strike while rugby league enjoyed a wave of national popularity unprecedented in its history.

Television's big potatoes deal which locked us in with the Channel Nine network for seven years, came ten months' later. The choice, really, was no choice. Channel Ten who had held the rights to cover the game ($42 million for three years) had fallen flat on their faces, reneging on the deal. In reality, Kerry Packer's Channel Nine was the only game in town. The newspapers guessed $70 million, and were close enough to the mark. There was a period of great controversy over Nine's truncated Sunday night replay, via which viewers received only 42 minutes out of 80, the match squeezed into a 'television hour' between 6.30 and 7.30pm. It was an issue that would never die—with Nine refusing to relent, and critics never letting the matter drop.

Yes, we took something of a pasting over the deal, with the Broncos prominent in that. We were asked again and again why we had signed for such a long period—seven years. Well, the truth of it was that Nine, and Packer in particular, wanted us to sign a contract for *ten* years. Our preference was three years.

With no other bidder we had no real bargaining power, and finally we met at seven. When we had signed the previous contract with Ten, all three commercial networks were in the market, putting us in the box seat. Now Ten were out of business, unable to pay us the agreed money, and Seven were in liquidation. The climate was vastly different. That's what backdropped the arrangement we finally reached with Nine. It was one about which I had some personal reservations—the reduced Sunday night match coverage, particularly. I never really liked that. Nine produced figures which indicated the game was producing better ratings at 42 minutes than it had when they showed the full match. But I got the message pretty clearly from many, many people: if they were going to watch a game of football, they preferred to watch the *whole* game.

The forces that were to toss us like a tiny boat on a stormy sea were now in place, unbeknownst to us. In brief, they could be identified this way:

- The success we had had. We were to be victims of our own achievements, when greedy eyes turned on us in 1994.
- The bold decision to expand; to make rugby league, for the first time in its life, a truly national sport.
- The Channel Nine deal, locking us in uncomplainingly, and with an Optus pay TV rider later added. This allowed no room for flexibility when the News Ltd approach came to us through the front door in early 1995. As people with a traditional belief in honouring the agreements we made, we were pretty much in Kerry Packer's hands. Any decision to do business with News Ltd/Super League virtually had to be his.
- The arrival of the Broncos into the competition in 1988, bringing new elements of unease, discontent, secret corporate ambition and ultimately, wicked treachery.

As we headed blithely on, thrilled by the successes that rugby league had had and full of enthusiasm for what lay ahead, the time-bomb was ticking around these ingredients.

If we made a mistake in all of it it was that we didn't listen with a keen enough ear to the ticking . . .

26

THE
GATHERING
STORM

In hindsight, one of the worst decisions we ever made at Phillip Street was the one that allowed the Brisbane Broncos into the competition. Right there, in one generous gesture by the League in the interest of expanding our horizons, was sown the seeds of the Super League treachery. The mid-to-late '80s was a time of much soul-searching at League headquarters. The game was a restless, growing beast and we wrestled with the double dilemmas of team reductions (in Sydney), and expansion (outside Sydney). In mid-1984 we were seriously looking at chopping a team from the competition, and starting with a 12-team competition in '85. An alternative proposal designed to spark debate made interesting reading in July 1986. The *Daily Telegraph* reported:

> Australian Rugby League supremo Ken Arthurson has proposed a 'super league' to replace the present mid-week cup competition. Arthurson has suggested a super league comprising four or five combined teams from Sydney, two from Brisbane, three NSW country teams, Queensland Country and Auckland. 'You could amalgamate Manly/North Sydney, Eastern Suburbs/South Sydney, Parramatta/Penrith and so on,' Arthurson said.

Hmmm. Sounds a bit familiar.

Arko

Eventually, as history records, we chose to take the expansionary path with our premiership. I will go on the record now and reveal that I was extremely dubious from the start about letting the Broncos in.

At different stages three different groups were bidding to win the franchise rights to get a Brisbane side into the premiership. We had agreed, in principle, that it would happen, that there would be a Brisbane team in the Winfield Cup. At the end, the two groups left going head to head were the Broncos and the Jeans West syndicate. My personal belief was that the Jeans West proposal was clearly the superior of the two. To an extent I was swayed by Ron McAuliffe's view; he was strongly, and bitterly against the Broncos' proposal. He was right.

But we did let them in, after a good deal of toing and froing up there, and gave them free access. We gave them virtually a licence to print money in that one team–one city set-up. They joined (with Newcastle and the Gold Coast) and initially did a good job, tapping into a city's hunger to have its own team in the 'big league'. But realistically though, I reckon your grandmother could have run the club. Sponsors were just about battering down their doors to get on board. And Paul Morgan, Barry Maranta and John Ribot and those blokes were walking around with their chests puffed out at what a great job they were doing, and what geniuses they were. The real test would have been to put them with Souths or Wests or Balmain . . . and see how they went then. Almost from the start they were too self-centred, too greedy . . . just didn't give a bugger about anybody else.

The same 'Porky' Morgan was to come out several years later and state unequivocally that he was the architect of Super League. When I first met Morgan, I thought he was good company. We got on well and I used to enjoy having a beer with him. My feelings now are very different. The bloke was driven absolutely by money—by the 'greed is great' principle. He made a statement to the press a couple of years back which sums him up: 'I'm not interested in being involved in anything from which you can't make a dollar.' At the start I misjudged him. I never thought the bloke I knew then would end up doing the things he did.

Things soon soured between Porky and Phillip Street. I remember a night in a crowded room at ANZ Stadium, with the sound of a heated argument behind me. Morgan was going at it hammer and tongs with John Quayle.

Then I heard him say, 'You guys in Phillip Street are a bunch of crooks!'

I swung around. 'What was that?' I demanded.

And Quayle said to him, 'Now you repeat in front of the chairman what you just said.'

Morgan stammered and stuttered and dodged around, declining the invitation.

We were swayed by the views of the QRL representatives on the ARL board in giving the Broncos the nod for a place in the competition in 1988. There had been some real dithering in Brisbane over the issue including a meeting at which Bill 'Biggles' Hunter, a former air-force pilot, just couldn't make up his mind on whether Brisbane should have a team in the Sydney competition or not, so declined to cast a vital vote on the issue. I think Biggles genuinely just couldn't face up to what was one of the biggest decisions ever put on the table up there, and I guess that was honest enough, even if he faced some ridicule as a result of it. Bill Hunter extolled the virtue of a team coming to Sydney, and then declined to vote when the count was 5–4 against.

The Broncos had the QRL representatives' support, ahead of the Jeans West submission—although McAuliffe, no longer on the ARL Board at that stage, as I have said, was bitterly opposed. I think the QRL guys were influenced by the fact that the Broncos were to be backed by home-grown Brisbane blokes, whereas the Jeans West application had its roots in Western Australia. I think there was also some internal politics involved. McAuliffe was linked to the Jean West group (suggested as club chairman), and there was an element of a strike-back at Ron in the QRL support for the Broncos. Despite my misgivings and my belief that the Jeans West proposal was the better of the two, I took the view that Queensland's wishes should be respected, and that they should get their way. I think it would have been wrong for NSW to overturn the wishes of

Queensland when it was about something that so deeply affected football in that state. And that's why I didn't push against the Broncos being given the nod. Underneath I was very disappointed; I honestly thought the other bidders had clearly the best offer.

If I had my time over and could change that decision, would I do it? Would I ever . . . would I ever! Because to change what we decided in 1988 would have changed rugby league history, and left the game to head down the path on which it was already so successfully placed.

I have no respect at all for the way the Broncos management conducted themselves, or for the decisions they ultimately made. I'm not blaming the players in any way. There are some fine blokes among them, and some champion footballers. And I have the deepest respect for the loyalty and enthusiasm of the Broncos' army of supporters. It's Morgan and his fellow travellers who have to live with what they did . . . and the dreadful damage to rugby league that was the consequence of their actions.

Everything was so sweet for the Broncos, from the moment they stepped into big time football. They drew huge crowds, their sponsorship returns were spectacular, they were soon making millions. In double-quick time they became the first club to ever actually make a *profit* out of rugby league. They had been handed free of charge a licence to print money . . . and all they wanted was more and more.

Almost from the start they were at loggerheads with Phillip Street, and especially with our marketing division and its chairman, Graham Lovett. In the interests of a level playing field for the game (the game itself always being the subject of primary concern in decision making) we had long before settled on a 'pool' system, with profits distributed equally to the clubs. The Broncos didn't want that, they wanted the bloody lot to themselves.

The arguments raged almost weekly, over this point or that. I recall a conversation I had at one stage with Porky Morgan when he, John Quayle and I were in discussion in my office in Phillip Street. In frustration I said to him: 'The trouble with you and your people at the Broncos is that it is always just a

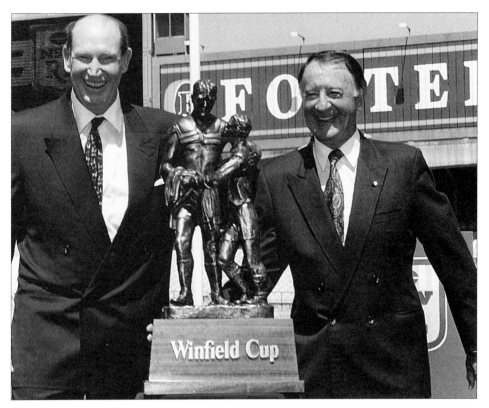

Above: A fateful day in 1993 as Channel 9 boss Kerry Packer and Ken Arthurson flank the Winfield Cup, celebrating 9's signing of the contract which gave the network the rights to televise rugby league. The smiles were to fade and the relationship crumble during the period of the Super League Wars.

Arko with the man who preceded him as NSWRL chairman—the much respected Tom Bellew, an important figure in the modern game's success story.

Right: Ken Arthurson and Barbara Barnes, married Sydney 3 March, 1987.

Below: A sparkling Queensland morning in the Whitsundays brought an impressive haul of reef fish for Ken and Barbara during a 1990s holiday break.

Opposite page, top: A photo resonant of future events as Peter 'Bullfrog' Moore aims an antique pistol at Arko. Ex-ARL Board member John O'Toole is the man in the middle. Moore's decision to join Super League threatened a lifelong friendship.

Above centre: Arko (front), the *Daily Telegraph*'s Peter Frilingos (middle) and NSWRL marketing man Graham Foster become intimately acquainted with some of the locals on a trip to Broken Hill for a Tooheys Challenge match.

Left: 'Judge' Arko hams it up; a place for him on the Federal Court bench would have been handy for the ARL in 1995.

England's Maurice Lindsay *(above left)* News Ltd's Ken Cowley *(above)* and Super League's John Ribot—big players in a huge story. (Photos courtesy of Action Photographics)

Arthurson declared himself deeply hurt and disappointed with two of the great players of the game, Mal Meninga *(above)* and Laurie Daley *(right)*—mainly with things said after the pair switched to Super League.

The way it was in 1995—press conferences, meetings, pressure. *(Above)* Quayle and Arthurson surrounded by the media after the Burchett judgment. *(Left)* A brief relaxed moment for two men who fought shoulder-to-shoulder in a fierce and unrelenting battle. (Photos courtesy of Action Photographics)

Yeah! Arthurson was gracious in 'victory' after the Burchett judgment, but couldn't resist a gesture of triumph. (Photo courtesy of Mirror Australian Telegraph Publications)

Weighed down by the burden of pressure Arthurson found himself 'blinded' too one morning—by a clever photo taken at an ARL press conference. (Photo courtesy of Action Photographics)

The realisation hits home as Ken tells the media of his retirement plans in early 1997. After 50 years in the game, fulltime is near. (Photo courtesy of Action Photographics)

question of, "What are you doing for me lately".' From the very first time we at Phillip Street did something that didn't suit them we were seen as the greatest pack of bastards who ever drew breath. That's how it was with the Broncos, almost from day one.

There were arguments over various issues, with the Battle of the Brewers, Powers v Fourex, one of the big ones. Powers backed the Broncos into the competition, and excellent sponsors they were, too. But the fact of it was that Fourex held sway with the QRL and the Lang Park Trust and under the terms of their deal the Broncos couldn't advertise Powers at the ground. They sure tried, though, doing their best to bend the rules in every possible way. They harped and nagged and criticised. Funnily enough, Fourex ended up being a Broncos sponsor anyway in the long run. It was another example of an old truism which was to be repeated again and again during the ARL–Super League war: When a business deal walks in the door, morality and friendship fly out the window.

The Broncos were constantly critical of the ARL and NSWRL, conveniently forgetting that it was the generosity of the members of those Leagues that gave them the chance in the first place. They conveniently forgot too, that we supported them in the move from Lang Park (Suncorp Stadium) to ANZ Stadium despite the fact that the QRL bitterly opposed such a move. Phillip Street's support was on the principle that every team in the competition had the right to say where their home ground was to be.

More than once things got so bad that we toyed with the idea of expelling them. Some of the things printed in the newspapers were more than hollow threats. In hindsight we would have been a helluva lot better off if we *had* expelled them. They just kept breaking the rules, to suit themselves, fuelled by the greed and avarice of big business at its worst.

Newcastle and the Gold Coast joined the competition at the same time as the Broncos, both of them offering commitment, loyalty and the utmost respect for the rules of the competition which they joined. Newcastle was a 'natural', despite the resistance that had existed for years among older officials to any move to the Sydney competition. Essentially, it was a rejoining of history. Teams from Newcastle had taken part in the first rugby league premierships of 1908–09, and the city had never been anything less than a great rugby league centre. They were instantly competitive, a real success story. More than that, I will never forget the loyalty of Newcastle folk to the ARL cause during the hard times of 1995–96.

The Gold Coast was a struggle. We needed another team to make a viable 16-team competition, and Gold Coast were the best chance. Finally some true-blue rugby league men, headed by John Sattler, Peter Gallagher and Bob Hagan, got together and made the possibility of a team up there a reality. Those guys were just terrific and the League owes them a debt of gratitude for the way they jumped in and filled the breach, starting a club for which life has always been a battle to date, but which is now making steady progress in its new home base at Carrara on the Gold Coast. The Broncos treated the Gold Coast club badly from the start. There was no way they wanted another Queensland team anywhere near them, and they set out to make life as difficult as they could. The same thing happened when the decision was made to add a second Brisbane-based side, for season 1995. Wallowing in self-interest, the Broncos opposed it all the way. Their attitude was a disgrace in a city of the size of Brisbane which can certainly accommodate two top-level football teams.

In so many ways 1988, the year of Australian bicentenary, was a momentous season in football. It was for me too. I went along one morning to the Governor's residence in Sydney's Botanic Gardens to receive an Order of Australia award, which was a moment of great pride for myself and my family. I remember well, too, a rainy night in March when we first played on rugby league's glamorous new home ground, the Sydney Football Stadium. The Stadium was instantly controversial. The expert advice given to the Trust was that when it rained 80 per cent of the fans would stay dry, and the other 20 per cent would get wet. I guess we all know by now that the original percentages quoted are off the mark. The problem with the original assessment seemed to be that it didn't allow for any wind. Most days there is wind, and it soon became obvious that if you went to the SFS when it was *both* wet and windy . . . the 80/20 estimate didn't stand up.

Accepting its deficiencies (and many of the early ones have been seamlessly ironed out), the Stadium really is a magnificent place to watch football, and a tribute to the energy of the then NSW sports minister Michael Cleary, who pushed it through. I won't forget that first night, when Saints played Easts and the rain bucketed down. As I walked down the race for the opening ceremony a voice boomed from the crowd: 'Why don't you put a bloody roof on the place, Arthurson!' Jeezus! That's one thing they *couldn't* blame me for.

But when you search for the events of historical significance that year the arrival of the Broncos far surpassed the opening of the $66 million stadium in the impact the Broncos were eventually to have on the game. Almost from the start the Broncos just wanted it all, wanted the whole joint to themselves. Given a free kick in front in 1988, they quickly became the only (big) money-making team in football. The fact of it is that rugby league is a very expensive hobby. Anyone going into it who thinks he is going to make a lump of money is having himself on. It has always been a struggle in Australia and only the generous subsidising of the sport by the Leagues clubs has sustained it and enabled it to grow into what it now is (or was at the end of season 1994, anyway). The president of the Washington Redskins got it right when someone asked him one day if it was possible to make a small fortune out of sport. 'Easy,' he replied. 'Just start with a large fortune.'

The Broncos man in the hot-seat at that time was, of course, John Ribot, who had once been John Ribot-de-Bresac. As chief executive of the club he was caught between the demands of a voracious board, and the checks and balances we tried to impose from Phillip Street. I had known Ribot for many years before he became top man at the Broncos. In 1982 I bought him for Manly, signing him from Wests where Roy Masters had resurrected his career by switching him from lock to wing in an inspired piece of coaching. Ribot blossomed as a winger; he was a beauty—big, strong and fast. He played with considerable distinction in his two years at Manly (1982–83), and was an affable and popular club man and a darned good footballer.

John was a bloke I always got on well with and liked, and when he became a delegate to the League on the entry of the Broncos to the competition, I did my best in the background to help him. I am greatly disappointed that he chose eventually to take the path that he did, to Super League. I had plenty of time for the bloke and it was sad for me to accept that he had turned his back on our side of the game, and gone with the News Ltd raiders. I always felt that he was pressured, influenced by the money-and-success hungry Broncos management which flanked him.

My memories of him were happier ones—of an outstanding wingman, winning matches for Manly, and Tests for Australia. But from fairly early days with the Broncos his relationship with Phillip Street was not a particularly comfortable one. I recall being in my office in town one afternoon when I heard the sound of raised voices coming from John Quayle's office. I headed across there, the voices growing louder. Quayle and Ribot were shouting at each other, in the midst of a furious argument. The pair of them sounded as if they were close to blows.

I went in. 'What's going on here?' I said. It turned out the pair of them had been arguing fiercely over a Broncos-backed bid to take a premiership grand final to Brisbane.

'Aren't you guys interested in finance?' Ribot shouted at Quayle.

I answered for him, 'Yes, of course we are, but finance isn't the be all and end all of everything. The game, and what is right for it and wrong for it, will always be more important.' Ribot couldn't see it.

I often had the impression that Ribot was being pushed by other forces—after the Broncos had come into the competition and also after he became Super League's chief executive. Through those years he said many things with which I strongly disagreed. I do appreciate however that when you're fighting for a cause you are honour-bound to preach the gospel of that cause.

I bumped into him at Brisbane Airport one day a few months ago and we chatted lightly for ten minutes or so. Not about football, of course. There would have been no point in that. I don't agree with the direction that John headed, but, as I have said, people have to make their own decisions, and I accept that. I'm sure that Ribot and I will always have a civil relationship. There is some mutual respect there from years ago, and of course it doesn't all evaporate. There are plenty of people on the Super League side I wouldn't want to talk to. Ribot is not one of them.

John is a fundamentally decent bloke. He is not without ability in some areas. But at Phillip Street he created many of his own problems. For one year he was voted on to one of the League's most important committees—the Premiership Policy Committee. Ribot doesn't know this, but when there was a coup, which bumped him off that committee after 12 months, both John Quayle and I voted for him to stay as a member.

Ribot got his chance (and an important step forward for the Broncos) when the North Sydney Bears chief executive Bob Saunders was dropped from that committee. There was reasonable speculation that Saunders had paid the penalty for Norths' president David Hill, who had some ups and downs in his dealings with the League. After Hill, a talented bloke with a sizeable ego, publicly criticised the League and its dealings with the Winfield company, he was carpeted by the NSWRL. Bob Saunders, his CEO at Norths, was voted off the Premiership committee for a year, then back on when Ribot got the shove.

There were varying theories for Ribot's downfall, one of them being that he was getting too full of himself, too uppity. A black mark against him was his blind resistance to the suggestion of a second Brisbane team coming in. At least one fellow official went public with his criticism of Ribot's parochial approach to the task at hand on that committee, claiming that virtually *every* topic was viewed in the light of what it would mean to the Broncos . . . instead of to the game itself.

When it was all blowing up, I asked Peter Moore one day: 'Why do you want to get rid of him? We need blokes from outside . . . we don't want it run just by blokes from Sydney.'

Arko

'I'll tell you why,' said Moore. 'The *only* thing he cares about is the Broncos.'

And mainly that was it; Ribot got the chop because people were so crooked on the Broncos, crooked on their constant whingeing.

It's a funny game, rugby league. Within not so many months John Ribot and Peter Moore were together in the bosom of Super League.

Partners in crime? Well, it's not an unreasonable description of what took place in early 1995.

27

BATTLE ALERT!

Among my souvenirs of the Super League war which has just about wrecked rugby league are 40 pages of confidential notes. They provide a compelling chronology of a devastating story. One of the first notations is this: '12/93—(Paul) Morgan speaks with (Ken) Cowley regarding breakaway competition.'

A little further down is the following: '4/94 (John) Ribot presents "first proposal" to Cowley.'

There it is in a few words: the beginning of a sporting disaster. It was back in December '93 that the seeds of Bronco treachery were first sewn.

The scrapbooks kept for me by my personal assistant Pam Parker over the years list 28 August 1994 as the day I was first injected into the story that became one of the biggest in Australian sport. The story is from the *Courier-Mail* and is headed 'ARTHURSON BLASTS MORGAN: SUPER LEAGUE PUSH IRKS ARL CHAIRMAN' and begins:

> Australian rugby league chairman Ken Arthurson last night blasted Broncos chairman Paul Morgan for throwing his weight behind a super league conducted by private enterprise.

I expressed views in that interview that were entirely consistent with what I have believed all along—that I was not against a 'super league' but that the game must never be allowed to leave the hands of the people who were its rightful custodians—the ARL. 'To turn your back on the game of rugby league for the mighty dollar you'd be a pretty poor sort of individual,' I told journalist Steve Ricketts.

The whispers were in the air by then. The well-connected Tony Durkin, Queensland editor of *Rugby League Week*, was out of the blocks very early indeed with a major feature story: 'WORLD SERIES LEAGUE', which appeared in the magazine on 2 March. An early Steve Crawley piece in the *Australian* was also pretty revealing in the light of future events. The *Daily Telegraph Mirror*'s Peter Frilingos penned a comment piece headed: 'SUPER LEAGUE: IT WON'T WORK'. Frilingos wrote of Super League as: 'The most stupendous game of chance ever promoted since league kicked off in Australia in 1908.' This is of particular interest considering Frilingos's later pro-Super League stance.

'Be not afeard: the isle is full of noises,' wrote Shakespeare in *The Tempest*. And so it was in rugby league in Australia in 1994 as the late months of the year ticked over. The only thing was we should have been afraid . . . very afraid.

One of the worst things while all this speculation was building, while the air filled with rumours, was that we were deep in negotiations with News Ltd. They had expressed interest in sponsoring the competition in the wake of Winfield's pending forced departure at the end of 1995. Winfield had given us the green light to talk to other prospective sponsors. Under a News Ltd deal the proposal was that the premiership would be called the Ansett Cup. Graham Lovett of Sport Australia and John Quayle were handling the negotiations in the main and late into 1994 we believed it was just about a *fait accompli* that we would soon have a new and powerful sponsor on board.

We had opened our records and financial statements to News Ltd. And we had opened our hearts—telling them what our plans were, our hopes for the game. They were privy to just about everything it was possible to know about rugby league in 1994. And that's the unforgivable thing. That while they were talking to us they were also in quiet negotiation in the background with the Broncos about the possibilities of a Super League. People have asked me whether I thought News were *ever* fair dinkum about the Ansett Cup idea—or was it just a dummy they threw us to get the information they needed? Well, I'd like to think they *were* fair dinkum, but after all that has happened since, I have my doubts. They were in there wheedling out all the knowledge they needed for what lay ahead. I find that appalling.

The deal with News foundered on the conditions we had put, or so it seemed. We offered the premiership sponsorship/ naming rights to News at around $8 million, with a cash component of $4 million. And the fact was that News, via information conveyed from Ken Cowley to Graham Lovett, accepted the proposal. In essence it was to be a three-way arrangement, involving News, Ansett and Coca-Cola. Later came the turnaround—with News backing away. In eventually rejecting the deal, Ken Cowley said the cash component was too high. How amazing that is in view of the hundreds of millions that have been flushed down the drain ever since.

At Phillip Street there was a sense of excitement about having News Ltd as partners in the game. We already had close ties with them through our licensing and marketing structure, and a full-scale involvement seemed a logical extension of that. For all those reasons we were as candid as it was possible to be in handing over the information they required to make their decision. We told them every single thing they needed to know about how the League worked. And they kicked sand in our faces . . .

Graham Lovett was the man in the middle in much of it, caught in a fairly awkward position. He had a foot in both camps, being actually employed by News Ltd, but also a member of the NSWRL board, too. Lovett and Quayle were to have a serious falling out over the situation eventually, and in time, of course, Graham Lovett resigned from the League Board, writing to me on December 12: 'Given my relationship with News Ltd and the unresolved question of the Super League and the ARL/NSWRL, I consider there is no alternative but to withdraw from consideration of reappointment to the Board of the NSWRL for 1995.' In my view Lovett handled things fairly and with integrity. He had done a remarkably good job in the marketing of the game and when the negotiations with News began I have no doubt that he entered into them in the best possible faith. He was as disappointed as anyone when the deal collapsed.

Arko

And in Lovett's strong defence it was he who first drove it home to me that the Super League thing was serious . . . deadly serious. That was in England, October 1994, where I had flown to attend the first Australia–Great Britain Test at Wembley.

Back home by then, other factors were emerging. Canberra were later to defend the Super League path they took with the claim that they had reached a final point of frustration with Phillip Street over a claimed lack of support in their attempts to hang on to star players Ricky Stuart and Bradley Clyde in the wake of rumoured huge bids from the Kerry Packer-supported Easts. Les McIntyre and Kevin Neil came to Sydney to see me about it, and express their concerns. They told me of the dilemma they believed they faced—of Easts luring the two players away with offers that were just too huge to refuse. I told them that I wasn't happy about such a situation if it was the case, but there was nothing I could do. It had been ever thus in rugby league, clubs now and then signed players from other clubs, sometimes paying far more money than they should have.

At that meeting something happened which neither Neil or McIntyre could ever deny—they swore they would never participate in a competition which wasn't under the control of the ARL. I'll be frank—I shared their concerns about Stuart and Clyde. Of course they didn't want to lose two such players. But under the League's rules, what could be done? Our game ran on a free-market basis. Neil told me subsequently that he had rung Ken Cowley and Cowley had said to him: 'Don't worry about it—we'll buy them for you.' And that was how News Ltd got the Raiders into the net.

It was in the luncheon room at famous Wembley Stadium on the day of the first Kangaroo Test of the 1994 tour that Lovett convinced me that trouble was truly afoot. His words to me were something along the lines of: 'This Super League business is definitely going on, Ken: it's going to happen.' He told me that News Ltd's David Smith was in England at the time, investigating the structure and finances of the English Rugby League.

I considered his words, and expressed my concerns. 'I think I should fly home and see Ken Cowley,' I said.

'Yes, I think you should,' said Lovett. 'He's going away

194

sometime in November so if you don't catch him pretty quickly, you won't get to him until December.'

It was Lovett who set up the appointment for me, on 10 November. From London, I rang John Quayle and told him of the developments. 'Let's get a meeting of all the clubs set up for when I get back,' I said. 'Meanwhile, sound out the clubs . . . see where they stand.' From that conversation, too, came the decision that we would have a five year commitment agreement drawn up, to be signed by the clubs. I stayed on for the second Test then flew home in some frustration, with the Ashes in the balance at one Test all. It's a little known fact that Ken Cowley subsequently offered to fly me back to England for the third Test. I was appreciative, but declined.

Before I left England I took the opportunity to talk to English League boss Maurice Lindsay about the Super League rumours, registering my concerns with him. Maurice swore that he had had no approach from Super League. He seemed to know nothing about it which was a surprise—considering that everyone else and his brother in league seemed to have got drift of the rumours. 'Maurice Lindsay has assured me that such a scheme (Super League) would be furiously resisted by his organisation,' I told the Australian media after my talk with him. Maurice assured me that if there was an approach he would certainly do nothing without first sitting down and talk-ing to us. 'Maurice, make sure you do that,' I said to him.

The meeting in Sydney on 10 November was held in Cowley's office at News Ltd and attended by Quayle and myself. Just four days before, the Fairfax-owned *Sun-Herald* had run a feature with an uncannily accurate headline in their sports sec-tion. '$500 MILLION RL HIJACK', it read, topping a sensational story by Alex Mitchell, which told of Rupert Murdoch's plan to 'revolutionise' league through a 12-team competition. On 10 November Cowley shared his version of the news: 'Yes, it's true, we've been working on the possibility of starting a Super League.' At a subsequent meeting I recall Cowley pointing to a folder at least three inches thick on his desk. 'We've been look-ing into this for some time,' he said. 'That's the full story right there . . . one day I'll let you see it.' The initial briefing was fairly

Arko

sketchy—of News Ltd's belief in a reduced, high-quality competition of 12 teams. Cowley indicated that they planned to make a full presentation to us 'later'. 'I would like to take rugby league to the rest of the world,' he said. 'If you come with us we will make the code a much stronger code. I love the game, Ken, I want you to know I'd never do anything to harm it.'

In the course of the meeting I said to Cowley: 'Ken, there's a problem with you going ahead with any of this. We have a legally binding contractual arrangement with Channel Nine—even if it was only a handshake we would be morally bound to stand by it.'

He replied: 'We're looking for pay TV rights. You can still have free-to-air rights.'

I suggested to him: 'Why don't you go and see Kerry Packer. Sit down and talk with him and if he's happy about it, well, we can have further talks.'

The meeting was amicable enough, but with an underlying tension. At one stage Cowley commented: 'Look at John Quayle over there, glowering at me.' And it was true that Quayle's approach that day left little doubt that he was filthy about what he was hearing. John is a bloke who wears his heart on his sleeve. He sat there with a steely stare, saying little. I tried to appear calm, even if my mind was racing with the possibilities. It was a fact-gathering exercise on our part, and there was nothing to be gained from aggressive or angry behaviour. I remembered the old saying: 'You get more flies with honey than you do with vinegar.' So I kept it calm and relaxed, and the thing was that I liked Ken Cowley, had always enjoyed a good relationship with him, and respected the man.

Later that day Cowley rang me back. 'I've been to see Kerry Packer,' he said. 'I didn't get much joy, in fact he almost threw me out of the office.'

Packer rang later in the day with a similar message. 'We've got a contract, and it's got nothing to do with them,' he said. 'And we want nothing to do with them.'

Nineteen of the 20 ARL clubs met four days later on 14 November, with the Auckland Warriors the only absentees. My recollection is that John Quayle and I spoke to Paul Morgan and Barry Maranta either before or after the meeting, and they both indicated they had had nothing to do with Super League, and would not be in any competition that was not under the auspices of the Australian Rugby League.

Maranta claimed in a later statement that he had asked me: 'What happens to clubs like Balmain and Souths?' and that I had replied: 'Oh, they'll just have to go.' He added that he was not sure if anyone else had heard me say it. The reason for that is that I bloody well *didn't* say it. It was a figment of his imagination, and I reject it emphatically. I said all along as chairman that I would never be party to forcing clubs out, or forcing them to amalgamate, even if I held the belief that natural processes would lead to a reduction in the number of teams in Sydney. In the end all 20 clubs signed the commitment agreement, the Broncos some time after the others. Relationships between the League and the Broncos had dipped to historically low levels. We were well aware they were the driving force behind Super League. I warned them they were at risk of exclusion from the competition because of their disloyalty. Obviously they didn't take kindly to that.

The thing was not dead, not by a long way. Through the weeks that followed, weeks of summer when rugby league should rightly have been on the back-burner, the whispers and rumours continued. There were stories in the paper almost every day, some speculative, some obviously containing News Ltd 'insider' information. In November in the *Australian* Steve Crawley wrote an article from the heart of Super League and ended: 'And despite the protestations of ARL officials, it will happen.'

My own confidential papers record much toing and froing, meetings, telephone calls, and faxes. They tell of continued contact between Super League operatives and club representatives. They leave no doubt that News Ltd were completely unfazed by the fact of clubs committing themselves long term to the ARL through the agreements they had signed. At a time when the game should have been bursting with anticipation for what lay ahead, it was in turmoil. On 1 December we announced a record $12.5 million profit for the season just ended. Rugby league was in the best state it had ever been in, yet was under fierce and covert assault.

I will declare quite openly now that at the time I was in no way totally against the concept of Super League. I could see that there were worthwhile things to consider in what News Ltd were investigating. And the fact was that we had already made our decision that we would look at 'rationalisation'—the reduction in the number of Sydney-based teams—at the end of the first two seasons of the 20-team competition. We would revalue and reassess. I thought that at 20 teams the competition *might* prove too big and unwieldy, but only time, and the functioning of the 1995 and '96 comps would tell us that. I had told our clubs that the issue of amalgamation was going to have to be confronted, although I would never force mergers. I certainly wasn't completely out of tune with what News Ltd were talking about.

On 30 January, 1995 John Quayle, Peter Moore and myself met Ken Cowley, Graham Lovett and David Smith at News Ltd. I asked Peter Moore to come to that meeting because he was a senior member of our board and also one of the top club chief executives. At the meeting there was more of the same—a general presentation of what Super League stood for, although this time there was a slide presentation too. Cowley indicated that News were not prepared to divulge financial details unless we signed a confidentiality clause—something that was never done. Again, the meeting had a certain edge to it. Peter Moore later recalled John Quayle's 'body language' that day—of the League's general manager half turned away from Cowley in apparent distaste, obviously disliking intensely what he was hearing. The ongoing tension that existed between Cowley and Quayle and Ribot and Quayle was a growing fact of life of those days pre the explosion. Quayle was used to saying what he thought and not holding back. What was happening with Super League alarmed him greatly, and his attitude when in the presence of any of the pro-Super Leaguers showed it.

Six days after that meeting came the World Sevens at the Sydney Football Stadium and the extraordinary machinations of that afternoon, of which I told you at the start of my story. The storm clouds were gathering over football's world, dark and menacing as the lights went out on the SFS that evening. Club officials examined their consciences and talked to their fellows as the following Monday loomed large—a day on which the sort of loyalty that the game of rugby league had been built on would be put to its sternest test.

28

D DAY—
6 FEBRUARY

Almost until it kicked off, there were doubts that News Ltd would go ahead as planned and make their Super League presentation to the meeting of the representatives of the 20 ARL clubs who awaited them on the first floor, 165 Phillip Street. It was Monday, 6 February 1995 the first of many crunch days in the battle for rugby league's future. It had been 24 hours since I had delivered the news to Ken Cowley that I wouldn't be supporting News Ltd's proposal. On the morning of the sixth I was having telephone conversations with Cowley almost up to the scheduled starting time of the meeting, repeating what I had told him the previous day—that I simply couldn't turn my back on the clubs who had been so loyal. Super League's plan meant the certain death, or significant diminishment anyway, of clubs. I wouldn't be supporting his proposal. But I urged Cowley to come along all the same. I wanted the clubs to make their own decision. Finally, he decided. 'We'll be there,' he said.

I met Cowley and David Smith before the meeting and told them that I had approached the clubs and they had agreed to listen to the proposal. Among those clubs were several who had signed confidentiality agreements with Super League and already had held talks with News. Among them were: the Broncos, Raiders, Reds, Knights. All declared they had signed only in their quest for further information.

On the second floor Phillip Street, I set the scene as well as I could. I knew there was an undercurrent of anger and discontent and I was firm in my opening words. I told of the previous meetings with the Super League people, of the proposal they had put to us and how I had told them I would make arrangements to place their plan before the representatives of all the clubs, 'So you would know exactly what was happening and then would be in a position to make up your own minds as to what direction to take.' I directed the meeting:

> 'Gentlemen, I want to make it very clear to you that I expect you to pay these people the utmost respect and courtesy when they join us. Certainly ask any questions you like. There may well be things you don't agree with and if you don't agree with anything, then say so. But my request of you is for respect and courtesy.'

The story of what followed has been told many times, although not always with complete accuracy. Ken Cowley addressed the meeting of 50-odd club delegates, a short preamble of seven or eight minutes.

From what I can recall of Cowley's address, he said something like this:

> 'I love rugby league . . . I can assure you I would never do anything to harm the game. Super League is not a corporate attack on the game in Australia . . . News Ltd has evaluated the game and seen a different vision to the Australian Rugby League. However, any role which News was to play in the game would not result in the ARL losing control of the administration of the game . . . it is not intended for News to own the game. Whatever happens we will not start up a rebel League.'

Both Cowley and Smith made that point—that there would not be a rebel competition. There was 50 witnesses to that. Facing a potentially hostile crowd, Cowley spoke well and with apparent sincerity. David Smith, however, didn't do anywhere near as well. I had found Smith OK in the dealings I had had with him. But this was a tough meeting, and frankly, he went over like a lead balloon.

His submission was backed by a slide presentation of News Ltd's plans, and Smith came across as arrogant and dogmatic. Instead of appealing to the delegates' sense of what was best for the game and how an already outstanding game could be even further improved, he adopted the stance that the game was in bloody awful shape and there was no real alternative but to take it along the News Ltd path. He talked about how all the mistakes 'you people' were making would be rectified under the new deal.

Reduced to its bare bones, the News Ltd proposal essentially was for a nationally based Super League competition, backed by a 'second level' competition in which existing clubs would retain their identities. All of it would be supported by extensive pay and free-to-air television coverage. There would be groupings of clubs in Sydney to support 'Super' teams, with the traditional teams then playing in the second tier competition, which was proposed as a very viable competition in its own right—but a 'feeder', also, to the Super League. Many people—then and later—could see value in elements of the News Ltd proposal.

But, I could feel the antagonism growing in the room as David Smith held the floor. 'Jeezus, you could have fooled me!' I said under my breath as Smith intoned rugby league's fallen state. The fact of it was that the game had never looked healthier: radio and television ratings were at record levels; crowds were booming; the financial indicators were at unprecedented heights. In fact our game was the envy of just about every other sport. We were leaders in marketing, promotion, drugs policy, player safety and most other things you could think of.

Yet here was this bloke telling us we were stuffing it up, that we didn't know what we were doing and that we had no option but to follow his way! In simple terms David Smith got it badly wrong that morning. Given his time again, I'm sure he would approach it very differently. At the meeting a week earlier Smith had seemed more relaxed. He had told us then that he had already spoken to a number of clubs, and that some of them had indicated their readiness to join the Super League concept. I guess Smith must have known he had blown it on the morning of the sixth. When he and Cowley left the meeting, the atmosphere was as cold as ice . . .

The thought sits firmly in my mind that if Ken Cowley, or even Rupert Murdoch himself, had made the submission on behalf of News Ltd, the outcome *may* have been different. People have suggested that if Packer *hadn't* come to the meeting it may have led to a different result, too. Well, I'm not sure, and we'll never know. Feelings were running pretty high, and in the main they were heavily stacked against News Ltd. Some words of David Smith's stick in my mind. During the meeting a club delegate put the direct question to him: 'If the Rugby League does not support your proposal, would you go ahead without us?' Smith replied: 'News Ltd will not start a rebel League'—the point that Ken Cowley had already made.

There is a belief that Kerry Packer, as Channel Nine boss, was always going to be part of the meeting that day. That is simply not true. What happened was that during the luncheon break which followed the submission by Smith and Cowley, Norths chief executive Bob Saunders said to me: 'Don't you think it would be a good idea if Packer came down and told the meeting what he told you yesterday . . . about not doing any deals with News Ltd? I know everyone believes what you said, but sometimes it's nice to hear it from the horse's mouth.'

I thought about it and replied: 'Yeah, I have no objections to that.' I pulled John Quayle aside, and he agreed it was a worthwhile idea. He rang Kerry Packer during lunch . . . and that's how it happened.

I spoke to Packer when he arrived that afternoon, and strangely enough, he seemed quite nervous about addressing the delegates. But when he got up, he spoke with considerable force. His message in effect was: why would you want to sell a business like this to a media outfit (News)? 'If you want to sell the business, *I'll* buy it off you,' he said. He added: 'I'll tell you what, don't ever sell your souls to people like that.' It was in answer to a question from the floor that Packer issued his strongest and most publicised statement: 'I just want you all to know that I've got a legally binding contract with you people and if any of the clubs go against it, I'll sue the arse off you.'

It has been claimed since that some people were intimidated by Packer, and by what he said that afternoon. In my view that is just an excuse for the weakness shown by blokes who were already demonstrably on side with News Ltd and the company's Super League plans at that stage. A couple of big hulks like John Ribot and Kevin Neil admitted they were intimidated, to the extent that they didn't get up and ask the questions they no doubt wanted to ask. That is to their eternal discredit. Both said subsequently that they *wished* they had got up. Well, I wish that too. It was an open forum to debate the pros and cons of an issue that could have a profound effect on rugby league. It was pretty pathetic—that blokes like them no doubt had matters to raise on behalf of their clubs . . . yet couldn't bring themselves to do it.

The meeting was a shocker for the representatives of Canberra and Brisbane clubs, driving forces behind the Super League concept. Apart from their failure to tackle Packer, or the issues raised by his stance, they were also having to wrestle with an embarrassing realisation—even though it was hardly fresh news—that Kerry Packer held the pay TV rights to the game, until 2000. This was an arrangement confirmed a fair while before—brokered with the full knowledge of Graham Lovett who was in regular contact with News Ltd—and covered in John Quayle's address to the chief executives' conference the previous November. Somehow with blokes like John Ribot and Paul Morgan this fact of football life had gone straight through to the keeper. When the revelation re-surfaced at the 10 February meeting, Morgan, Ribot and Barry Maranta just looked at each other. Under the terms of his free-to-air contract Packer had first option on the pay TV rights, and had picked them up. On this issue John Quayle prepared a letter for me to send to Ken Cowley confirming that the rights had already been settled well before that day, and if John Ribot hadn't been aware of it, well, he should have been, because he had been made aware along with everyone else. Maybe it was just a situation of a lack of communication within that club. I never sent the letter that Quayle prepared, I rang Cowley instead, and told him the situation over pay TV rights was a matter of fact and record.

He said to me: 'I've been told it didn't happen.'

And I replied, 'Well, you have my assurance that it did.'

He said: 'OK.'

As Mike Colman's excellent book *Super League—the Inside Story* records, John Ribot seemingly never accepted that assurance.

The facts are these: Nine's pay-for-view option was exercised more than a *year* before the crunch meeting of 6 February. John Quayle informed club chief executives of that in clear terms in a speech he made at their annual conference in November 1993.

I'll admit that the meeting of 6 February was a trying affair for everyone, including me as chairman. There was some fiery debate, with Peter Moore copping a hammering from Nick Politis (Easts) and George Piggins (Souths). Rumours were circulating that Canterbury were already locked into discussions with Super League. Moore was accused of having declared that he would be happy to sit down and talk with Super League. The Bullfrog got up and denied the claims—telling the meeting that all he had done was written Super League a letter indicating that he would be happy to look at any proposal, but only on the understanding that any competition that was the outcome of all that was taking place must be under the control of the ARL.

There was a full, frank and robust discussion and at the end of the meeting, with Packer on his way, I said,

> 'Gentlemen, you have heard the proposal from News Ltd. Everyone who wanted to ask a question has been given the opportunity to do so. I have asked anybody who had something to say to get up and say it. I am of the view that some of the ideas put forward have some merit and deserve at the very least our consideration. Now, I am not calling for a vote *en masse* to what has been put to us. I propose instead to ask you all individually for your thoughts.'

And that's what I did. I went to each of them and asked the question along the lines of: 'Do you believe we should accept the proposal of Super League—and will you remain loyal to the ARL?' One by one I looked each delegate in the eye and one by one they got up and swore allegiance to the ARL and declared they were not in favour of the Super League proposal. Not *one* of them said they weren't supportive of the ARL or that they supported what David Smith had proposed. The answer from Keith Barnes (Balmain) was typical: 'Mr Chairman, my club does not support the Super League proposal. We would not be in any competition that was not under the control of the Australian Rugby League.' And so it went, around the room . . .

Sitting on the table, if such a result proved to be the outcome of the day, was a revised version of the loyalty agreements signed back in November '94. I got League lawyer and close friend of the game Colin Love to get up and explain the differences between this and the original agreement. In reality this document was only a 'fleshing out' of the first one. The delegates were given the agreement to take away, with a 48-hour deadline for signing—time enough for discussion within the club, independent legal opinion, or whatever they wished. There has been talk that the clubs had to sign the agreements under duress; that they were pushed and bullied into doing it. That is a sneaking, snivelling, bloody lie. All of them had the opportunity to go back to their boards—which they did. In any case they all signed, including the Broncos after a day or two's fiddling over technicalities. They were worried that the League might go back to the old 'gate sharing' arrangements, rather than letting clubs keep their own gates. Obviously that wouldn't have suited them. I allayed their fears by giving them assurance covering the couple of areas of their concern, and offering them written confirmation.

At the end of the meeting, late on 6 February, I said this to the delegates: 'Thank you, gentlemen, I appreciate what you have done. Most of all I appreciate your loyalty to the League. While ever we stand together, nobody can tear us apart. All the Rupert Murdochs in the world can't break us if we stand loyally and solidly together.'

I was exhausted. But for me the work was a long way from finished. Inside and outside the Leagues Club, one floor down, roamed huge packs of media people. The press conferences that followed were huge, the ongoing enquiries seeming endless. I was completely drained at the end of it—although that was something I would get fairly used to in the long months ahead.

There was another job to be done too. I had to convey news

of the outcome of the meeting to Ken Cowley, to pay him that courtesy. A potted summary of our telephone conversation is as follows:

KA: 'Ken, I just wanted to let you know that the clubs have unanimously resolved to reject the proposal which you put to them this morning.'

KC: 'Ken, I am disappointed in that. I think that it is a great opportunity for league, but we are certainly not discarding the idea, and we will be pursuing it in the future. I want you to know that any further negotiation or approach will be made through the front door of the Australian Rugby League.'

KA: 'Thank you Ken, I appreciate that.'

The 'front door' reference was to come back and haunt News Ltd and its managing director. Cowley ended the conversation with the words: 'I'm going to ring Kerry Packer and congratulate him.'

I put a great deal of faith in Ken Cowley's words. My concerns about what might happen in the game were at rest to an extent. I took comfort in the belief that any further negotiations would be done on the reasonable basis of open discussion and consideration. At the NSWRL board meeting which followed some days after my conversation with Cowley I told our people, 'I believe Cowley has accepted our decision and that we should show good faith.' I told them of his declaration that any further approaches would be through the 'front door'. And in a show of our own genuine good faith I expressed to the board my belief that we should pursue the renewal of our licensing arrangement with News—even though such an arrangement would have been more lucrative for us if kept in house—and that we should continue to pursue sponsorship contracts with Ansett and Traveland. Our gesture to them couldn't have been any more open or friendly.

The morning of 7 February the *Sydney Morning Herald*'s seven column story on the events of that gruelling day carried the strapline: 'Flash score from the super league: Packer 1, Murdoch 0.'

But the war wasn't over. It was only just beginning.

29

APRIL
FOOLS

At the ARL in the months of February and March 1995 we
waited for the other shoe to drop. News Ltd had been
rebuffed at the Phillip Street gates, but we figured that very
likely they were just over the next hill, regrouping. The activity
had gone from overt to covert. No-one was knocking on the
front door anymore, but there was quite a crowd around the
back, whispering.

Only later, via the notes gathered for the vast legal battles
that ensued, did it become apparent as to just how much plot-
ting took place before the 'Pearl Harbor raid' of March
30–April 1. These are just a handful of the entries, which feature later in this book in 'The Super League Secret Files'—an
extraordinary chronology which tells perhaps better than anything else could of the dark and treacherous deeds that were
taking place right through that time:

February 7. (Kevin) Neil tells *Canberra Times* that once Packer
told the meeting he had pay TV rights 'it was the end of the
story'.
February 13. Kevin Neil meets Ken Cowley.
February 17. Lunch at Oskar's Restaurant, Coolangatta—Paul
Morgan, John Ribot, Ken Cowley.
February 21. David Smith meets with Peter Gow at News Ltd.

Arko

Late February. Ribot presents Super League II proposal to Cowley and Smith (proposes a competition independent of ARL).

March. Chart/plan of attack/war room document—relating to the week beginning 27/3.

March 2. Meeting in Brisbane, North Qld club reps and News Ltd.

March 14. Fax from David Smith to Mal Meninga. Confirming details for flight to Sydney for confidential meeting with News Ltd.

March 14. Meeting at the Ansett Managers' Lounge, Sydney, between Kevin Neil and John Ribot.

March 23. Ribot alleges that in a meeting with Rupert Murdoch the latter approves of Super League II.

March 27. Memo to Ken Cowley from David Smith re plan for the week.

March 27. (Peter) Gow lunches with Arthurson and swears he's had 'absolutely no involvement with Super League'.

March 28. News Ltd letters to coaches from David Smith. Includes, Anderson, Lang, Monie, Mulholland, Sheens—requesting services as coaches for SL.

March 30. Flight schedule for News Ltd people involved in signing up clubs and players.

Oh, yes, there was movement at the station all right. And none of it at the front door. The above selection, I'm sure, gives no more than a glimpse of what was going on.

In reading the secret papers that recount the gathering storm of Super League you will note that Cronulla chairman Peter Gow—who is Elle Macpherson's father—is mentioned more than a few times. During March the rumours reached my ears that Gow was a strong player in the Super League thing. I quizzed Bob Abbott, who has such close Cronulla connections.

'Gee, I wouldn't think that would be right,' said Bob. 'I'll ask him if you like.' Bob came back to me a day or two later. 'Mate, that bloke's not involved at all,' he said. 'Why don't you get him in to have a bit of lunch?'

So I did. We went to lunch, Gow and I, on 27 March and he

swore to me that he had had nothing to do with Super League. History reveals to me that I have probably never been told more bald-faced lies than I was that day. Gow was in it up to his ears. A week or so earlier I had had an amicable lunch with Kevin Neil and Les McIntyre at which they had pledged their loyalty to the ARL. Les's later departure to Super League hurt me. I'd always thought of him as a fine old country rugby league bloke, as solid as a rock. He was a life member of the NSWRL, and deserved to be.

The best description of the atmosphere in rugby league in the months of February–March 1995 was of an 'uneasy calm'. Deep down, everyone was edgy. Almost every day I would hear stories of clubs having dealings with News. Invariably, when I tackled them, they would deny it.

But we headed on with teeth gritted, to a season that should have been rich in promise. We launched it with a slap-up dinner at the Entertainment Centre in Sydney, hooking up with the four new clubs via giant TV screens. Mal Meninga, Australia's captain and not so long back from his history-making fourth Kangaroo tour, took to the stage to launch league's brave new world of 1995. Within a week or two he would be gone, and that was one of the deepest cuts of all. Mid-dinner the curtains swished open to reveal the lush sounds of Yanni and his orchestra. Rugby league had never been more ritzy.

Then, to acclaim a moment in history, a planeload of officials, journalists and assorted friends jetted out on the weekend of 10–11 March—bound for Auckland, Townsville, Brisbane and Perth. There, at one venue after another, they watched history being made as the four new clubs became part of the Winfield Cup and of a premiership that had been part of Australia's sporting life for 87 years. It should have been a wonderful, memorable trip, and for some it was. But Super League managed to reach out across the land and spoil even that significant triumph. En route to Townsville on the Saturday, *Sun-Herald* sporting editor Ian McKinnon disclosed to John Quayle that the newspaper the next day would be running a major story that Super League was 'on'. Quayle winced . . . and all of us waited.

Arko

There has been a theory aired that rugby league had become 'too comfortable' in the richness of its successes in the 1990s, and that the glamorous launch of early '95 and the jetsetting, champagne-sipping tour of the premiership's opening weekend was a reflection of that. We have been likened to the last days of the Roman Empire—of dining too well and too often. We have been accused of going 'soft' and thus being vulnerable to the predators in the shadows. I refute those claims. I know that John Quayle and I had great plans for the future. We would sit endlessly talking and planning things that might make a darned good game even better. I honestly think that the only time we let our guard down—the time we could have done more—was when the Super League rumours first started. But then we were in such serious and apparently harmonious discussions with News Ltd about sponsorship and the long-term future of the premiership that we *did* feel comfortable that we were on the right track. But all the while the lifeblood, the countless bits of information of what we were, how much money we had, and how we ran, were being fed to those who were to become the enemy. Maybe we can plead guilty to being a bit naive . . . to trusting what seemed to us a close business partner. If we fumbled, that was it.

On the week ending Saturday 1 April, the lid blew. Suddenly pandemonium was upon the game. Canberra had signed . . . and Canterbury . . . and others. The newspapers were full of it. It was the beginning of what I was to label 'The Pearl Harbor attack.'

April Fool's Day 1995 is a day I will never forget. With the stories and rumours raging around us, and separation of one from the other just about impossible, we held an emergency board meeting at the NSW Leagues Club. It was the day that Peter Moore, one of my closest friends for 30 years, resigned.

I was in at the League very early that morning. Peter rang home and told Barbara that he needed to see me, and she told him that I was already at Phillip Street. Our meeting in the board room on the first floor had just begun when there was a knock on the door. It was Peter.

'Could I see you privately for a few moments?' he said to me.

I excused myself and we headed across to one of the adjacent

League offices. There, Moore said to me: 'I'm sorry to tell you this, mate. But I'm going to have to resign. All my (Canterbury) players have signed to go over to Super League. I have no option but to step down.'

I was rocked by the news. 'Have you given it plenty of thought?' I asked him (I didn't know then that Peter was about to cross over to Super League himself).

He said he had.

'I'm sorry to see you go,' I said. 'Obviously you have given it a lot of consideration and you feel you have no choice.'

And that was it. Four or five minutes, a few words, and it was over.

We shook hands, and I went back to the meeting. There I broke the news of Moore's resignation. I could tell that some of the board members were pleased. Doubts and suspicions about Peter had existed for some time. My own feelings were mixed. I had lost a great friend and ally, but Moore's situation at Canterbury had made it inevitable that he would have to cut his ties with Phillip Street. In the months following it became a sore point with some people in the game that he and I kept in some sort of contact. But the friendship had been a close one for so long—an important one to us both—it was no easy thing to throw away. The Peter Moore situation was hard for me—we had always been there for each other when things were tough. It was a very personal blow to me to realise he wouldn't be alongside to help fight the battle.

I accept what Peter Moore tells me about what went on—which essentially was that what happened was not his doing and was done initially without his knowledge—because of our friendship. He has always said to me since that once his players and coach (Chris Anderson) had decided to go across, he was left with no alternative. I have said to him: 'If you tell me that, I have to accept it, but you've got to understand why no-one else is accepting it. No-one who knew you could ever accept that such things could happen at Canterbury without your knowledge, or without your stamp of approval. Here it is—the biggest thing that's ever happened in the history of the club and you're telling people you didn't know anything about it.'

Arko

I am aware that Gary McIntyre (the Canterbury Leagues Club chairman), a bloke who has disappointed me greatly and who is no friend of Moore's, was in the thick of it. He is not a bloke I trust or like, not the bloke I once thought he was. And there is irrefutable evidence that he was in close and covert co-operation with Super League. McIntyre compounded all of it by coming out with a ridiculous document in 1997, purporting to tell the full story of why Canterbury went to Super League. I've never seen anything so full of holes or errors.

For a time there was some awkwardness between Peter Moore and I, but we kept the dialogue going. In 1995 after the blow-up, we talked spasmodically of the possibilities of compromise, and how it might be brokered. Peter and I met three or four times over the couple of years, and talked now and then on the phone. I'm sure he carries some guilt, whatever he feels his role was. His downfall in the game saddens me. He had been a loyal contributor to rugby league over the years, and a clever one. Now he has so many people bitterly turned against him, but my friendship with him will remain. I think he was wrong in what he did . . . but that's only my personal view. Saying it doesn't mean he *was* wrong, and that I'm right. Frankly, I'm still finding it hard to accept that he's not still around, fighting the good fight for the ARL.

Moore was one of several people skewered in the glare by what happened. People with some sort of stance in both camps. Graham Lovett, who I talked of before, was another. Brian Walsh, our talented promotions man was another—very much on our side of the fence, but in a situation where he managed one of the game's elite players, Andrew 'ET' Ettingshausen, who was to cross to Super League with his Cronulla teammates. My personal view is that both Lovett and Walsh handled a difficult situation fairly and ethically. I don't know if everyone shares that view, but it's mine.

Friendships were tested, and in some cases shattered. One to fall apart was that between John Quayle and the *Telegraph*'s chief rugby league writer Peter Frilingos. There is no doubt that Frilingos had been seen as an enthusiastically pro ARL man over the years, to the extent that he was sometimes looked on as being too *much* our way within his own organisation (News Ltd). It is also an historical fact that Frilingos had some sort of conversion on the road to Damascus and apparently in a single day went from being ARL-positive, to a keen supporter of the Super League concept. I could, and can, live with that. As I have said, people have to make their own decisions in life . . . and then live with those decisions. I've got to say with Frilingos that he's always treated me OK, and always faithfully reported what I have said to him. But he had a very close working relationship with John, and when he switched boats mid-stream, they fell out very badly. Terminally, in fact. The Super League raids caused a lot of that sort of thing.

That weekend of 1–2 April was a nightmare. Almost every second brought a new rumour. In the occasional quiet moment I found myself sitting there thinking, 'God, surely they're not going to try and destroy this game of ours after all the wonderful success we've had?' We were on our knees. This dreadful deed, this disgraceful corporate raid—the signing of our players in stealth and the dark of night—had knocked the stuffing out of us. For an hour or two we were on the canvas. But rugby league is a game of picking yourself off the floor now and then, and as that long Saturday unfolded we were back on our feet . . . and moving. All the time I kept thinking of Ken Cowley's assurance about coming through the front door.

The lists of the players signed in Super League's secret raids was jolting. They included some of the finest players in the game. The way it was done was no less than shocking—the lingering TV image of (Super League's) Michael O'Connor climbing through a window like a thief in the night a pretty fair reflection of the way things were. But I don't particularly blame the players. They were pawns in a much larger game. And the manner of their signing was a bloody disgrace. Picture it: footballers herded into some hotel room in the depths of night, denied contact with managers or families or legal representatives, pressured to sign on the spot. The tactics were nothing short of despicable. Justice James Burchett saw all those things in his later Federal Court decision. Better than anyone he understood the principle that it was morally wrong for anyone to benefit from the sort of deceitful, dishonest behaviour that was News Ltd's stock-in-trade. That his fellow judges were eventually to *reward* such behaviour angers me still.

But no, I don't hold grudges against the players. The offers were big, the News Ltd pressure enormous, the peer pressure a factor, too. It would have just been nice though, if one of the top blokes had put his hand up and said: 'Hang on a minute. Rugby league under the ARL has given me my chance in life . . . I'd like some time to think about this.' None of them did . . . except a solitary teenager . . . Adam Ritson from Cronulla who showed his quality when he insisted on the chance to get some outside consultation. News to their credit at least allowed him that, and so it was that Ritson chose to come back to the ARL. The terrible illness that Adam was to suffer later, ending his football career, was one of life's great injustices. The young bloke was headed for marvellous things in football, and I'll never forget his quiet strength during those difficult days of '95. I'm so sad about what happened subsequently in his life. He was a wonderful footballing talent—certainly destined to wear the green and gold.

It was Adam who was unlucky enough to be in the hot seat on the day of the infamous exchange between Paul 'Fatty' Vautin and the *Daily Telegraph*'s strident right-wing columnist Piers Akerman. At that press conference held in the somewhat gloomy surroundings of the shell of what was once the Tatler Hotel in George Street—the place where the NSWRL was born in August 1907—Adam Ritson was put through the wringer by the media, simply bombarded with questions. In retrospect it was not a great choice of venue, although I understood the reasons behind it . . . getting back to grassroots and all that. It was when I felt the grilling of Ritson was getting to the unfair stage, and closed the meeting, that the celebrated exchange took place between Vautin and Akerman. Fatty Vautin, chairing the meeting, got stirred up by Akerman's abrasive approach (Fatty is a red-head after all), calling him a 'fat heap of s——' and then declaring, 'I'll f—— give it to you in a minute' as the two eye-balled each other. I had no idea who Akerman was, then, I just knew he was some little fat guy being rude. Akerman was later to go back to the paper and tell his editor that he had just been abused by 'someone called Fatso Vaughan'. I didn't condone what Vautin said and I told Fatty subsequently that he shouldn't have said it. But the bloke was so obnoxious and rude and discourteous, that at the very least I could understand . . .

It wasn't the only explosive meeting of that time. The Cronulla public meeting of 10 April was also to hit the headlines. The whole thing was something of a charade. The Sharks were gone for all money by then, Super League signed, sealed and delivered. It was more for show than anything else when they put on their 'public information' meeting. Anyway, there we all were—Super leaguers on one side of chairman Peter Gow, the ARL on the other. Gow just sat there like a Lowe's dummy, didn't say a word all night. Ribot was there, preaching about 'world vision', and I was there, doing my best to get across the ARL's more down-to-earth message. The Super League 'vision' bullshit is one of the great red herrings of Australian sport. All this crap about 'taking the game to the world' . . . the fact is the game was already out there in a strong way via pay TV. And do you reckon people in China or plenty of other places are going to be hanging there waiting until they get Adelaide v Townsville on their screens? It was rubbish . . . a blind to disguise the true motive—which was to secure quality sporting fodder for Murdoch's Foxtel pay TV network.

The meeting at Cronulla is remembered mostly for the words of Mal Meninga who stunned everyone when he declared he'd never got anything out of the game, and the ARL had done nothing for him. You could have knocked me over with a feather. There were derisive boos and catcalls from the audience and Johnny Raper bounced up from the floor and tackled Meninga on his words. Headlines were the certain outcome.

The meeting was pretty much a disgrace. Cronulla's marketing man Rickard Fisk acted as moderator and after closing the meeting following questions promptly allowed (Super League's) Barry Russell to get up and address the meeting. I just said to him: 'You're joking.' Fisk rang me the next day and apologised for letting it happen, but my suspicion is that it was prearranged.

My own inclination was to forgive Meninga to an extent. He was a bloke I'd always had plenty of time for—as a player and a person. I thought he had probably fumbled his words in the tension of the occasion, and hadn't really meant what came out. But you know what? After Super League had kept him locked away for a couple of months he emerged to do a television interview, the occasion presenting him with a perfect chance to take back what he had said. Meninga managed only to stick his foot deeper into the bog by making another ungracious statement, although he did admit that his Cronulla statement had, 'probably come out the wrong way'. Interviewer Roy Masters made the point to him, 'But the Australian Rugby League were good to you on the Kangaroo tour. They paid for your family to go over and be with you for the last part of the tour . . . it was a nice gesture.'

Meninga's reply: 'Well, don't you think they should have?'

Meninga had the chance to be gracious and dignified in his handling of that interview, and to regain at least some of the ground he had lost. He failed.

Meninga's role in the whole thing saddened me a great deal. The game had been good to him, and he had been good to the game. There were plenty of people who reckoned he shouldn't have gone on that fourth tour, but we stuck solidly behind him. I never accepted the theory that he shouldn't have gone. We were proud and pleased to have him as our captain. I have not seen the bloke since the Cronulla meeting. His words that night diminished him forever in the eyes of many people. The letter that followed from the 'Immortals' (Bob Fulton, Reg Gasnier and Johnny Raper) must have bruised him even more. He had the chance to balance the ledger, redress with some dignity the mistake he had made. Yet, he didn't do it. Now he has no choice but to live with the consequences of some ill-chosen words and sentiments.

The secrecy and deceit of so much that went on still appals me, even years later. I am often drawn back in my mind to Cowley's 'front door' assurance and one day when we were talking at the height of the war in 1995, I tackled him on it. 'Well, the action we took (the raids on our players of March 30–April 1) was designed to enable us to then come through the front door,' he told me.

It's an explanation that doesn't hold much water. Like

plenty of others, Ken Cowley became a casualty of the Super League wars. At the start of it he was one of the most respected figures in corporate Australia. But inevitably, with the 'front door' quote and others ('I love rugby league. I can assure you I would never do anything to harm the game.') imprinted forever against his name, his reputation was diminished. I am not happy about that. I have always had a high regard for Cowley. Basically, I think he's a very decent person. I suppose in serving a hard taskmaster like Murdoch he had a job to do. The sad thing is that he was damaged by it . . . as was just about everything else in the game that had been rugby league.

30

LIES AND WHISPERS

My personal view of the Super League chaos is that if Canterbury hadn't gone—hadn't jumped to Murdoch's cash—the thing would never have got off the ground. The Bulldogs stand uniquely in the whole thing, as the only 'traditional' club to take the bait. They had been a member of the League for 60 years when Gary McIntyre, or whoever it was, sealed the deal with News Ltd in the last days of March 1995. All the other Super League catches were relative new chums— the soul brothers of 1967, Cronulla and Penrith, 1982's Canberra, 1988's Brisbane and perhaps most painfully of all, the 1995 newcomers Auckland, Perth and Townsville . . . on their way barely before a ball had been kicked. That was loyalty for you. And it really hurt. It was through the generosity of the traditional Sydney clubs that these newcomers were invited into the game. They had been knocking on the door, almost breaking it down in their enthusiasm to get in. Yet the instant the first words were uttered about Super League's bullshit vision, they were gone. It was pretty deplorable behaviour— ranking high on the scale of the (many) atrocious things that were to happen in 1995–96.

I remembered back to late 1992 when we made the big decision to take *four* new clubs on board in 1995, rather than the one or two that people had expected. We stuck our necks out then, chancing our arm on a big expansionary sweep when we could have taken a more conservative path. The vote was heading to Auckland and South Queensland, but the feeling was strong that North Queensland and Perth had done so much fine work in getting ready that they were darned hard to knock back. And to knock either or both of them back could have meant a lost opportunity—perhaps one never regained. So we went out on a limb, and announced we would bring all four teams in for the 1995 season, adding a rider in the minutes that we would review the situation at the end of the 1996 season. That's why the defections of April '95 cut us to the heart. If there were ever people who should be ashamed to look at themselves in the mirror, it was the men who guided Auckland, Perth and North Queensland's fortunes that year. Of the four of them only the Crushers stuck with the ARL, and not before Super League had had a crack at them, as they did at just about every club.

People such as Kevin Neil (Canberra) and Porky Morgan (Brisbane) disappointed me greatly. I had always got on reasonably well with those guys, and they were blokes who had looked me in the eye and sworn they wouldn't participate in a competition unless it was under the control of the Australian Rugby League. I can only presume that the blokes who made those sort of comments to me had their fingers crossed at the time. Following is a record of what Morgan said to me on Saturday 1 April 1995 via a phone conference line with John Quayle and two solicitors, Colin Love and David Kennedy. Love's file notes read:

> 11.45 a.m., KA phones Paul Morgan. Morgan and (Barry) Maranta both deny involvement with Super League. My recollection is that Ken Arthurson then received a telephone call from Morgan which was on loudspeaker and in words to the following effect:
> Morgan: 'I understand you've called a board meeting about the Super League raid. I'm just calling to give you an assurance that I know nothing about it. I swear to you that the Broncos are behind the ARL all the way on this.'

When the phone call ended, John Quayle said, 'I don't trust him. I think the Broncos are in it up to their necks.'

And Ken replied, 'Well, what can I do? You heard the man. He's just rung me personally and he swears on a stack of bibles that the Broncos have nothing to do with it. I will just have to accept him at his word.'

It was breathtaking stuff. The Broncos had already done the business, in fact *started* the business. Morgan was always arguing that we never did anything for the Broncos, claiming that everything they put up was knocked on the head—which wasn't true. Later, he was to admit to being the architect of Super League.

But the Broncos weren't the first club to jump. That dubious honour belonged to the Bulldogs—half of the team and coach Chris Anderson signing at the office of News Ltd's lawyers Atanaskovic Hartnell in Goldfields House, in the heart of business Sydney. That was 30 March, the Thursday.

The offices of the NSW and Australian Rugby League at 165 Phillip Street, Sydney have always been lively places. In the early days of April 1995, they became a madhouse. The events of April Fool's Day were an immediate call to battle. We determined that if we were to preserve something of our game we would have to move with great speed to sign as many players as possible to counter Super League's raids. We moved within hours, co-opting the two men who knew footballers best—national coach Bob Fulton and NSW coach Phil Gould—to head the fightback.

Phillip Street will never see scenes like it again. The place was just rocking, crammed with players and agents and our people trying to bring some order to it all. Mobile phones were a dime a dozen, and every so often huge plates of sandwiches or Chinese tucker would arrive as we did our best to feed the masses. It was a mad, bad time. There were constant media interviews. And at any time of the day and into the evening you could just about bet that either John Quayle or I would be in the process of being buffeted, jostled, badgered or questioned by someone. The staff were marvellous—loyal and uncomplaining. People like Pam Parker, Micki Braithwaite and Dianne

Arko

Blunden worked brilliantly to keep it all together. It was a strange, unreal time. So many people stood fast and strong, while others were found wanting when the pressure was on. It was just like war. It *was* war.

Quayle was a wonderful ally and mate through it all. He didn't take a backward step, and committed most of the hours of his life at that period to the cause. He was painted as the 'villain' from the other side of the fence, and there was talk that any compromise would have to be without Quayle. I made it very clear I would never be in that. Our friendship and working relationship strengthened through those demanding months. We were friends, we trusted each other implicitly, and we were loyal to each other and the game. Individually and together we were prepared to make the hard decisions. I don't think it's immodest to say ours was a good and successful partnership from 1983 onwards. And in 1995–96 it developed new strength, new steel. I'm sure neither of us will ever forget our shared experience.

In one fell (foul!) swoop with their actions in the autumn of 1995, Super League had pushed player payments to crazy, unsustainable levels. It was quickly common knowledge that players such as Canberra's Laurie Daley, Ricky Stuart and Bradley Clyde were on $700,000 a year. The now Easts Leagues Club chairman Denis Muddle called Phillip Street 'The Lolly Shop' and so it was as bemused players came in, signed contracts and went away with more money than they had ever dreamed of. Football players will never again be in a position of such strength.

Ricky Stuart was one bloke who at least came back to us to meet and talk, after signing with Super League. I think that deep down Stuart, and certainly his manager John Fordham, would have been happy to find a way back to the ARL. But it was no easy thing. All Stuart's Canberra teammates had joined Super League—and that is pressure of a most extraordinary sort on a player. No doubt News Ltd made use of it very skilfully.

I was disappointed with Andrew Ettingshausen. He had been such a role model for our game, such a figurehead. He had been great for the game and the game had been bloody good for him. Yet, like Stuart, he was at a club that had gone Super League and that made it tough. My disappointment in Andrew lay primarily in a letter which appeared under his name in the *St George Leader*, bitterly criticising the ARL, and in my view, unfairly so. I accepted his decision to go, to join Super League. I was disappointed in Andrew's decision to be critical of a game which had been good to him. Very likely he was under pressure to 'go public' with some propaganda, but I thought he did the wrong thing. Sadly, a little further down the track Laurie Daley managed some permanent damage to his reputation with some inflammatory and dumb statements. I don't know who was advising him—but they should hang their heads in shame. 'I was treated like a dog (by the ARL),' said Laurie at one stage. Well, Jeezus, if flying business class across the world, living in five star hotels, being clothed, fed and looked after, being paid $700 a week living expenses tax-free, getting his grog free from the sponsors and earning quarter of a million dollars a year or so via the ARL's game is being treated like a dog—well, I think most people would say, where do I sign? Daley, trotted out as some sort of spokesman, was damaged in the eyes of many people by the ridiculous things he said. No doubt. And that's a pity. I have always found him a decent young bloke.

The propaganda war waged by News Ltd against rugby league was a bloody disgrace in a society like ours where you're entitled to expect some sort of balance in the media. But the fact of it was that News had no choice but to peddle lies and misinformation, because the truth was that the game had *never* been in better shape than at the end of the 1994 season. Crowds were at record levels, TV ratings were extraordinary (seven of the ten top programmes for the year were rugby league matches), radio ratings were sky high and the game's finances had soared to record heights. Nationally, the public acceptance of rugby league as a major Australian sport had never been more widespread. And ahead there was only high expectation. The move to the 20-team comp was a giant step, certainly. But we had checks and balances in place—and the shared belief that the reduction of the number of clubs in Sydney would be part of the next few seasons.

Arko

What was done to us in the interest of commercial greed was the most disgraceful thing that has happened to any sport or organisation in my lifetime. And not for a second should anyone ever think that what Murdoch did was for the 'good' of rugby league. It was done for the good of the Murdoch organisation, that's all. These are the words that sum it up: pay TV, power, money, commercial greed. Rugby league is a perfect sport for TV, with its close-centred action and its explosive nature. Murdoch wanted it. Simple as that. Anyone who believes that Rupert Murdoch awoke from a deep sleep one night and said, 'Gee I'd like to do something for the game of rugby league,' would deadset have to believe in the tooth fairy. The only people who didn't believe that were those who were being so handsomely rewarded that they were blinded. The irony was still to be realised back then—that for all the rhetoric they peddled, News made a god-awful mess of the whole thing, costing themselves hundreds of millions of dollars and failing to create anything even vaguely representing the 'vision' of which we heard so much. By mid-1997 it was becoming apparent that they had got what their actions deserved. In a most unusual twist, the giant corporation themselves had become victims of the Broncos original grab for cash. The sad thing was, though, that they had dragged league into the quicksand with them. Murdoch's mob had some victories along the way, sure, but never the big one they sought. It was apparent from very early indeed that the Murdoch boast of the war being over in 24 hours in the wake of the 'Pearl Harbor attack' was hollow indeed.

The offices at Phillip Street had to be seen to be believed. Day by day after the first flurry, the legal eagles took over. I'd come into the office some days and there'd be clusters of serious men in suits. 'Jeezus, who are these blokes?' I'd say to Quayle. 'Lawyers,' was almost always the answer. Both Quayle and I had agonised over the money side of it. In our years at the helm we had built the League's reserves to the highest levels they had ever been. Total reserves of the ARL and NSWRL were in the vicinity of $20 million when war broke out. Our original budget for the legal costs was $3 million. I recall that one day I asked John Quayle the question of legal costs—and we were up to $8 million! All the while our hard-earned reserves were draining away . . .

Forces gathered behind us in those early days, with Channel Nine, to a lesser extent, and Optus digging into their coffers to provide the financial wherewithal. Optus have always been simply sensational in the strength of the support they have provided. At the heart of their operation was a very cool customer indeed in Geoff Cousins, one of the unsung heroes of this whole story. Cousins never flinched in his support for the ARL. Through that time he demonstrated to me that he is one of the most highly principled people I have ever met. When he said he was going to do something—he did it.

It was very much against my wishes that the decision was made in those crazy days of trying to shore up the game, to delve into English football, and sign some of their key players. The money flung at that little campaign was outrageous. I refused to have anything to do with it. Money was being paid to managers over there, and it looked very much to me as if they were just going for their life and having a lend of us. Frank Stanton, a man experienced in the ways of English football and footballers, flew over from Sydney to bring some commonsense to the campaign. It was only later that I became aware that 'Operation UK' had been authorised by James Packer. I think that most of the things we did in that time, we had to do, but this was a futile costly exercise . . . succeeding only in trawling in a few players, rattling the Pom administrators a bit . . . and not much more. I'd hate to see the bottom line cost of it.

Sometime later I saw James Packer in London and I said to him, 'I think this is a scandalous waste of money and as far as I'm concerned we won't be paying it back.'

D'you know what his answer was? James just looked at me straight and said: 'I don't blame you.'

The whole circus was a bonanza for the player managers who had sprung up like mushrooms in the game. For some reason Super League had chosen largely not to do business with managers, but to go direct to players. That would seem to have been a fatal flaw, considering that some managers could

Arko

'deliver' whole tribes of football players. For the managers—Wayne Beavis, Steve Gillis, Sam Ayoub and the rest—it was Christmas come early. They were certainly there in the thick of it as the ARL fought back.

I am pleased to say that players coming to see us were not put under the sort of desperate pressure that Super League heaped on them during the Pearl Harbor raid. Not that it was easy for anyone in the atmosphere prevailing. But not once did we deny a player his request to speak to his manager, legal representative or his family. More than once, the place full of managers with their flash cars parked somewhere beneath, I thought how different things were. Signing a player in earlier years was often the most informal affair. I'm sure that many genuinely have been signed on the back of beer coasters over the seasons. Often during my years as secretary the written contract wouldn't be drawn up until long after the handshake had been made. And that handshake was more than enough. I doubt that blokes like Mick Cronin *ever* signed a contract. Once you had the word of a bloke like Cronin—not that I ever signed him—well, that was about as solid as any arrangement could ever be. Often there was just a letter of intent, then a gentle progression towards the contract, with no-one worrying too much, knowing that the deal had been done and dusted. Gradually it changed, and reasonably so, with footballers getting expert help and advice in their dealings. Jim Comans, who was to have such an impact as the Judiciary chief in the 1980s, was probably the first solicitor to get involved with looking after a footballer's business. He was certainly the link when Manly signed Malcolm Reilly back in the 1970s. Others followed, notably men such as Colin Love, who took over Jim's business. The pair were friends, astute lawyers in their own right, and perfectly equipped to look after sportspeople because of their own sporting backgrounds. They spoke the language.

The bounce back of the Canterbury four (Jarrod McCracken, Jason Smith, Dean Pay and Jim Dymock) to the ARL put a significant shot across the Super League bows early in the tussle. They were four of the best players in the game, who came back to talk to Fulton and Gould. It was found in

226

court that they had signed their Super League contracts under duress—a pointer to how business was done across the board at that time by Super League. The money involved in Super League signing them—and then us resigning them—was crazy. But I think it was a firm tactical strike for the ARL, sending a tremor through the opposition, and proving that there was still a tonne of fight left in the dog yet.

Every new day in that spring seemed to bring something extraordinary. Early on I was guest panellist on the now-famous *Footy Show* edition on which John Ribot copped something of a serve. I was happy to debate the issues involved, but kept out of the fireworks. And there sure were some—with 2UE's Ray Hadley taking to Ribot with great gusto. Hadley, who I rate the best football caller I have heard, was not particularly against News's concept of a Super League. But like a lot of people what he was really furious about was the *way* they had gone about it. He really went for Ribot in what Super League were later to call an 'ambush'. Hadley was to pay a price for that night, and for his strong pro-ARL stance, which really was no more than an honest reflection of what he believed. When Super League had done their little deal with Channel Nine and the jerseys were being dished out for the 1997 version of *The Footy Show*, Hadley missed out.

The Packer camp sent down a very experienced trouble-shooter to Phillip Street in the first week of April '95 in Graham Richardson, to drag our campaign together with Fulton and Gould. Before long Richardson became known as the Prince of Promises. 'Richo' the tough political scrapper seemed to revel in it. He worked bloody hard and very effectively. Later on he got caught in the web of the people he worked for and I suppose had no alternative but to go along with decisions made—when Nine and the League drifted apart. As a very skilful politician Richardson was beautifully placed to do the job that had to be done in that early April. Politicians are great with words, great at speaking the language that people understand, great with promises—and Richo played his part for sure in helping us hold it all together. The title of Graham's biography is *Whatever it Takes*, and that seemed about right, having watched him so skilfully in action. I was certainly grateful for his help at that time.

I have never discussed with Graham what happened subsequently—Channel Nine's treachery in going back on their word and getting into bed with Super League. I would like to think that having fought the fight that he did for the ARL, he would have been devastated by that. So too, I would imagine Channel Nine head David Leckie who stepped down from our board, on which he had been a good contributor, when Nine did their first deal with Super League, and the channel's boss of sport, Gary Burns. Right to the end I was telling people there was no way Channel Nine was going to jump. I remember reading in a book years ago a story about Packer ditching some people who had stood by him for years. 'That's not the Kerry Packer I know,' I said to myself at the time. I can only presume that whatever Channel Nine did, and whoever did it—whether it was James or anyone else—that the decision must have had Kerry's imprimatur.

Packer himself was never again a visible player in the whole thing after his dramatic appearances of 5 and 6 February 1995. The big man came in, said his piece, then disappeared from view. Murdoch was barely seen at all, apart from an ill-conceived television appearance on *Witness* during which he showed his complete lack of knowledge about rugby league—the game for which he was supposed to have this wonderful vision. It was during this interview that Jana Wendt sought his response on the 'Packer 1, Murdoch 0' newspaper headline, bringing the reply, 'Oh, I think that is only a half-time score.' I would venture to say that Rupert Murdoch has never seen a game of rugby league. I certainly haven't bumped him on the hill lately, having a pie and a beer. Packer, at least, is a sporting bloke.

At a sportsmen's luncheon on the Gold Coast some months after the drama had started I gave a talk, and in questions from the floor afterwards was asked about Packer. 'Kerry Packer doesn't seem too much involved, we haven't heard anything about him,' the bloke said.

I answered, 'No, you're right, as a matter of fact he has been conspicuous by his absence.'

The *Australian* picked up the things I had to say, and ran a story the next day, leading to a sharpish exchange between myself and Brian Powers. Powers had not read the article and had the impression I had said more than in fact I had—and had been critical of Packer. We sorted it out, but I said to him: 'I am not withdrawing what I said about Kerry.' I could understand what many people were saying—that Packer had stormed in, loaded the gun, then disappeared, leaving the skirmishing to everyone else.

There was some solid criticism of the League when the news emerged later in '95 that Bob Fulton and Phil Gould—plus Mal Reilly, coach in the absolutely vital strategic city of Newcastle— were granted huge loyalty payments by the ARL. I'll just say this: Gould and Fulton did a damned fine job for us, working about as hard as two blokes can work. They have my thanks for that. I will only add that I wasn't party to the payments made to them. You must understand that in that crazy time things were happening so fast and with outside 'agents' involved in the dealings, that the League's control on the reins was not as firm as usual. I said at the time that the game couldn't afford the sort of money that was being spent. In relation to Reilly, Gould and Fulton, even I, as chairman, was unaware of just how large were the payments, although I have read various guesses, with the bottom line total running into millions. Money was coming from different places (Nine, Optus), through different hands. At the same time Super League were throwing around their millions, too. Between us in a disastrous couple of weeks we pumped up the player and coach payment market to simply ludicrous levels. It was a game out of control, and it will be years before some of those contracts of '95 run their course, and sanity can prevail.

For the first and only time since I became chairman I felt during the crazy period that things were happening in the game that were beyond my control. Handling a mountain of media demands daily ate up my time and my energy. Meanwhile in the background the phones never stopped ringing, the lifts never stopped opening with a new batch of players . . . and all the while the sound of cheques being torn from cheque books provided the theme music.

31

TOMORROW, THE WORLD

I was sitting in James Packer's office at Australian Consolidated Press in downtown Sydney on the day Super League announced that New Zealand and England had jumped. That was a bad, bad day for the ARL, and devastating for me personally as I struggled to try and come to terms with the disloyalty involved. Maurice Lindsay, the ERL boss, at least had the courtesy to ring me when they signed. The cash-strapped Poms landed a deal worth around 87 million pounds ($200 million), and according to Lindsay had absolutely no choice but to take it. But as for that bloody Graham Carden in New Zealand . . . words just about fail me. He and his fellow travellers had sold the New Zealand Rugby League to Super League for a song . . . a few million bucks—and had not even had the good manners to talk it over with the game's lifetime partners across the Tasman! Carden didn't even pick up the phone. His rush to complete the deal was not only a treacherous act but revealed him as a poor businessman. I can still barely believe it all these many months later. New Zealand and Australia had been bound together when rugby league began in the two countries. The seminal matches in Sydney in August 1907 between the New Zealand All Golds and NSW led *directly* to the birth of the new game. Yet 87 years on, with many battles fought, and triumphs shared this way and that, they had dumped us like a bag of rubbish, with the shots being called by a lightweight like Carden.

It's a funny thing, you know, but I reckon if you take just a handful of individuals and events out of the equation, Super League would never have happened. Porky Morgan is one, Canterbury's 'jump' against all the traditions of what that club should have stood for, another. And I'd say that if you took Graham Carden out of New Zealand, the Kiwis would never have switched. Ditto for the entrepreneurial Maurice Lindsay in England.

The progressive loss to Super League of New Zealand, England, France . . . then the Pacific countries where we had worked so hard to get a foothold, was shattering for us. But in some ways the injustice of it all—of snatch and grab raiders stealing away something that was patently not theirs—only stiffened resolve within the ARL to keep fighting.

Within a year or two there were signs of disintegration of the international scene under the Super League banner. A Great Britain trip to the Pacific islands and New Zealand in 1996 was an absolute farce—with a dozen players being shipped home from New Zealand early to save money. In its 87 years international league had no precedent for that.

Bogged down in endless legal wrestles, of which more later, and submerged in Super League's tireless and empty rhetoric, the 1995 season was a disaster, with just the occasional light now and then shining through the gloom to give it a lift. From the moment News Ltd announced their decision to challenge the loyalty agreements signed by the 20 clubs in February, rugby league became rugby legal. And all the while Super League chipped away at our clubs, hawking their 'vision'. In turn Illawarra, Newcastle, Balmain, Norths, the Crushers and St George knocked them back—with the Saints, particularly, on the brink at times. Through consideration of a possible merger with Sydney City Roosters (Easts), there was further trauma to be contended with inside the club. For long weeks John Quayle didn't see a football kicked, so intense were the seven-days-a-week demands as the legal aspects of the war started to take shape. I kept turning up for games . . . the one pure thing left . . . finding them a release from the pressures of the week. But it was an eerie, unreal feeling.

And yet, there *was* some gold among the dross. When Paul 'Fatty' Vautin took on the assignment of coaching a seriously weakened and apparently outgunned Queensland side for the 1995 Origin series, there was some sniggering behind hands. Nobody, absolutely nobody, gave Queensland a chance. The selectors by then had chosen their course of picking exclusively ARL players for the representative games, and the fact was that with the Broncos gone to Super League, the majority of the highest-rated Maroons were out of play. It all looked so one-sided that even some Queensland officials were pushing the case for Super League players to be included. Fatty didn't want a bar of it.

'Look,' he said. 'I'm only interested in blokes who genuinely want to play for Queensland and who have some pride in pulling on the jumper. I don't want the others. We couldn't win it with them anyway.'

What happened subsequently—a Queensland clean sweep—almost defies belief. It was a magnificent achievement, by Vautin and his men, built on all the old traditions that had made rugby league what is was: courage; loyalty; pride in the jumper; an attitude of never-say-die, and a belief that any team you play, no matter who they might be, are only made up of 'blokes with two legs who will fall when tackled'.

The achievement of Australia's World Cup team in the Centenary Tournament at the end of that unsettled, unhappy year was another glittering jewel in the murk. I rate it one of the finest performances ever by an Aussie side. From the moment Bob Fulton and his team stepped onto (Super League) English soil they were treated almost as lepers, certainly as second class citizens. Everything was a battle—no-one offered them any encouragement or help. And it was on right to the last. I wasn't at the official World Cup celebration dinner after the Aussies had won the final over England, but I'm told that even then the Australians were shoved somewhere up the back of the room, and left alone. That sort of treatment is to Maurice Lindsay's eternal discredit.

Maurice was unhappy with me from the start. He had urged me with some desperation to ensure that there were Super League players in the side. But our selectors took the attitude of (a) rewarding loyalty and (b) picking their teams with the (ARL) future in mind. We had gone through (another) court battle to reach that point, with our selectors being instructed to consider Super League players. My understanding is that they did exactly what they had been ordered to do, but felt so strongly about our own future representative sides in a sorely divided football world, that they chose to stick with the ARL loyalists. So we landed in England as an all-ARL side.

'You can't win it,' Lindsay told me on arrival.

'Won't we?' I responded. 'Let's wait and see.'

And we did win, beautifully and against the odds—after falling to the Poms in the opening match. It was a significant and special achievement. And I know it was a bitter blow to the Super Leaguers, to have such a tournament staged in this brave new Super League world . . . and to have a bunch of ARL interlopers come in and take the prize.

The World Cup tournament was played in a sort of uneasy, temporary peace, I was still the International Board's director general then and at the meeting we held in London before the Cup was played I said to the delegates: 'There really is only one important thing at the moment—that we all get behind the Centenary World Cup and make it as big a success as we possibly can.' I continued, 'Gentlemen, it is pointless discussing some of the matters we have listed here on the agenda because the future is so clouded for all of us. The World Cup is the thing— and that should be our focus.' And that's the way it was at a meeting that was a little tense, but courteously conducted. We put our heads down and sorted out the nuts and bolts of the tournament, including the finances.

At the time I write these words the ARL is still waiting for a large pool of money owed from that 1995 event. There is every indication that the League has been badly dudded by the Poms. The estimate of Australia's share from a tournament that was a considerable success was 800,000 pounds. We were given one payment, of 500,000 pounds, and no more. Maurice

Lindsay has been quoted as saying what a great financial success the Cup was, but all requests from Australia to view the books and accounts have been ignored. Lindsay has indicated that all payments have been properly made from the receipts of the Centenary Cup. It looks to me far more likely that for the first time in the history of the game one rugby league country has welshed on another.

A chunky little five eighth with a big heart provided some old-fashioned emotion at the end of the year, when Super League Canterbury won the premiership, over Manly. The off-field battles were forgotten for a time as the Bulldog warrior Terry Lamb celebrated the end of a truly great club career. What a way to go out, at 34 years of age and with 328 first grade games on the board. The 17–4 grand final win belonged to Lamb.

Only problem was after all the tears and farewells and emotion . . . Terry Lamb came back to football in 1996.

32

SO NEAR,
AND YET . . .

As the battle raged in 1995, I always felt that the link between Ken Cowley and me kept a slender lifeline pumping between the two sides of the game. Even as the war became less and less about football and more and more about legal argument, we tried to find common ground. I'm sure Ken was 100 per cent genuine in his efforts. I know that I was. During the time when both sides were in the trenches we met on a number of occasions, and talked many times by telephone. We met in my office, we met in Cowley's office at News Ltd, and when it got to the point that every time we moved we were besieged by media people, we met on three occasions in an apartment in Macquarie Street. We were still meeting right up to the moment when the Burchett Federal Court case kicked off. All the while rumours blazed—of this settlement or that, of a deal just around the next corner—but always as elusive to pin down as a shadow.

I can reveal now that on two separate occasions we were on the verge of reaching the compromise position that the game needed. But the pattern proved to be frustratingly the same anytime Ken and I drew close to an answer that might have been acceptable to everyone. I would leave the meeting, filled with quiet hope that, at least, we had got somewhere. Then, next meeting it would be as if we were starting all over again.

Somewhere in the background Ken Cowley was receiving advice which seemed specifically designed to kill any chance of compromise. There was something nasty in the woodpile, and I always had my suspicions about the Broncos and Canberra. Especially the Broncos. Having got their breakaway wishes, they weren't much interested in offering any olive branch.

The two proposals on which we got close were these:

1) THE TWO-TIER PLAN

This was a proposal designed to buy time, to give the game its chance to find the answer it needed. The idea was for two divisions of ten, with promotion and relegation (two teams) between them. We talked about this set-up existing for two seasons— 1996–97, and then in 1998 moving to the creation of a 14-team competition, with amalgamations reducing the team numbers. The two year time span would have given the necessary time for clubs to come to terms with both the *idea* of amalgamations, and the necessity. Both competitions would have been viable and competitive. Both would have had extensive television coverage, and would have fulfilled the voracious appetites of the two pay TV networks. I believed that the promotion and relegation clause added the necessary 'edge' to both competitions.

The plan foundered on a totally unreasonable Super League demand. After we had discussed the idea at some length, and promisingly, Ken came back to a meeting with the condition that the Super League clubs could *not* be subjected to the possibility of relegation under the two-tier system. They had to hold guaranteed places in the 'top' division. This of course was bloody ridiculous and unfair. If you have promotion and relegation, it must, of course, embrace *all* teams. It had to be a level playing field—there was no system in the world that worked any other way. It was the end of Plan A.

2) THE POWERS PLAN

When it became apparent that Ken Cowley and I weren't going to find the answer we sought for the game, I suggested one day that PBL boss and Kerry Packer confidant Brian Powers should join us, in the hope that an extra contributor could help break the impasse. Via the talks that took place between the three of us, I believe we got to the very brink of settling the matter. The idea that evolved became known as the Powers Plan. This had as its arrival point a sophisticated 14-team 'super' competition—the participants decided on the basis of performance over seasons 1996–97, during which the 20-team structure would remain in place. After the two years, as in Plan A, there would be amalgamations. There would also be the retention of a second-level 'feeder' competition in which clubs could maintain their identity, while still having a stance through franchise arrangements in the 'super' competition.

I took this plan back to our clubs who had given me their full backing to negotiate with Cowley. I knew there could be no settling of anything without the concurrence of the clubs. I had promised that, and my further declaration as chairman had been that I would have no part in forcing traditional clubs out of the competition or ordering amalgamations. If there were to be such decisions, they had to make them themselves. In 1995, the ARL clubs were heading down the path of accepting the Powers Plan. No firm commitment had been made, but my gut feeling was that the plan would have gone through. Even a hardliner like Souths' George Piggins said to me he believed there was merit in the proposal. George, incidentally, never flinched from his belief that if there were to be amalgamations or rationalisation of any kind, then the ARL should be making those decisions. I agreed with him. At ARL level the Powers Plan was looking good.

When Powers, Cowley and I next met at the Astor Apartments, in Macquarie Street, it was the same story as before. The veil had been drawn over Super League eyes, yet again, and suddenly the Powers Plan was not acceptable. That was pretty well the end of it. We had a plan on the table that to any reasonable eyes looked workable. By then it was pretty apparent that the Super League version of compromise was spelt s-u-r-r-e-n-d-e-r. To them, it was no two-way street, which compromise has to be. In fact, I'm convinced that the forces working in the background wanted no part of any settlement.

The worst part of all was that the people killing off football's hopes for peace were not 'outsiders'. They were football people. Ken made it clear that he felt loyalty to the clubs and people who had joined Super League. I countered: 'Ken, you're talking about people who have been with you a few months. I'm talking about clubs and people who have been with us for nearly 90 years.' Not 90 minutes, 90 years.

I believe Ken Cowley was taking bad advice, from people with personal agendas, and closed minds. His situation was not easy, and I was sympathetic to that. He was trying to deal with about four major corporate matters at the one time, including Ansett negotiations and the matter of Fox Films trying to secure the Sydney Showground area as its base. Football was only one thing on his list, and he obviously depended a good deal on the advice of people around him. The advice they gave him was poor, and unhelpful to the game's secure future.

As you will read now and again in this book, my unwavering position in all of it was that whatever happened, the ARL had to run the game. Ken Cowley and I talked about that. I told him that I would be more than happy if a separate finance committee was set up, one that could have plenary powers in the money side of the game. And as far as I was concerned, News Ltd could have a free hand to set and run the marketing strategies. However, Super League's version of the ARL 'running' the game and ours differed quite markedly. Essentially they wanted the ARL to be their lackeys—to run all the hard bits like juniors, schools, referees, judiciary—while they ran the big game. In other words they wanted us to do all the hard yards, while they put the ball over the line.

The discussions I had with Ken Cowley were always reasonable, and amiable. The waters were muddied by the presence of the complicated question of pay TV ambition and rights, and of shifting media relationships between the Packer and Murdoch camps. But inevitably, at the end of the day, the sticking point we hit was football-driven. That was the worst feature of it all. Football-wise I never thought that Super League came at it from a position of strength. The competition they had cobbled together was in no way the right 'mix'—and especially in Sydney.

In attracting only Canterbury, Cronulla and Penrith, they were left with significant deficiencies in the city that is the heart of world rugby league. The geographical mix was poor and the important element of tradition was missing. Their bargaining position came from the power they could muster through the backing of News Ltd, not from any sort of hot-shot football competition, because they didn't have that . . . or 'vision'.

Somewhere along the track in those ongoing negotiations with News/Super League, via Ken Cowley, I was made an offer to join them. Acting as an intermediary, Peter Moore conveyed it to me. He told me of an opinion offered by Ken Cowley, that, 'We would like Ken (Arthurson) with us. He could assume a supervisory role, a position overviewing the game.' The term used for this role was apparently 'past governor' and the work, not too hard—just keeping an experienced eye on things from the top level. The money suggested was $300,000 a year. It was never a chance.

It is a matter of record that my salary package at the League was $145,000 per year—out of which I paid my own superannuation. In one of the more disgraceful episodes the News Ltd press tried to make capital out of the relatively modest salaries that John Quayle and I earned—salaries that were not within cooee of what their own executives earned, or what they had thrown at an army of football players and Ribot and various other officials they had conscripted. Cowley's own salary figure of $1.7 million was subsequently published. When the *Telegraph* realised that our salaries were not in the same ball park as the Super League figures, they sunk to the depths of publishing an article about how my wife Barbara was paid $13,000 a year (out of my salary!) for secretarial and hostessing duties. That was about as low as it got. The arrangement was approved by the League's auditors, and the fact was that Barbara rarely stopped working for the League in a variety of ways. Whenever the game had international or interstate visitors she was involved in catering, functions, and helping look after the people from out of town. Yes, I plead guilty, as chairman, to having a company Lexus from the League, although my own wish was for something less expensive.

Arko

The *Tele* even sent a photographer out to take pictures of my house. In my street we have a neighbourhood watch programme, and a neighbour confronted the photographer. The bloke left his card and when I rang him later, he apologised. The story I was told was that they were sending a feature writer out to see me, and the photographer had beaten the gun. No doubt they were trying to get some story on me living in a fancy house. The fact was I had lived in the same house on Collaroy Plateau for 20 years.

So many things happened that made me question the morality of the Murdoch organisation. Yet my only meeting with the man at the helm—Rupert Murdoch—had been a harmonious and enjoyable occasion. It had happened a year or so before the 'troubles' when I was holidaying on Hayman Island. My time up there happened to coincide with a News Ltd conference on the island, and when I ran into Ken Cowley he invited me to go out on a cruiser with them one evening, for cocktails. On board that night, Ken introduced me to Rupert Murdoch and we had an enjoyable talk—much of which centred around the near-worldwide TV network that he had in place. In our chat Murdoch pledged to me that he would get behind rugby league and support it on his overseas networks such as Star TV. In fact that happened, although they didn't pay a cent for it. Considering all the later hullabaloo and rubbish about taking the game to the world, the fact was it was already out there. The fact that they didn't pay us for it was indicative of the reality: that people in India and China were not going to be hanging off the ends of their lounges waiting for the rugby league to come on. They'd never heard of it and would very likely never care about it.

I was impressed with Murdoch that evening. I must say that I thought he came across as a very humble sort of bloke, relaxed and friendly on what turned out to be a most enjoyable occasion. I have always admired him as a businessman. In the Super League matter I can only presume the obvious—that he was very, very badly advised, by people with personal vendettas and agendas.

33

WINNING
IT

Through the months of spring 1995, Justice James Charles Burchett sat in a courtroom in downtown Sydney for 51 days, listening to the story of a sporting disaster. All of us got very used to Court 21A of the Federal Court Building in Macquarie Street. At issue was Super League's challenge to the loyalty clauses signed by 20 clubs in February that year. At stake was the future of a game which had been part of Australian life for most of the 20th century. The guts of it was News Ltd's bid to have the ARL commitment and loyalty agreements set aside under sections 45 and 46 of the Trade Practices Act. We had cross claimed against News on a variety of issues.

I suppose everyone there got to feel that they came to know James Burchett pretty well—if from afar. To a layman like me he seemed a man of great legal knowledge—a man of considerable understanding, and acutely perceptive to the small things. More than once I thought to myself: 'Fair dinkum, if I was ever in trouble, he'd do me. He knows his stuff.' I had never met the bloke, and probably never will. But his fair and considered handling of the case made it even more amazing to me when three of his colleagues a year or so later managed to overturn *every* decision he was to make. I will go to my grave never getting close to understanding that.

Arko

I had three days in the box, and plenty of days listening and looking on, so I got a pretty fair sense of Burchett, the man. I remember telling Ken Cowley one day that I was going to go into the box, give evidence—something he decided not to do.

'You're crazy,' said Cowley. 'Our blokes will really "go" you . . . they'll cut you to pieces.'

'They can go for their lives,' I told him. 'I've got nothing to hide.'

In fact I went in feeling quite relaxed. There were a couple of pluses—the first being the certainty that the bloke questioning me wouldn't know as much about rugby league as I did. The second was that I *didn't* have anything to hide. I was just going to tell the truth, tell the story the way it was. So I went in with a positive attitude—and even though I found the experience long, and demanding, I never felt that the task at hand was outside my control. Three days the cross-examination lasted, ranging back and forward through my life in league, and the events that had overtaken the game that year. Only John Ribot was in the box longer than me and there is no doubt he took more of a pounding than I did.

During the long wait, I was constantly heartened by the demonstrations of public support for the ARL position. It seemed to me that the response of ordinary people was overwhelmingly in favour of the ARL and the traditional game. At times it reached extraordinary levels. My head was forever on television and in a strange sidelight to the whole thing, I became more recognisable—at 65!—than I had every been in my life. Just about whenever I ventured into public people would stop me in the street—workers on building sites, little old ladies, mums pushing prams, blokes in suits. 'Good on you, Arko,' they'd say. 'We're with you . . . we're with the ARL.' I can remember walking up Pitt Street one day with Colin Love, and being stopped again and again. 'I just can't believe that,' said Col when we finally reached our destination. I can tell you the support gave me strength, and reinforced in me the rightness of what we were doing. In particular I'll never forget the people of Newcastle—the wonderful, unflinching support they gave the ARL. Novocastrians will do me any day when the going gets tough.

I'm sure everyone on both sides of the fence was happy when the 51 days in court ended. I was satisfied that the League's view of things had been conveyed accurately and thoroughly. I was quietly confident that justice would prevail, and I approached the summer with hopes high. Then, Channel Nine's shock decision that it would do a deal with Super League came on 24 November as a sour and jarring note. Kerry Packer was subsequently to go to bat personally and publicly for Ken Cowley following the towelling that Cowley (and News Ltd) was to take in the Burchett judgement. The case for football's future hung in the balance, yet already our loyal 'allies' were in bed with the enemy. It was a decision that still astonishes and angers me. My old mum used to say that when poverty walks in the door, love flies out the window. Well, with these people, it's pretty apparent that when a business deal walks in the door . . . it's friendship and loyalty that fly out the window . . .

There was nothing we could do about Channel Nine's treachery, or about the Burchett decision, except wait for the latter. And it was a wait that dragged right through summer, to the afternoon of 23 February 1996. But what a day that was for the League when it finally arrived—a justification of all we stood for and believed in. James Burchett's brief and succinct summing up of the thoughts contained in his 220 page judgement delivered as much as we could ever have hoped for. Such was the tension in Court 21A that it took time for the full meaning of the dry legal words the honourable Justice was intoning to sink in. I got my steer from Colin Love, sitting alongside me.

Colin turned to me with the words, 'She's right.'

'You beauty,' I replied. It was all I could think to say. In judgement after judgement, James Burchett destroyed News Ltd's case.

Afterwards, there was pandemonium. There were tears on our side . . . and widespread joy. But I quickly called my people together and said to them: 'Let's not gloat or carry on about this. That's not the way we should be. The fact is there are still plenty of problems with the game, and we should realise that, and act accordingly.' I advised our people to act reasonably and with some humility. In the many media interviews I conducted that day I shared the belief that the League should sit down and try and work out an agreement with News Ltd. The game had been in a major prang and to get it back on the track we badly needed the support of someone like News Ltd.

It was not until later that I read Justice Burchett's scathing criticism of such people as Ribot, Moore, Cowley and Barry Maranta. It gave me no great satisfaction. I certainly wasn't in the business of gloating over other people's discomfort—and especially, in some cases, people who I respected and liked. The stinging criticism was widely aired in the media—of deceit, dishonesty, corporate immorality. Sharp, painful themes which must have cut to the bone. I don't intend to recycle it here, but the words and phrases were surely like knives to the recipients—'completely corrupted', 'clandestine', 'connivance', 'unreliable'. Suffice to say that I was grateful enough that in the big picture of his judgement Justice Burchett had seen through the whole charade of News Ltd's claims. In his own reserved, dignified way he had identified the 'vision' as the bullshit it was—and blown it out of the water.

The night that followed the judgement was something of a blur—a happy time back on the second floor of the NSW Leagues Club, with handshakes and hugs. It was no wild party though; I think we were all too drained for that. But there were a few beers and some smiles that had been missing for too long. Along the way, something happened that I had never experienced in my life. I was serenaded! One of the League staff, young Christine McNamara, took my hands and sang 'Wind Beneath My Wings' in a sweet, clear voice. It was a special night, a night when people on the ARL side relaxed and enjoyed themselves for the first time in months.

It was late when I got home. But my mind was still at full gallop. The tumultuous events of the past year cascaded through my thoughts. There was no chance of sleep, but at least lying there, I felt a tremendous lifting of spirits. I knew it wasn't over, though. I knew they would be back with their appeal, and then another if they had to. By that time my health had become a concern, although I hadn't made too much fuss about it. But I knew that I had to be there at the end—at the moment when the legal machinations had squeezed the last drop, and settled this ARL v Super League issue forever. I had to play the 80 minutes.

During the time of the 1995 premiership semi finals, on a single day it had hit home to me just how great a toll the ongoing battle had taken. I was in a meeting at the League one morning, sitting alongside Graham Richardson, when suddenly excruciating waves of pain pierced through my chest. I excused myself and went and sat outside the room. Pam Parket brought me a glass of water and Richardson followed me out after a while.

'Do you feel all right?' he asked.

'No, as a matter of fact I feel bloody crook,' I answered.

People around me had seen the signs before I had. More than a few said to me later they had been concerned at my appearance in the many television appearances I was still being forced to make. The strain that was building in me—a combination of anger, frustration, worry and general stress loaded on in the long days and nights—was showing.

For a while before that day I had been getting occasional chest pain. I would wake at 3 o'clock in the morning with this tightness gripping my chest. It was an odd feeling, but it came and went in no particular pattern. I didn't have too much time to think about it and I just battled on. I presumed it was some form of indigestion.

But the 'attack' that morning at the League really shook me, and I knew I could ignore it no longer. I made a doctor's appointment for the next day, and that night I lay awake feeling every little twinge, and wondering if my next breath was going to be my last. Dr Alwyn Keighran gave me the once-over, sent me home with an order not to lift anything or exert myself in any way. Then I was on to a specialist, Dr Grout, who then put me in hospital for a couple of days, where I had a range of tests. The good news was that my heart was OK. The bad news was that I was suffering rather seriously from stress 'wear-down'. The general opinion being that the fact I'd kept myself physically fit over the years had helped me get through, but that the warning bells were now ringing loudly.

Arko

The advice was stern and strong: if I didn't cut down my work load—and substantially—then I was heading for very serious trouble. The fact was I had been working enormously long hours, surrounded by negatives—by lies and deceit, by personal friendships that had collapsed, by hate and bitterness in some cases. It was not a healthy environment.

It was because of the expert medical advice I received that I made my decision to step down as executive chairman of the ARL—to the less 'formal' (and unpaid) role of non-executive chairman. I had talked it over at length with John Quayle, such a friend and confidant through the whole thing, and we were both aware of the need for me to fade back a bit. But it didn't really work. The change was more in name than anything else. People still wanted to see me, get my views—at all times of the day and night. I was just as busy. The only difference was that I wasn't getting paid.

In the early hours of 24 February 1996, I was feeling no pain. We were back in the driver's seat in football, as the Australian Rugby League (or its equivalent) had been since 1908. But already, in another place, the decision had been made that Super League would appeal to the full bench of the Federal Court against Justice Burchett's decision. There was no sign of the fat lady just yet . . .

34

LOSING IT

In the weeks that followed the ARL's stunning victory in the Federal Court under the firm hand of Justice James Burchett, it was as if the lunatics were running the asylum. For us the judgement meant in simple terms that a 20-team competition would go ahead in 1996—although News Ltd had wasted no time in lodging an appeal. That had been announced at 8 p.m. on the night of the decision, via a Ken Cowley press release. That was about the only solid thing that the Super Leaguers did at that time. Most of the rest of it was fairyland stuff. Almost every day, it seemed, brought some crazy scheme or statement from the Super League side of the fence. Obviously they had been knocked for six by Burchett's judgement—and there was a wild casting around to try and find an answer that might ease a way around it. Sadly, some of the players became pawns in the game, controlled like marionettes to say and do stupid things. Laurie Daley in particular was especially badly advised, and painted himself into an embarrassing corner with some of the things he said. 'There's a possibility of playing in England, playing rugby union or playing Aussie Rules,' he said. 'But I have made my decision . . . I won't be going back.' At one stage I think he even called us 'Nazis'.

For my own part, relief was the overwhelming emotion. The basic thing that sustained me through all of it was that if you were honest and up-front in the way you conducted yourself in life, then you'd get through. I was sustained by the belief that we were fighting for something that was right. I was appalled by some of the things I had heard in court; appalled by the lies told. But no-one could have played a straighter bat than Burchett. He conducted the proceedings with dignity and fairness and in my view he cut right through to the heart of it in his judgement. I had faith in the justice system when we started, and I had faith now that it was over. Well, for the time being anyway.

The Burchett decision essentially left the Super League players with two choices. They could either come back and play football under the ARL banner, or they could sit out. Covert Super League forces tried to contrive a third choice with their 'Global League' concept . . . one of the greatest pieces of bullshit it has been my misfortune to run up against in half a century in the game. For those who believed in the tooth fairy, the easter bunny and goblins at the bottom of the garden, this was to be run by Maurice Lindsay on behalf of the players—with no involvement from Super League. Oh yeah? Global League, Maurice informed us, was to be backed by the English League. I was more than pleased to offer Lindsay some advice—that instead of gallivanting around North Queensland (which he was at the time) he should get back to his own patch, which was a shambles. He had far more to worry about than telling us what we should be doing over here. I offered the view that the English Rugby League couldn't sell blankets in Alaska and told the media: 'His muddled attempt to create a rebel competition against the ARL has shattered his reputation in this country beyond belief.'

This was a bastard of a time. At one point John Quayle offered himself as a sacrificial lamb, telling the *Sun-Herald* he would resign if that's what it was going to take to get the game back together. I would have no part of that. There was no way that Quayle should have been victim of what had taken place. The handing down of orders by Justice Burchett on 11 March, 1996, proved to be the penultimate strike against the rebellion. Most significant of all was Order 15A—a 'no pay, no play' direction. Either the Super League players played in the ARL competition—or they wouldn't get paid. But, still they held out . . .

On 22 March, the game sank to one of the many low points it touched during 1995–96, when seven Super League clubs forfeited their first round (ARL) premiership matches, because their players had declared themselves unavailable. It meant the cancellation of six of the ten scheduled matches. These were rugby league's first forfeits of modern times and historians reached way back into the past to recall the occasion of 1909's premiership, when Balmain forfeited to South Sydney in protest at their final being played as a curtain-raiser to a representative match.

The opening weekend, thin on football, was a pretty dispiriting event. But I was heartened by the feeling that existed deep within the 'real' football people. At Steelers Stadium for the Illawarra–Wests season's opener I was cheered loudly when I addressed the crowd and told them:

> 'I didn't think I would ever see the day when players went on strike because their clubs didn't have the guts to tell them what their contractual obligations were. These players are people who have been made wealthy by the game. Now they are turning their backs on a game that has given them everything.'

Eventually the players came back, and so too their clubs . . . because they had to. On 26 March the Full Bench of the Federal Court killed any chances of a rebel competition starting in 1996, and by the next day the majority of the players were back, although some were still dragging their feet. If the players were to be paid in 1996, they had to play football. It was as simple as that. Some held out—notably Manly's Mathew Ridge who didn't make his return until May, and Gorden Tallis, who having taken the Broncos' bait, chose not to come back to St George at all and sat out the season, thus missing playing in a grand final.

On the weekend of the first round I had a chance meeting with NSW captain Laurie Daley, via radio station 2UE. Daley had been one of the most outspoken of the players, saying far more than perhaps he intended. But I had determined that there would be no hard feelings and no retribution when we finally got the game rolling in '96.

Arko

When chance brought us together on the airwaves, I told Daley: 'I'll give you my word that you will be given every consideration, that nothing will be held against you as far as representative football is concerned.'

'Thanks mate,' said Laurie.

'Probably we've both been a bit embarrassed about talking,' I told him. 'I'm glad we've had the chance now.'

I was determined that the gesture of conciliation from the League—for an absolutely level playing field for all players in 1996—would be carried out.

And we certainly kept our side of the bargain in that rather sad and struggling year. As I had promised we picked Super League players in all the representative games, and they responded with commitment and full-blooded efforts in the early games (City–Country, State of Origin) as footballers should. But it all fell apart when we tried to stage an Australia–New Zealand Test series—against the wishes of the Super League-aligned NZRL. At that point something happened which I never believed would be possible in Australia—rugby league players declined the green and gold jersey of their country. Eight Super League players selected in the side chose to withdraw. They were: Andrew Ettingshausen, Brett Mullins, David Furner, Steve Walters, Steve Renouf, Laurie Daley, Glenn Lazarus and Wendell Sailor. I have no doubt that their collective decision was made on the urging of their boss, News Ltd. There is no doubt the players were under strong pressure not to play. But at the end of the day you've got to be your own man. When it comes to playing for your country I wouldn't give a bugger if ten Murdochs or ten Packers were trying to tell me what to do. It wouldn't cut any ice with me, I'll tell you that. The day the players said 'no' to the Aussie jumper ranks with me as one of the most hurtful of them all. Whoever within News Ltd was responsible, whoever insisted that the players be pressured into not playing, should hang their heads in shame. Since 1908 rugby league players have fought for the dream of the green and gold jumper. To win one was to climb football's highest mountain. Now blokes were turning them down . . .

In 1997 I was angered to hear Glenn Lazarus's words after

Super League staged their 'Australia v New Zealand' match, a pale shadow of what international football should be about—and which they had the temerity to call a 'Test', which it wasn't. Lazarus said he had no sympathy for (ARL) players who hadn't been given the chance to play in the match, because the ARL hadn't provided Super League players with that opportunity, anyway. That wasn't true. In June 1996, eight Super League players had been chosen to represent their country—and declined.

That 'Australia–New Zealand' game of 1997 should never go into the record books as a 'Test'. It was a 'Test' in inverted commas, the way responsible members of the print media presented it. It should never be added to the genuine Test record of those who played in it.

The season limped along, never seeming quite real. On 23 May, the hearing of the Super League appeal against the judgements of James Burchett began before the Full Bench of the Federal Court—Justices John Lockhart, Ronald Sackville and John von Doussa. On 2 July I announced that I would be standing aside as executive chairman of the ARL, to allow a restructuring of the Optus Cup competition. 'I've taken the ball up so many times I've run out of puff,' I told the media. In reaching my decision I had been guided by an old philosophy: 'It's better to go when they want you to stay, than stay when they want you to go.' On the neatly typed press release my future looked quieter and clearcut—but it never really worked out that way. I found myself as busy as I had been all along. In court, the submissions of the two sides heard, the Federal Court judges reserved their decision and retired on 6 June to consider rugby league's fate . . .

I suppose it would be fair comment to say that my last season at the helm in rugby league ended fittingly. On Sunday 29 September Manly, who I believe have been the best team for a couple of years, ground out a tough and professional 20–6 grand final victory over St George—the club's sixth premiership, and Bob Fulton's second as coach. Geoff Toovey's incredible bravery—to play the match with a broken cheekbone *and* win the Clive Churchill Medal as Man of the Grand Final—

lifted the game well above the ordinary. It was one of the most courageous performances I have ever seen.

All the while the great shadow hung over the game . . . and now we didn't have long to wait. The following Thursday came the news—the appeal decision would be handed down the next day. I slept barely at all on the Thursday night. I was uneasy; something, somehow, didn't feel right. By all that was good and fair dinkum we should have wrapped it up the next day, won the appeal and been cleared to take the game of rugby league on and into the next millennium. After all, no company surely was entitled to profit from identifiable deceit, dishonesty and immoral behaviour, was it? But there had been hints in the media that News Ltd were feeling good about what was coming up and I approached the day with some trepidation . . .

The morning was tough. John Quayle and I mainly just paced up and down, watching the clock tick over. On the stroll to the court I said to him: 'Mate, we can't possibly lose. I mean, the loyalty contracts for a start would have to be enforceable. They would have to be valid for starters, we're not going to lose that.' But in the court my feeling of unease grew. Apart from the legal eagles, not one of the Super League mob was there. This could either mean they were anticipating a thrashing, or something else . . .

It is too painful for me to dwell at length on what we heard. I got the drift straight away when the reading of the judgement began. Then the smirks started to appear on the faces of those in the other camp. On and on it went—astonishing, unbelievable . . . genuinely shocking. One by one they turned over *every* decision that James Burchett had made. I was to say many times later that it was like playing the same team twice, under the same set of rules, with the only difference being a new referee, and winning 100–nil the first week, then losing 100–nil the next.

Sitting in that court that day was one of the most devastating experiences of my life. How could it be? I asked myself the question over and over as Justice Lockart droned on. Justice Burchett, a respected and reputable judge, had sat and watched and listened and soaked it up for 51 days. He had taken in every moment, every piece of evidence, observed the body language;

he knew who was telling lies and who wasn't. And after weeks of deliberation he had reached his decision, his strong words effectively crushing the company whose behaviour had been found to be so treacherous and disgraceful along the way. Now these blokes, without access to the nuances of the evidence, had thrown every bloody thing out the window.

In his original judgement Justice Burchett said that even if there had been a breach of the Trade Practices Act he would not have granted relief because of what he saw as the dishonest behaviour of News Ltd.

The appeal had been conducted on dry, legal arguments—fine points of law, and arcane technicalities. News Ltd didn't touch on that at all, or try to get Justice Burchett's scathing views turned around. They were prepared to cop that sort of humiliation in the interests of the bigger picture. And the Appeals Court was obviously unconcerned with a principle that I would imagine 99 per cent of people in the street would value very highly indeed—that of the morality of a company or organisation being able to benefit from dishonest, secretive or deceptive behaviour. Under the appeal decision that's exactly what happened.

I was furious, hurt, bewildered. This wasn't justice as I had grown to understand it in Australia. Here was reward being given to a mob who had been *proved* to have acted dishonestly and deceitfully. Where was the justice in that?

In the many interviews that followed, there is no doubt my face said it all. In the immediate aftermath, I felt as if I had been run over by the Southern Aurora, but I stood there, facing the biggest media army you've ever seen, and did what I had to do. I expressed my bewilderment, and assured everyone that we would continue fighting for what we believed was right.

Back at the League we all just sat down and licked our wounds and tried to make sense of it. But we never flinched. The determination was still there. It wasn't over yet and the mood was one of: 'We'll be back in the ring tomorrow. We might be down today, but we're a long way from being out.' There was never a doubt that we would go all the way to the wire—and bid to take the matter to the High Court.

The Super League propaganda machine switched to full

throttle in the wake of October's Federal Court decision. From their rumour mill we were assaulted with whispers, red herrings and innuendo—and in some isolated cases even fact. It's one of the few wraps that I can give Super League—that in the area of peddling misinformation, they are Olympic class. The tactic was always to divide and rule, to spread stories about particular clubs being on the verge of jumping, and so making other clubs nervous and vulnerable. At different stages, according to the stories doing the rounds, it seemed that every ARL club was targeted by a Super League organisation well aware of the serious deficiencies that existed in the make-up of their own competition. I am proud to say that our clubs knocked them back in every single case—with St George lured with the bait of a Melbourne franchise, and Parramatta the last of them to declare they were sticking fast with the ARL. Already ARL determination and will was restored after the disappointment the Federal Court had dealt us. On 8 October, Optus, such staunch backers, pledged $120 million in funds over the next five years. Two days before, the *Sun-Herald* had come out with a sports section on the front page of which was a tombstone carrying the inscription: 'RIP Australian RL. Born 1908. Died 1996.' They couldn't have been much further off the mark.

The court skirmishes continued. Six Penrith players, plus Anthony Mundine (Broncos) and Rod Silva (Bulldogs), began action in the Industrial Court to challenge the validity of the ARL loyalty agreements. Two days after that we lodged the necessary papers with the High Court, seeking leave to challenge the findings of Messrs Lockhart, von Doussa and Sackville.

I knew deep down that from my point of view, the blast of the whistle signalling fulltime on my career as a rugby league administrator wasn't far away. My hope was that the High Court would take our appeal on board. Seeing as how one respected judge (Burchett) had seen an issue as black and the Full Bench had seen the same issue as completely white, I was hopeful that a higher authority still would see the need to make a final judgement. As summer neared, we awaited this last throw of the dice . . .

35

FINAL
MINUTES

On 15 November 1996, the High Court took less time than it takes to play half a game of football to knock back our appeal against the Federal Court verdict. We were out of the game in just over 20 minutes—leaving rugby league with no choice but to get itself ready for the madness of a two-competition structure in 1997. It was another decision I struggled to come to terms with. How could one judge be so 'wrong', then his peers, guided by the same laws, confronting the same issues, be so 'right'? For a layman like me, if there was ever a case for final adjudication, then this was it. But the ref said no—and whether we liked it or not we had to accept his decision.

Rugby league was a profoundly changing game. A few days earlier John Quayle had decided that he had had enough, and resigned as general manager of the NSWRL and chief executive of the ARL. His decision, made with characteristic Quayle firmness, rattled rugby league's already shaky facade. It was, however, no shock to me. It had been in John's mind for some time and we had discussed it over a period of weeks. John increasingly felt that he wasn't getting the support he needed from some people inside the game. He felt that some of the people he was doing his darndest to fight for were not giving much in return. A job chance came along—a couple, actually—and in the interests of himself, his family, and his health, there was no way I could advise him not to do what he did. Perhaps from a selfish point of view I could have talked him out of it . . . but there was no way I was going to do that. I had too high a regard of John Quayle—both the man and the administrator. He had fought a bloody good fight for rugby league. He had paid his dues.

John Quayle's decision to go hastened my own exit. John was aware of my thoughts on my own retirement being not far down the track, and had always said that he didn't want to be there when I wasn't. His final legacy to the game was a beauty. Days before he made his decision to go he had clinched the Optus support package—the lifeline for the ARL clubs to carry on to 2000 and beyond. But even when it happened some of the clubs were quibbling about the deal he had brokered for them. He wasn't looking for pats on the back—just a little support. In the end, he had just had enough.

The clock was now ticking on my own future, and it was a funny feeling. I had good days and bad. The boys from Manly rugby (union) club put on a luncheon in my honour, and made quite a fuss, with people such as Alan Jones saying some very kind things. I was honoured under the rugby club's 'True Sons of Manly' programme. This was a real buzz and especially considering that it was a gesture from one football code to another—and even more so in the historical context of rivalry between the two rugbys which traced all the way back to 1895. I appreciated it greatly.

Such was my feeling for the district I lived in that these local honours truly meant the world to me. At Brookvale Oval one afternoon they had named the new grandstand after me in an occasion of some pomp and ceremony and great emotion. That was a supreme honour, considering my links with the place. I remembered it back in the very earliest days when it was little more than a cow paddock. Midway through every year it would have degenerated into a dust bowl, such was the traffic that galloped across it in any football season. The ground has been part of my life, for most of my life: I can still see in my mind's eye Souths' Johnny Graves parting the 'huge' crowd there one afternoon—about 11,000 of them—to kick the winning goal for the

Rabbitohs against Manly. These days it is a model football ground, the grass lush and green and with a capacity of 28,000. I am proud to have played my part in the rise of this special place. Proud, too, to have my name plonked on the fine grandstand at the sou'-western end. I used to smile to myself at the prospect of Super League teams coming there to play Manly and the players raising their eyes to see the Ken Arthurson Stand. The man who many perhaps perceived as 'the enemy' would be watching over them.

It was just before Christmas 1996 that I had to contend with the aftermath of an embarrassing story in the *Sunday Telegraph* headed 'Arko advised me to join Super League'. It was a story about Peter Moore which gave the impression that I had given him the nod to link up with News Ltd in 1995. Nothing could have been further from the truth. The fact was that Moore had already *been* with Super League for six months or so when he rang me one day. He had been offered a job as a recruitment officer with them, and the idea appealed. Peter was also in line for a superannuation payment running into hundreds of thousands of dollars if he chose to leave Canterbury.

'What do you reckon?' he asked me.

This was my advice: 'If it's something you really want to do, and you're happy to do it—go for it.'

That was all. That was a wickedly dishonest headline, giving totally the wrong impression. Bloody mischievous . . . and too stupid for words. I'll tell you now that if I had to name the events of the Super League war that were most hurtful to me, these two would be near the top of the list: The Canterbury decision to jump ship. And Peter Moore's decision to go with them. Peter and I had been shoulder to shoulder in rugby league for 30 years, allies—one for the other—when the going got tough. So when it came to this, the biggest fight in the history of the game, it was really hard for me to accept that we were on opposite sides of the fence.

As if I would ever have advised Peter Moore to join Super League. My advice to him came as a friend, months after he had made his initial decision.

On 22 December 1996, the newspapers carried the first

indication that I was considering getting out. At that stage the time frame was fairly relaxed. 'Either April or October,' I told the media.

At this point I approach the completion of the loop in this book on my life . . .

On Friday 17 January 1997, Channel Nine made the formal announcement of a deal with Super League. I had heard the rumours on this, but had defended our 'allies'.

'Not when the chips are down . . . they won't do it,' I had said to people who suggested that treachery was in the wind.

But on the Friday afternoon I took a phone call from James Packer. I was having a break in Queensland at the time and I can still remember his opening words: 'Ken, it's James Packer. This is a call that gives me no pleasure to make . . .'

He went on to tell me that Channel Nine had made a 'business' decision to link with Super League in 1997. At that stage he made no mention of the Monday Night Football component— the hijacking of the concept that had worked so well for us.

'I'm disappointed,' I told him. 'I take it you will be honouring the agreement you have with the Australian Rugby League?'

James Packer assured me that Channel Nine would be doing that.

The news on the Monday Night Football hijack came a day or so later. It was a case of not only being knocked down but having the boot put in as well. Business had come through the door—and friendship and loyalty had flown out the window. I offered the opinion that under the circumstances, David Leckie (Channel Nine's chief executive) could no longer be a member of the board of the NSWRL—and by the Monday, Leckie had resigned via a two-line letter. That was a shame. I had regarded Leckie's contribution as very valuable indeed during the short time he was on the board. He and I have not spoken since that time, nor have I spoken to anyone else from Channel Nine, but knowing David as I do, I'd be surprised if he had been supportive of Nine's decision to get into bed with Super League.

In his well-publicised interview with Ray Martin in 1997, James Packer was to come out and lament rugby league's troubled state, and express his belief in the necessity for a one-competition format. Can I just pose this, a thought which I believe gets to the very nub of the whole two years of madness? Why the bloody hell couldn't Murdoch senior and Packer senior have arrived at that point two years before? Christ, that makes me furious! Their failure to reach an agreement which everyone now expects to happen put rugby league and the game's community through two years of agony. Their failure to strike a deal on the issue it was all about—pay TV—has done the game untold damage. It has fractured lifetime friendships, destroyed the game financially, and driven away its loyal fans in vast numbers. It has caused the substructure of the game to crumble alarmingly, to the point that rugby league may never get back to what it was at the end of 1994. Just imagine what a sport we would have had now if the $500 million or whatever it is had been poured into the game *itself*, instead of flushed down the drain in ludicrous, inflationary payments to players and multi-million dollar support of the legal community. Just imagine . . .

In quieter moments I roved back in my mind on aspects of our approach to the running of the game at the ARL. Had we been *that* wrong, had we contributed substantially to the dreadful thing that had been done to league by the News Ltd raid? The answer to that is that there is no doubt we had erred now and then, made decisions that in cooler light down the track we mightn't have made. We were human: we weren't perfect. But I honestly believe it's just about impossible to present a case which suggests that the NSWRL/ARL *hadn't* done a good job and a responsible one when anyone took time to examine the standing of the game of rugby league at the end of season 1994.

Channel Nine's move dragged me down about as far as it was possible for a fundamentally positive person like myself to go. I just started to feel that I couldn't take it any more. And when I started to think like that, I was also figuring . . . I'm not going to be much use to anybody if I'm in this frame of mind.

The game was badly, chronically bruised by then. A flurry of publicity early in '97 involving North Sydney players misbehaving at a one-day cricket match in Sydney lowlighted by images on national TV of Jason Taylor being led from the SCG soaked in beer, didn't help either. It should also have been over and done with in a day or two—having been so widely aired that it required swift and strong action from the club. Unfortunately, Norths dithered . . . for what seemed weeks, before they finally creaked out some action. And all the while the media needled them, as they always would. Something had happened and people were looking for an answer. Norths responded tardily and the whole thing was a salient lesson to the clubs which will take rugby league into the future. The message is clear: if you have an off-field problem, confront it with speed and strength, then let the fans know exactly what you have done. It was a fumble by Norths, and all of us have those. My opinion of the North Sydney club remained unchanged: a decent, loyal, professional outfit doing their best for rugby league.

More than ever, any time footballers play up off the field and get themselves into the headlines, it is an offence against the game they play. Too many people have drifted from the game already, to other sports, other interests. Sadly for some people, some dedicated fans have learned that there *is* life after football. They're going to be damned hard to get back. And the certainty is that mug behaviour from supposed sporting role models is only going to drive more away. If I have a final word to players it is this: if you want to keep playing rugby league, and earning good money from it, think hard about what you do away from the playing field . . . very hard.

By then, 40-year-old Neil Whittaker had been appointed, and was preparing to come on board as the new chief executive of the NSWRL and ARL. He was a fine choice, with a background which was equally solid in both the game of rugby league and the corporate world. With Neil to start in February I felt I should give him a month, to help as much as possible in the easing-in process. This was a new deal in rugby league and I wasn't going to stay too long. Neil Whittaker and the new NSWRL chairman Warren Lockwood, a solid, decent bloke from St George, had to cut the cloth their way. It was the beginning of a new era, and my decision was only to stay a respectable period, then go. Both of them know I will always be on hand until the day I die, to help in any way I can. I am only a phone call away . . . or in Neil's case, about a minute's walk. By chance we live only streets apart in Collaroy Plateau.

36

FULLTIME

On a Tuesday night in January 1997, I tossed and turned for hours, finally, near dawn, arriving at the very brink of my decision. As I drove down the hill to The Spit that morning and over and up and on towards Phillip Street, my mind was still at full gallop. I had talked it over the day before with my old mate Tom Bellew—my resignation as chairman of the NSWRL. My thought then was to stay on as ARL chairman for a time, and Tom favoured that line of attack. But during the night and into the early morning of Wednesday 22 January, I moved closer and closer to the thought that I would get out—completely. My health was a real concern now, for the first time in my life. Channel Nine's decision to link with Super League had flattened me. And I was missing John Quayle. We had genuinely been a 'team' for many years and especially in the trench warfare of 1995–96. He was gone, and the longer I thought about it, the more I knew it was right for a complete changing of the guard at Phillip Street. Driving to the city that morning I figured that to resign *twice* from jobs I had loved doing would be double the torture. Far better to cut clean—to leave the NSWRL and the ARL in one strong, decisive step on one day. By the time I drove in from Elizabeth Street to my spot in the car park under the old building as I had done so many thousands of times, my mind was made up.

So it was that at a board meeting of the NSWRL that day I announced my resignation. I had told only Tom Bellew beforehand. I would stay until 28 February, then leave them to it— albeit with promises of my support, if needed, until the day I died. I had been 52 years in the game if my 'serious' beginning in league could be traced back to joining the Freshwater D grade side in 1945. On the same day, a loyal ally in Greg Mitchell, executive assistant to John Quayle, also resigned. The press release told my story succinctly. It read in part:

'The fact is that I stepped down . . . because the demands of the job were taking their toll on my health. Doctors had advised me to ease my workload and that is what I had tried to do. But the reality is that the workload has increased, it is inevitable that it will increase further and I need to step aside. It is not in my interests or the game's interests for me to be fighting the demands the job will make on my time. I'm not leaving the country, I'll be around if anyone needs my advice . . .'

Later that week I talked Bob Fulton out of stepping down as Australian coach. 'Stay a year at least,' I advised him. 'It's in the best interests of the game if you do.' The times were changing.

The month that followed galloped by in something of a blur. For me it was a time of reflection and now and then the arrival of a gulping moment of realisation that it was really going to happen. I left football on the last day of February, one of the tougher days of my life. Nothing seemed quite real as I sorted through drawers in my office on the fifth floor, picking through the things I would take and keep. In the afternoon the staff came to my office for a drink, and we battled to keep our chins up . . . me especially. There was forced laughter and some tears and sadness. Leaving those people was a terrible wrench for me. They had been so loyal, so uncomplaining during the hard times of the past two years. The troubles had bound us all closer together than we had ever been. Adversity does that. Many kind words were spoken, including a nice tribute in the media from John Ribot. I appreciated that. I had always liked the bloke . . . just wished he hadn't done what he did.

Later, came two low-key official farewells, then an ARL dinner in Brisbane, and a splendid night in Sydney when friends from all the corners of my life came to say goodbye. Kevin Humphreys and John Quayle spoke beautifully on that night and I will never forget the warmth of the occasion and the good feelings and good wishes that Barbara and I took with us.

I left football disappointed, and with not much more than faint hope for the future. It was not the way I would have chosen to go. In the previous two years many things I had believed in had been challenged and in some cases destroyed forever. The game that had been my life had been tossed around like a cork on stormy waters, its very long-term existence threatened by those unholy partners-in-crime: Bronco greed and the ruthless corporate ambition of News Ltd.

Before it all began I had had faith in the Australian justice system. No more. I will go to my grave never understanding how the law could reward proven dishonesty and deceit. Some of News Ltd's behaviour through the whole thing was positively un-Australian—and James Burchett nailed that with deadly accuracy. I support fully the principle of fair competition and free trade in our society. I have no problem with a new company moving in alongside another, and starting in direct competition. But News Ltd did far more than that to the Australian Rugby League. They came in and *stole* our stock—our players, our clubs, our assets, our logos, our traditions . . . even our league-playing *countries*. And they did this via the means of treachery and deceit and in the dark of night. And for that they get rewarded? If that's our justice system, leave me out . . .

Once I had *some* faith in politicians. I was sure there were honourable ones, good among the bad—people of principle who were there genuinely to serve, and to help build a better society. The Super League matter did nothing to support that faith. The silence of politicians during the hijacking of rugby league was despicable. In Canberra, there is a politicians' rugby league group. In name, anyway. Well, where were they when Murdoch was stealing the game? Nowhere to be seen, that's where. In England the pollies showed far more guts, making a real fuss on matters of strong principle when the Murdoch takeover was on. But if there was ever evidence that Australian politicians are scared of upsetting the Murdochs and Packers of the world, it was during this business. They didn't give a yelp, although I applaud the later strong reaction by Anthony Albanese the ALP's MHR for Grayndler in NSW when Telstra—a government instrumentality—put $20 million or whatever it was into Super League. That was a disgrace—public money being put into a breakaway organisation. I would urge the government never to drop their guard on the important principle of rugby league being available to fans on free-to-air TV. I am not filled with confidence on that score, the fact being that when Packer or Murdoch bark, politicians have a tendency to jump.

The Telstra principle applied when the RSL sold out to Super League for $20,000 over the Anzac Day 'Test' in '97—which, of course, wasn't a Test match at all. I would quietly remind the men who made that decision that the spirit of Anzac is about loyalty, comradeship, bravery and blokes standing up for each other in times of crisis. And I would suggest that there wasn't a lot of any of those qualities on display when Super League launched their silent raid on a game which had been an Australian institution for 90 years—and which had provided succour for people back home during two world wars.

In my view Super League would get an 'A' in only one, solitary area of the whole thing: their ability to keep pumping out the rhetoric and propaganda. Via their extensive publicity machine they have proven breathtakingly good at that. They were superb too in the art of creating uncertainty, in planting seeds of doubt. Inevitably they would undermine any major ARL promotion, by feeding the media with some rumour or other on a 'major' issue, stealing newspaper space, and unsettling. 'Destabilise' is a word that comes to mind.

As I have made clear, I supported some of the fundamentals of what they were on about when they came to us in 1995. But the truth of it is that much of the 'vision' presented is a giant con. This garbage about taking the game to the world . . . when you stop and analyse it, it means absolutely nothing. It gives me some bitter satisfaction to see them stumbling as I write these final words. Their competition is not going well in mid-1997—and why would it when they so seriously underestimated the importance of Sydney and its traditions in the bigger picture of Australian rugby league? News fell for the 'outsiders' vision of people like the Broncos and Canberra—and now they are paying dearly for it. It is only fitting that the Broncos are paying heavily for it, too. That their administration team failed to grasp the reality that people turned up in huge numbers to matches in Brisbane because they wanted to see the Broncos take on the 'enemy' of the traditional Sydney clubs, is a true indictment of their lack of insight into rugby league.

News Ltd are very likely wishing the whole thing to buggery. If they could turn back time to pre-1995, I reckon they'd tell the Broncos' plotters to go jump in the lake. They would want no part of it. The Super League wars have sorely damaged News. Their senior executives have been discredited and the total bill, so far, must be up around $300 million. I would imagine that the strong 1997 rumour of Murdoch telling them to 'Fix the bloody thing . . . or else' would be spot-on. It wouldn't surprise me if News reached a point where the decision is made to throw no more good money after bad—and the plug was pulled.

It heartens me greatly that 'little people' have taken a stance against what News Ltd/Super League did to a game which was so much a part of so many people's lives. I couldn't begin to add up how many people have told me that they no longer buy the Murdoch *Daily Telegraph*, which was the main mouthpiece for News Ltd propaganda throughout. One bloke of my acquaintance summed it up to me when he said: 'Look, I know it doesn't mean a bloody thing to Murdoch (not buying the paper), but it sure makes *me* feel good.' Others have told me of their small, personal pleasure in knocking back a Foxtel pay TV approach, because of Super League. For my own part, I never buy a *Telegraph* these days, and I have not watched a Super League match on television. Within myself, I don't even acknowledge that it exists.

I have the sense now that some people at Phillip Street were waiting for me to go so they could push through a pet project or two. I was disappointed to learn, for example, that NSW

Arko

Country and Queensland have amended the rules of Peter Corcoran's mini and mod games for youngsters. That was something I would always have resisted. These two games were just about the best promotional vehicle rugby league had—a wonderful legacy to the game from Corcoran. They had been in place for 15 years or so, whetting the appetites of countless thousands of youngsters for rugby league, and easing them through the learning years and into the 'big game'. Peter's innovation was so successful that just about every other sport followed suit and developed their own variations. Mini and mod football added up to a truly magnificent innovation for rugby league. So why change them now? Why change a traditional thing which has been such a solid platform for the game's success? It's funny how some people in the game resist the efforts of men like Corcoran and Tom Bellew. Both men have been wonderful workers for rugby league, however both are seen perhaps as *too* pedantic and particular. But the game *needs* those sort of people—and desperately. It needs its devil's advocates to question and chide. Administration of any sport must be a thing of balance and people like Corcoran and Bellew are vital components in the mix. Good men, true rugby league men. It saddens me a good deal that decisions have recently been made to tamper with Peter's games. I can't think of one single thing that was better for league than the games he devised.

I think the players of the game have to be especially concerned and careful. They are richer than they have ever been in rugby league's history. They are also more vulnerable than they've ever been. I sense a distinct resentment in the community at the vast and ridiculous payments being made to footballers (although that situation is certainly not their fault!), and that resentment has translated to a significant 'turn off' factor among people who once followed the game. Blokes with a mortgage, not much money and a house full of kids, find little common ground anymore with BMW-driving overpaid footballers, who are nudged along by managers chasing ever-bigger contracts. More than ever before the players have to care for their game—in everything they do, on and off the paddock. They have to give value in all that they do.

And the future? Nothing is more under the microscope in Australian sport than the future structure of rugby league as the two sides edge closer to some sort of compromise. My firm view on it is this: that to merge or get rid of traditional clubs in the short term—i.e. for season 1998 as has been urged—is impossible. To do it would be to traumatise even more the loyal supporters who have stuck with rugby league through the worst months of its long life. The fans don't deserve that. I urge the two sides (ARL and Super League) to adopt a softly, softly approach. For 1998, nothing more radical should be considered than the two sides getting back together, in a competition of *no less than 18 teams*—two tiers if they choose to do it that way. If it was 20 teams . . . or even the existing 22, that wouldn't worry me. The dogma preached by Super League—of a 12 or (maximum) 14 team competition—should be ignored at this stage, and maybe forever. It should be just one more, of many, possibilities on the agenda as rugby league uses '98, and possibly even 1999, to come up with the 'right' decision for the game. There may well be a time in the future when clubs choose to link up in merger arrangements for the good of all concerned. But my plea to the game as this book goes to press is: not now— not rushed through in a month or two as Super League's propaganda machine seems to be urging.

So persistent are the slogans being trotted out—'12 is the perfect number', 'not enough players to go around for any larger structure', 'mergers will have to take place because it will need two Leagues clubs to financially support a club in the future', 'four (or five) Sydney teams is the maximum number'— that it seemed many people couldn't see the woods for the trees as the debate raged. The fundamental need in the whole thing is rarely discussed—that of costs within the game being slashed, by player salaries being reduced to acceptable levels. I know it can't happen straight away because of the lingering madness of some of the crazy contracts given to players during the war. But it *must* be done. Rugby league today has players earning three times as much as the Prime Minister—no wonder it has lost touch with the working class which was its heartland.

I know what I'd be doing—I'd be cutting the salary cap in

half. Straight away. Significantly reduced costs could do away with this perceived need to kill off or amalgamate clubs. In my view the only avenue for the ARL as it wrestles with the problem in '97 is to buy itself time with a well-promoted interim competition in 1998—why not two tiers of 10, with promotion and relegation between them?—and to make sure it doesn't fall for the snow job being attempted by Super League.

The News Ltd-fed talk of certain and quick compromise that surfaced in May 1997 seemed to me ridiculously facile. It will never be as easy as a few words on a newspaper page. The problem with News Ltd's view of compromise is that it has always been closer to surrender. In truth compromise is giving and taking; two-way traffic. And that's the way it must be. My faith in everything we believed in and fought for would crumble if there was any sign of meek surrender from the ARL. I don't believe there will be.

I have confidence in both Neil Whittaker (general manager) and Warren Lockwood (chairman) at the NSWRL. They are two good guys, capable men who I'm sure will always remain true to the principle that the ARL must run the game. Optus's pledge of long-term support gives the ARL the necessary back-up to head resolutely on, and find the right answer for the game. Super League, to me, seem to be placed on more shifting sands. Their head man, Ian Frykberg, however, seems genuine in his ambition to find a solution.

The certainty is that whatever is to happen for rugby league must happen with speed and firmness. I sense the game draining away, almost every day. Other sports are increasingly taking strength from rugby league's collapse. In Sydney, the other football codes—Aussie Rules, rugby union and soccer—have never looked healthier. And hanging over everything is the immense shadow of the 2000 Olympics, and the certainty that the Games have the potential to draw much away from all other sports in the three years ahead. Rugby league two and half years into the war that has crippled it is a seriously damaged sporting product. Super League have denigrated apparently unshakeable traditions such as Test and Origin football—with the pale imitations of their 'Tri-series' and pseudo-'Test'. They have done things that the 'real' game of rugby league would never do. I am still appalled by their actions in trying to hustle people away from a Swans match at the SCG with their offers of free tickets to a Super League match at the SFS. Considering our happy coexistence with other sports over the years, that was about as bad as things could possibly get, although not so far out of step with normal News Ltd practice, I would suggest. The Super Leaguers have undermined much of what rugby league was built on, and drew its strength from. The question must now be asked: Will the game *ever* get back what it once had?

My answer is, yes, one day it will. Rugby league was born in blood and conflict all those years ago and it has been a tough game for all its life. The game's history tells of league rising again and again when it seemed sorely in trouble, or, at times, almost down and out. Over the years it has breasted some big rivers. My prediction is that the game will rise again one day. Never, though, has it been in as much strife as it is now. The task is nothing less than a complete rebuilding of public faith and confidence. And the truth is that some of the 'market'—the people who were once its lifeblood—are gone forever. The answer lies only in a getting-together between the two sides. If they continue to fight . . . there will be nothing left to fight over.

My long-term confidence is based on the fact that the raw kernel of rugby league—the game itself—is still an immensely appealing entertainment. Even in the doldrums of 1997 there have been sparkling games . . . Parramatta–Sydney City, Manly–Sydney City, the Origin series . . . and from all reports the NSW–Queensland Tri-series Final. And that is rugby league's hope; that the game as pure sport is good enough to win back the lost ground . . . if the administrators can get the framework right. The decks have been progressively cleared for that. Most of the people who claimed the headlines during the height of the battle—Carden, Arthurson, Morgan, Moore, Quayle, Smith, Monie . . . and plenty of others—are gone from the playing field now, or so far in the background as not to matter. Ken Cowley will soon be out of it, too.

The arena is left to the new breed, and they are welcome to it. Writing this so close to my departure from rugby league, my own sadness hangs heavy. I know from experience that time is the great healer though, and a revitalised game, if it happens, will gradually soften the impact and the memories of the events of the years 1995–97—and revitalise me too. Some of the things won't ever go away. It is with absolute frustration that I think of Murdoch and Packer and their detached jousting via their minions while a good game bled. If only they had done their deal back then in February 1995 . . . If only they had cared.

But enough of that. Fifty two years it's been, and only two of them crook. I'd rather think of the others and the million images they reflect . . . of great players . . . wonderful games . . . of the friendships that make life worthwhile.

Rugby league, I won't forget you, and I won't abandon you. My plan for years to come is that I'll still be a face in the crowd at Brookie—the sun beaming down and the Pacific sparkling not so far across the way. Around me folk will be recalling Randall, and Eadie and Fulton and Reilly and the rest as they discuss some fresh-faced, up-and-coming kid.

When I left Phillip Street on the last day of February 1997, someone asked my how I would like to be remembered. I paused and answered: 'Only time will tell what the scoreboard registers on my performance.

'But whatever that might be, I know deep down that I've done my best.'

I'd like to think as a football man that it was a reasonable final blast of the whistle. I had played the full 80 minutes, given it my all, done the best I could.

I could do no more.

SUPER LEAGUE—THE SECRET FILES

The ARL v Super League battles in the Federal Court in 1995–96 were preceded by a trawling exercise which brought in vast amounts of material, adding up to a mountain of papers. Diaries, faxes, private notes and memos were subpoenaed by the legal teams involved. Ken Arthurson, at the heart of the ARL defence, believes the material gathered for the League's case gives a deeply revealing profile of how News Ltd and the Super League proponents went about their business in the period before and just after the Super League Wars erupted. Key excerpts from the huge body of material held privately on the ARL's behalf are published here, for the first time.

DATE	EVENT
10.12.93	NSWRL General Committee Meeting at which Ribot not elected for further term on Premiership Policy Committee
12.93	Morgan speaks with Cowley regarding break-away competition.
4.94	Ribot presents 'first proposal' to Cowley
14.6.94	Ribot writes to Cowley enclosing draft working brief for Super League
12.8.94	SUPER LEAGUE REPORT
7.10.94	Kevin Neil meets with Chris Anderson
18.10.94	Kevin Neil meets with John Ribot in Sydney
19.10.94	Memo from David Smith to Ken Cowley
22.10.94	First test at Wembley. Lovett advises Arthurson that Super League is going ahead. Arthurson advises Quayle by telephone.
27.10.94	Memo from David Smith to Ken Cowley
7.11.94	Morgan tells *Telegraph Mirror* 'We are not the pushers (of Super League) and we haven't been approached. I haven't seen a document.'
10.11.94	Arthurson and Quayle meet Cowley and Lovett at News offices.

COMMENT

Sets out the entire objectives/strategy for Super League. Says that News Ltd wants to establish an elite national competition between 12 privately owned teams (at least 4 owned by News to begin with), and to run an international World Club Series (involving NZ & UK). 'However, careful consideration needs to be given to the wisdom and practicality of aiming to start actual competition *six months from today's date*.'

This doc. contains handwritten notes in the margin which, combined with the narrative, point towards instigating team mergers (eg. Canterbury/St George/Illawarra/Cronulla) and moving some clubs into other geographical areas.

Smith suggests that *Rugby Union players* be allowed to play as 'part-time professionals' for Super League. Acc. to Smith, this would allow Union to maintain its current traditions etc but at the same time 'embrace the inevitable change'.

Possibilities for an English Super League. 'Create a Super League winter competition by amalgamating the 16 top clubs and London to 10 or 12 teams in a structure similar to that which will exist in Australia.'

Arko

DATE	EVENT
23.1.94	Gordon Allen Laurie Puddy and Steven Edwards meet Ken Cowley and David Smith at News
24.11.94	Gordon Allen meets Peter Moore
25.11.94	Memorandum of proposals from Port Jackson Partners Limited to David Smith
12.12.94	Australian Consulting Partners (ACP) 'Alternative Strategies' (part of overall ACP proposal for implementing SL)
13.12.94	Fax from Kevin Neil of Canberra to David Smith detailing Canberra Player Contract details
14.12.94	Meeting between News and Cronulla at which Sydney Sharks Super League concept discussion paper (prepared by Peter Gow, Robert Johnstone and Robert Walker) is discussed. Present: Peter Gow, Brett Crowley, Robert Johnstone (Consultant with Sports Management Australia) and Robert Walker (Consultant with Australian Corporate Investment), David Smith, Ken Cowley.
19.12.94	Letter from P S Moore to Ken Cowley
22.12.94	News sign Confidentiality Deed—for Canberra, Brisbane, Red, Newcastle, Cronulla.
22.12.94	Fax from Peter Orlay to David Smith
22.12.94	Meeting at Wickham Crescent, Red Hill, Canberra—Kevin Neil, Mal Meninga, John Ribot, Ken Cowley.

COMMENT

P2—'News have determined to go ahead in 1996 with super league with or without the ARL.'
P4—we would like . . . to gain access to your strategy documents.'
Given News Ltd's position with RL establishment, ACP suggests 2 alternative approaches '*that involve making early moves outside the ARL—an "early defection" strategy or a "rebel" strategy.*'

Presented to News Limited—basically a plea to News Limited to let Cronulla League Club join Super League.

'Our club passed a motion very recently that we support the concept of a Super League run by the Australian Rugby League in conjunction with News Ltd.'

Hand written fax advising David Smith to go to the UK to see the ERL and Wigan. '*Get back to Aus fast where the game is "in play"* . . . *The longer you leave the ARL preso now the game is "in play" the more time they have. Packer is currently preoccupied with Pay . . . maybe that will spill into next week . . . but probably not the first week of Jan.*'

Arko

DATE	EVENT
29.12.94	Letter from Brad Mellen of Newcastle Knights to David Smith
10.1.95	Fax from David Smith to Ken Cowley. Going to Canberra tomorrow re player contracts (Tim Sheens has the wobbles). Refers to 'the person I have in mind as GM of the Adelaide Club'.
18.1.95	Super League Proposal to Ken Arthurson for Day 1.
20.1.95	David Smith meets with Peter Gow, Brett Crowley, Bob Elvey and St George representatives Warren Lockwood and Warren Saunders.
30.1.95	Arthurson, Quayle and Moore meet Cowley, Smith and Lovett at News
late January/ early February 1995	Handwritten note referring to Super League clothing and designs
1.2.95	Fax from Peter Gow of Cronulla Sutherland League Club to David Smith. 'Further to our most recent discussion this communication is to confirm that the Cronulla Club wishes to formally apply for a Super League licence.'
2.2.95	Fax from David Smith to Peter Gow. Enclosed draft employment letter and Confidentiality Agreement ('Set up so that you and St George can sign without Illawarra'.)
5.2.95	Arthurson telephones Cowley to say he won't support News proposal at Club meeting.
5.2.95	Arthurson and Quayle meet Packer who undertakes not to make any agreement with News without ARL consent.
6.2.95	Meeting of Club delegates addressed by News and Packer

COMMENT
'In principle we have no problems with signing the confidentiality document that you have proposed, however we have some concerns relating to the legal ramifications that may occur from such signature.'

Proposes that existing clubs continue; 20 team competition stays; ARL role is maintained. 'Will you work with us to develop the proposal?'

Handwritten note of meeting—undated, 'Super League definitely starting 1996 with or without ARL.'

DATE	EVENT
6.2.95	Arthurson telephones Cowley to inform of outcome of meeting. Cowley assures News will come 'through front door of ARL'.
7.2.95	Confidential memo from David Smith to Ken Cowley. Refers to thanking Wayne Goss 'for having listened to us'. Names Kevin Neil, Paul Morgan/John Ribot, Peter Gow, Brad Mellen, Laurie Brindle and Alex Hamill as having been 'particularly supportive'. 'I do not recommend the Western Reds. They are still lying prostrate at the door of the ARL.'
9.2.95	All clubs return executed Loyalty Agreement.
21.2.95	Neil and Les McIntyre lunch with Arthurson and repledge loyalty to ARL.
Late 2/95	Ribot allegedly suggests to Smith that following meeting of 6.2.95 approaches will have to be made to players, coaches and referees directly.
Late 2/95	Ribot presents Super League II proposal to Cowley and Smith (proposes a competition independent of the ARL).
3.3.95	CHART/PLAN OF ATTACK/WAR ROOM DOCUMENT relating to the week beginning 27.3.95
2.3.95	Meeting at Michael's Riverside Restaurant, Brisbane, between representatives of News Limited including David Smith and North Queensland including Barry Taylor.
13.3.95	Shane Richardson (Cronulla) tells *Canberra Times* 'The bottom line is that we've signed a 5 year agreement with the ARL, and as far as I am aware that's what we are involved in.'

COMMENT

Daily schedule for a period of one week with tasks divided up between Smith, Ribot, Gow and Lovett. Details who to sign up, when and where.

Arko

DATE	EVENT
23.3.95	Notes for discussion produced by ACP.

| 23.3.95 | Letter from Robert Topfer to Terry Chamberlain of Clayton Utz (copy to David Smith). Refers to meeting with Meninga yesterday and terms of agreement reached with News Ltd. |
| 27.3.95 | Memo to Ken Cowley from David Smith re plan for the week |

27.3.95	Gow lunches with Arthurson and swears he's had 'absolutely no involvement with Super League'.
28.3.95	News Limited letters to coaches from David Smith. Includes Chris Anderson, J. Lang, J. Monie, Peter Mulholland, Tim Sheens—requesting services as coaches for SL.
30.3.95	Flight schedule for News Ltd people involved in signing up Clubs and Players
30.3.95	News commences players signings
31.3.95	Flight schedule for News Ltd people involved in signing up Clubs and Players

COMMENT
Current proposal—10 team national Australian competition including teams from Auckland, Brisbane, Canberra, Illawarra, Newcastle, North Queensland, Perth, Cronulla, Canterbury and Norths?; our first attempt was unsuccessful, a second, more aggressive approach is needed. Key elements—sign up all players at approximately twice current earnings; mount a legal challenge to the 5 year agreement which binds the clubs to the ARL. Credibly mount a rival superleague without the ARL establishment—even though the best outcome is for the ARL to call for agents.

Tuesday 28.3.95:
* *Phone Elias*
* *Phone Meninga*
Thursday 30.3.95:
* *Phone Bradley Clyde*—to reassure haven't forgotten.
* *Phone Brian Walsh*—to say relax about ET
Friday 31.3.95
* *Phone Peter Moore*—at 9–10pm to reassure that his team has been considered and to relax no matter what happens.

This schedule coincides with the CHART/WAR ROOM DOCUMENT and other schedules for the week beginning 27.3.95

Not only explains who was flying where and when but who was to be signed up on what day. Willie Carne, Steve Renouf, Lachlan Murdoch and the Broncos lawyer are booked under false names.

DATE	EVENT
3.95	CHEAT SHEET: Presenter's Outline to potential Super League players produced by Richard Farmer and Trevor McEwen in late March 1995
1.4.95	Fax from Sam Ayoub of Ultra Management Sports to Shane Richardson of Cronulla Sutherland Football Club. Reference to contract signed by Geoff Bell at 3.40 am on 1.4.95—claims that SL contract was signed under duress.
1.4.95	Letter from San Ayoub to Shane Richardson of Cronulla Sutherland Football Club (attached to back of letter from Sam Ayoub above). Reference to contract signed by Mitch Healey at 4.00 am on 1.4.95—claims that SL contract was signed under duress.

COMMENT

Outline of SL proposal to players and a question and answer cheat sheet for players to use in response to media questioning. The first half of the narrative is specifically aimed at tempting the players to sign up with News Ltd.

'If we reach an agreement here today, you will leave with a cheque in return for your signature on a Super League Playing Contract—we anticipate our 10 teams will be from North Queensland, Brisbane, Newcastle, Illawarra, Canberra, Auckland and 3 sides from Sydney. Under the game's current structure, you cannot earn additional income from merchandising. Your Super League Contract provides for you to earn 50% of merchandising opportunities. So if there is a Willie Carne cap or a Laurie Daley T-Shirt, you share the profits 50/50 with your club.'

The second half of the document sets out the likely questions players will be asked by the media, and News Ltd's preferred answers.

It clearly asks the players to lie about their involvement with SL:

Q. have you signed a Super League contract?

A. I currently have a contract with (name of your club) and I fully intend to honour that.

Q. Are you in negotiations with News Ltd?

A. There's no point in that when I have a current contract which I'm obliged to honour

DATE	EVENT
1.4.95	Meeting at the Perth Sheraton between Malcolm Noad and Cronulla representatives including Brett Crowley and Shane Richardson
3.4.95	Letter from Ken Cowley to Bradley Clyde of Canberra Raiders and Paul Harragon of Newcastle Knights. Offering them positions as full-time employees of News Ltd
3.4.95	Telephone discussion between Peter Moore and John Ribot
6.4.95	Letter from Ken Cowley to Directors of Canberra Raiders indemnifying against loss or damage resulting from action taken by ARL NSWRL.
7.4.95	Shane Richardson meets and telephones John Ribot '*Re Monday night/Mal Meninga*'.
10.4.95	Fax from Terry Chamberlain of Clayton Utz to David Smith. Payments of $10,000 per month to Meninga family from April 1 are to go into family trust.
10.4.95	Cronulla club meeting attended by Ribot, Meninga, Gow, Crowley, Arthurson, Quayle and Cronulla club members ('the public meeting')
12.4.95	Letters from Ken Cowley to all players signed with SL. Letter of Welcome to all new players; assurance that players signed with SL have full support and protection of News Limited.
20.4.95	Shane Richardson and Ribot meet Brian Smith. Richardson telephone conversation with Ian Robson of Auckland Warriors.
21.4.95	Notes of meeting with News Ltd

COMMENT
Includes conversations about Cronulla assisting in signing its players. Conversations about not disclosing the fact that Cronulla or its officers or employees were engaging in Super League activities.

Conversation about Canterbury participating in or assisting the establishment of Super League

John Ribot, Michael O'Connor, Mark Levy, Royce Simmons and Roger Cowan in attendance. 196 players now signed. Budgetary figures supplied to Cowan for the first 5 years on the undertaking that he would not distribute them. In the first year there would be a profit of approx $1.3 million.

Arko

DATE	EVENT
27.4.95	Letter from Brett Rodwell (player) to Lachlan Murdoch
1.5.95	Letter from David Riolo (player) to Lachlan Murdoch
5.5.95	Hand written fax from Peter Mortimer to 'Bullfrog'.
12.5.95	Numerous letters from Ian Robson to other CEOs announcing Auckland Warriors' decision to sign with the Super League rugby competition
17.5.95	Fax from Super League Limited to Rugby League South Australia
23.5.95	Letter from Ferris to Ken Cowley
20.6.95	Memo to Club Executives and Coaches
21.6.95	Meeting minutes

COMMENT
Reneging on contract signed with Star League, because it was signed under duress and was not truthfully told about the SL competition or rights under the contract.

Reneging on contract signed with Star League because signed under duress and without full disclosure of knowledge of rights under the contract.

Working on concept to lure amateur players from rural NSW into SL. Necessary to bypass CRL because they have a bad image.

Consequences of SARL's failure to comply with request from ARL; agree to provide RLSA a grant of $270,000

Appears that Knights and SL will go ahead next year, therefore for us to compete we will need financial assistance.

Subject: Player Pool.

Rugby Union players; Daniel Herbert—Broncos; Joe Roff—Cronulla; Mark Ellis—Bulldogs; Glen Osborne—Bulldogs; Jonah Lomu—Auckland/Wigan/Leeds/Bulldogs; Joost Van Westhuizen—Leeds/Bulldogs/North Queensland. The four clubs below indicated they were interested in the following rugby union players.

Perth Alan Prince, Matt Burke, Todd Lowden, Scott Bowen and Peter Mueller;

Newcastle Brian Lima, George Harder, Justin Mads and Jason Little;

Penrith Gordon Falcon, Justin Mads, Walter Little and A Mehrtens;

Nth Qld Too Vaega

'Michael O'Connor is available for an assistance in signing these players, or other rugby union signings.'

Michael O'Connor talked with 12 Norths players on Tuesday night; 6 affidavits from Brisbane, 3 from Penrith and 2 from Canberra; wear out the storm regarding the tenth franchise; must make sure that Jonah Lomu does not go to the ARL.

Arko

DATE	EVENT
14.7.95	John Ribot diary extract
Undated	'Sydney Premier League Competition NSW Overview'

COMMENT
Meeting with Mr Murdoch in Ken Cowley's office for 1 hour at
9.30 am
Marked 'Confidential' this document sets out a tiered structure
for the SL competition. 'The long term viability of the Super
League competition will depend on our ability to develop future
Super League players for our elite competition.'

A LIFE IN
RUGBY
LEAGUE

KENNETH RICHARD ARTHURSON, AM
Born October 1st, 1929.

Awards
1988   Received an A.M. in the 1988 Bicentennial Australia
        Day List of Honours.

Life Memberships
1967   Manly Warringah Football Club
1973   Manly Warringah League Club
1979   New South Wales Rugby League
1988   New South Wales League Club
1989   Papua New Guinea Rugby League
1979   Australian Rugby Football League

Administration
1956–61 Manly Warringah Football Club   Committee
1962   Manly Warringah Football Club   Honorary
                                         treasurer
1963–83 Manly Warringah Football Club   Secretary
1968–82 New South Wales Rugby League   Management
                                         committee and
                                         board

Arko

1974–   Manly Warringah League Club   President
1977–83 Australian Rugby League   Board of
                                              directors
1983–87 New South Wales Rugby League   Board of
                                              directors
1983–97 Australian Rugby League   Executive
                                              chairman
1985–   International Rugby League Board   Director
                                              general
1986–   Sydney Cricket Ground Trust   Trustee
1987–97 New South Wales Rugby League   Chairman
(Before becoming Secretary of the Manly Warringah Football
Club was administrator of the Police College at North Head.)

Coaching
1953   Parkes Rugby League Football Club Player/coach
1954   Manly Warringah RLFC   Third grade
1955–56 Manly Warringah RLFC   Reserve grade
1957–61 Manly Warringah RLFC   First grade

Rugby League Playing Record
1945   Freshwater Surf Life Saving Club D grade premiers
1946   Freshwater Surf Life Saving Club C grade premiers
1947   Freshwater Surf Life Saving Club C grade premiers
                                          (undefeated)
        Freshwater Surf Life Saving Club A grade premiers
1948   Freshwater Surf Life Saving Club A grade premiers
1949   Freshwater Surf Life Saving Club B grade premiers
1948–49 Manly Warringah DRLFC   President's Cup
                                          winners
1950–52 Manly Warringah DRLFC   Grade player
1953   Parkes Rugby League Football Club Player/coach
        (serious injury forced premature retirement)

INDEX